Seeing Young Children:

A GUIDE TO OBSERVING AND RECORDING BEHAVIOR

Dedication

To RML, whose pride in my accomplishment I would have
cherished above all others.

Seeing Young Children:

A GUIDE TO OBSERVING AND RECORDING BEHAVIOR

Second Edition

WARREN R. BENTZEN
State University of New York at Plattsburgh

 Delmar Publishers Inc.

NOTICE TO THE READER

Cover photo by Jeff Greenberg

Cover design by Nancy Gworek

Delmar Staff
  Administrative Editor: Jay Whitney
  Project Editor: Carol Micheli
  Production Coordinator: Barbara A. Bullock
  Art Coordinator: John Lent
  Design Coordinator: Karen Kemp

For information, address Delmar Publishers Inc.
3 Columbia Circle, Box 15-015
Albany, New York 12212

COPYRIGHT ©1993
BY DELMAR PUBLISHERS INC.

printed in the United States of America
published simultaneously in Canada
by Nelson Canada,
a division of The Thomson Corporation

1 2 3 4 5 6 7 8 9 10 XXX 99 98 97 96 95 94 93

Library of Congress Cataloging-in-Publication Data

Bentzen, Warren R.
    Seeing young children : a guide to observing and recording
  behavior / Warren R. Bentzen.

      p.   cm.
    Includes bibliographical references and index.
    ISBN 0-8273-4477-5
    1. Behavioral assessment of children. 2. Observation (Psychology)
  3. Observation (Educational method) I. Title.
  BF722.B46   1993
  155.4—dc20   92-27335
                                                          CIP

Contents

Preface

I have no doubt that anyone who has had a book published must feel very flattered and a tremendous sense of gratification and accomplishment when the publisher asks for a second edition. I, at least, am experiencing those feelings. Of course, I can't hold Delmar Publishers or my editor solely responsible for the decision to put out a second edition of *Seeing Young Children*. It goes without saying that you, the reader, have played a large role in the book's success, and for that I am also deeply grateful.

There are some major changes that I believe make the second edition a decidedly better book than the first edition. I won't cite all of them here, but let me mention a few of them.

The material presented in Chapter 2 (Overview of Developmental Theories) has been expanded rather significantly. Indeed, it may appear to some readers that *Seeing Young Children* is now closer to a full-blown human development textbook than it is to an observational manual. It is not our intention, however, to supplant any child or human development text or any text on developmental theory. It is simply our position that making more, rather than less information available under one cover increases our text's effectiveness by eliminating the reader's need to find other sources of information.

In Chapter 3, I have added to the discussion of the concept of "group" by adopting the perspective of Patricia Yancey Martin and Gerald G. O'Connor (1989), who identify the characteristics of small groups on the basis of four components. As I explain in Chapter 3, these components "provide a framework within which to put . . . observations of children's group behavior" (p. 50). Again, the goal is to permit more sophisticated and more accurate observation and recording than was possible with the first edition. It also adds to the reader's understanding of group behavior.

The observation exercises involving infants (Chapter 16) now cover the period of one month to twenty-four months, in contrast with the earlier range of fifteen to eighteen months. Consonant with this extended age range, significantly more information is provided about this period of the life span. A good deal of the discussion takes on the problem of defining infancy, and I offer definitions based on age or developmental level, behavioral definitions, and definitions based on function. This latter definition is pursued in some depth in terms of nine competency areas, a treatment we believe will be to the reader's advantage. I also discuss why the period of infancy is so important, a critical determination if one is to approach the observation of infants with confidence regarding the legitimacy of one's efforts.

The prefatory discussions to the observation exercises have also been expanded in some instances. Up-to-date information concerning physical growth and development includes quite complete descriptions of an infant's developmental milestones. Special attention is given to the development of the infant to reach for, grasp, and manipulate objects.

Of course, the observation exercises themselves have been changed to reflect the up-dated discussion of infancy. I believe that the addition of these significant amounts of information move *Seeing Young Children* closer to being a *primer* of infant development rather than just an observation manual. The addition of this new information is particularly justified by the fact that truly meaningful observation requires a base or foundation of knowledge and theory. If the chapters on developmental theory tell the reader "more about penguins" than he or she wants to know, that information can be skimmed over without detriment to the primary purpose of observing children's behavior.

Chapter 17, the young child from ages 2 through 6 years, has some additional information that I believe will enhance not only the observations but also the reader's understanding of the development that occurs during that period.

In the area of cognitive development and behavior, discussion of children's concepts of causality includes a slightly expanded discussion of finalism, artificialism, and especially the concept of animism, which is presented in terms of Piaget's formulation of the substages through which this concept develops.

I am particularly pleased to include in the second edition, information regarding the cognitive ability of mental representation. Certainly Piaget placed a lot of importance on the *symbolic function*, as he called mental representation, and it would be difficult to argue cogently that the ability to have words and other abstract symbols "stand for" various aspects of "reality" is not a critical feature of our mental life.

The discussion of play has, I think, been greatly improved over the first edition. Parten's (1932) classical description of play categories formed the basis of the observations of children's play behavior in the first edition. In retrospect, this was much too limited a view of such an important activity. The second edition incorporates, among other materials, Grace Craig's (1989) six categories or forms of play "that depend on particular characteristics and functions" (Chapter 17, p. 210). This new information describes and explains play much more completely, and I think more accurately, than do Parten's categories, although they can still be used to structure observations of play behavior.

The treatment of emotional development and behavior has also been extended. The core of this expanded treatment lies with the work of Stanley and Nancy Greenspan (*First Feelings*, 1985), who describe the stages of emotional development. Again, the importance of emotional development and behavior motivated the inclusion of this new material, which will allow more sophisticated observation and recording of this developmental/ behavioral area.

There are other changes that the reader of the first edition will easily notice. I sincerely hope that most of the revisions will be well received. I am certain that other changes could have been made, or some present ones left out, and I am happy to entertain those suggestions for the next edition.

For the second edition, my guiding philosophy is this: The primary objective of acquiring and refining one's observation skills is, in my own view, virtually independent of specific content. Given basic knowledge of "normal" development and behavior, one can learn to observe development and behavior that both conform and fail to conform to normative developmental patterns. To understand sickness, as the saying goes, one must first understand health.

Warren R. Bentzen
Plattsburgh, New York

Acknowledgments

The following reviewers deserve my sincere thanks for their invaluable assistance and advice in the revision of this edition:

Nancy Morse, Parkland College
Rosanne Pirtle, Marian College
Mark Benson, Virginia Polytechnic and State University
Gayla Roberts, Trinity Valley Community College
Joan Yoakam, Amarillo College

Author's Foreword

There is more to observation than what meets the eye. The ability to observe almost anything is the product of maturation and learning—and in some cases, of years of study and hard work.

The premise of this manual is that observation never just happens as a matter of course. Observing or "seeing" children involves who we are, what we know, and what we have experienced. Although we inherit the ability to see in a physiological sense (we have eyes that register images), seeing in a meaningful psychological and intellectual sense goes well beyond one's eyeballs. Seeing is more than physical sensation. Our physical seeing has to be transformed so that we can use the raw data it provides to function, make sense of our environment, and act on our perceptions.

My own thinking on observation has had to change because I once took "seeing" for granted. For these changes, I am indebted to the writings of Jean Piaget and Norwood Russell Hanson. Partly from reading and thinking about their thinking, I have become interested in observation as more than just "looking at" something, whether this "looking" be done in a formal or informal way.

This manual is not a theoretical book. Its goal is to acquaint you with the means of observing and recording the behavior of children and to help you try out those means.

The book gives more than instructions for "looking" at children and describing their behavior. It explains what observation is and how it relates to developmental theories. I hope that you will come to see how the subject of child development influences, and is influenced by, the observational experiences and skills you acquire.

There is one final concern with which I must deal. In an attempt to avoid the use of sexist language, I have randomly used pronouns denoting gender, referring to both sexes with equal frequency and without bias.

Part 1

Overview

chapter one
Introduction

Objectives

After studying Chapter One, you will be able to

- describe the differences between seeing in a physiological way and seeing in an observational way
- analyze the importance of observation to early childhood education
- analyze the importance of observation to science and to an individual
- examine the relationship between observation and the observer's personal and theoretical perspectives
- discuss in general terms what observation is and what it involves

Observation: Some Preliminary Thoughts

The scene is a preschool classroom, and you have come simply to visit, and to watch. You notice a small boy sitting at a table playing with a piece of clay. He is alone, and you want to get closer to see what he is doing. The boy (we will call him Robby) smiles as you approach, and asks you if you want to play with him. You say "yes," and he gives you his clay. As Robby watches very closely, you roll the clay into one large ball and then break it into two, roughly equal parts. You hand him his portion of the clay and tell him, "Now, we both have just as much to play with." Robby nods and smiles again, takes his ball of clay and rolls it around on the surface of the table. You take your part of the clay and proceed to flatten it out like a pancake. Robby is now very interested; he looks intently at your flattened piece and then shouts, "Hey, *your* piece is bigger! I want *that* one!" You are, after all, a guest, and you certainly do not want to quarrel with a three-year old over a piece of clay, so you trade your piece for his. He smiles once more and goes back to his playing.

You have just observed a child's behavior in a particular situation. You have received information through your eyes and your ears. But what happened? What have you seen? What could you say about the observation process you have just gone through? What could you say about Robby?

Had you seen Robby through the eyes of a trained preschool teacher, you could have seen a child in Piaget's preoperational stage of cognitive development. You could have seen a little boy who was unable to *conserve substance*. From that you would have seen Robby's inability to understand that if no clay was added and none was taken away, then the amount of clay must remain unchanged. You could have seen Robby being fooled by the outward appearances of the pieces of clay. Moreover, you could have predicted all of these things just by knowing that Robby was three years old. Questions and possible answers such as these are central to this manual. Think about observation and what it will mean when, in doing your observation exercises, you say, "I'm going to observe children."

One might think that observing something is a fairly simple task. This belief is given support by the vital role our ears and eyes play in getting information about our environment. Observation appears to involve seeing or hearing some stimulus or set of stimuli coming from the external environment.

There is a difficulty, however, when we think of observing just as seeing or hearing. A problem arises because humans are not cameras or tape recorders; we do not merely take in sensory information through the eyes and ears. If we did, we would be as unable as the camera and recorder to use that information. It is precisely because we can do something more with sensory information after we obtain it that observation becomes complicated. Furthermore, what and how much information we perceive varies from person to person, and even within the same person, from one time to another. And so it is that two individuals can be visually aware of the same object or event, but visually aware in quite different ways (Hansen 1958). Here is an example.

Mrs. Delgado has enrolled her four-year-old son Phillipe in a community childcare center. It is the center's policy and practice to involve parents in some of the curricular activities that take place there. This is done partly in the hope that parents can carry on in the home what the center is trying to accomplish in just a few hours each day. One might say that the center takes a broad "systems" view of childcare, believing that home and school are interrelated, and that what happens in one of those places affects what happens in the other.

Phillipe is relatively new at the center, having been there about a week. Mrs. Delgado is at the center on a particular Monday morning to help the staff but especially to observe her son's "progress" in the program. Phillipe is in the big block area with two other boys, and they appear to be building a "house" together. Mrs. Delgado watches closely, being especially alert to Phillipe's interactions with the other two boys. Phillipe, you see, is, by his mother's perceptions, shy and seemingly tentative about initiating and maintaining social contacts. As she observes her son's behaviors, she wonders what value there is in playing with big wooden blocks. Because she is very interested in his social behavior, she concludes that his present activity is more appropriate to building muscle strength and coordination than it is to fostering interpersonal skills. Furthermore, she doesn't want the center to ignore or underemphasize skills and abilities that require thinking and planning and talking—"cognitive" and language skills.

Mrs. Hafner, the center director and head teacher, is also observing Phillipe in the big block area. As she looks at him, she doesn't "see" everything that Mrs. Delgado sees, simply because, as his mother, Mrs. Delgado has had four years to get to know her son very intimately. Mrs. Hafner, on the other hand, has had only about three hours a day for merely a week to learn anything at all about the boy. But, Mrs. Hafner has at least one advantage over Mrs. Delgado: she can see and interpret events and behaviors that are relevant to Phillipe *in the context of the childcare center* that would go unnoticed and unappreciated by Mrs. Delgado. She can do this because she is professionally trained in early childhood education and in child development. Consequently, she "sees" all the boys in the block area acquiring and sharpening their spatial relations skills—learning how, for example, blocks of different sizes and shapes can fit together to form the particular structure they are trying to build. They are also acquiring a sense of weight and some understanding that size alone does not necessarily predict an object's heaviness or lightness. Big things can weigh less and be easier to lift than small ones—a somewhat large but light pine wood block as compared with a small but heavy cube of lead. Mrs. Hafner also will see the language and arithmetic skills that are being used—"Hey," says Phillipe, "give me *two* more blocks so that I can finish this bridge."

What Mrs. Hafner may not see, at least not at first, is the shyness and unwillingness on the part of Phillipe to enter into social situations. This may not be an immediate *interpretation* that Mrs. Hafner is likely to make, because she has not observed Phillipe in many other situations where he could exhibit his shyness. His mother, of course, might be inclined to "see" shyness in much of what Phillipe does in association with others.

The point of this hypothetical example is that Phillipe's mother and his teacher saw essentially the same *overt* behaviors as they watched him playing in the big block area. What we've depicted, however, is Mrs. Delgado seeing *only play* going on. She does not fully understand the value of play and the many kinds of learning that are taking place. Mrs. Hafner, on the other hand, does see *learning* taking place *in the context of a play situation*. Mrs. Delgado doesn't see spatial relationship or arithmetic skills being acquired and practiced, nor does she see Phillipe learning what she most wants him to learn—social interaction skills.

This use of the word seeing is a way of dealing with the observation process. It must be kept separate in some important ways from seeing in a physiological sense. When we look at an object, its image is projected on that part of the eye called the retina. For example, look at Figure 1-1. The image that figure forms on your retina will be identical with the image on someone else's retina. Physiologically, most individuals will see the same thing.

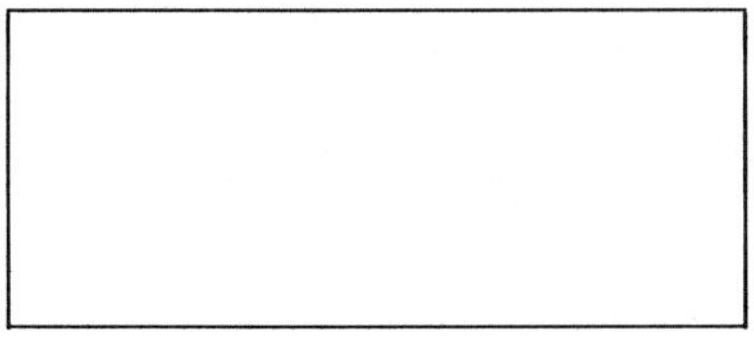

Figure 1-1 In a physiological sense, all persons with normal vision see the same thing when they look at this figure.

What distinguishes seeing in the observational way from seeing in the physiological way, also distinguishes what a physician and his patient see when each of them looks at an X-ray. Both the patient and the physician receive the same visual information; the X-ray picture is projected on each of their retinas. Because of the differences in their backgrounds and training, however, each perceives something different; each draws different meanings from the visual information taken in. The patient may see only shadows or vague outlines; the physician will see a tumor or a clogged artery.

The essential point here is that all of us look at and organize the objects and events in our world according to our past experiences, what we know, and what we believe.

Why Observation is Important

Goodwin and Driscoll (1980) give three reasons why observation is important in early childhood education. First, it allows measuring many behaviors of children that may otherwise be unmeasureable. Young children's verbal abilities are limited, which rules out use of traditional information-gathering techniques such as interviews and paper-and-pencil tests. The area of emotions is especially suitable to observational methods; the observer can see the child as he actually behaves, without the shortcomings of limited test-taking ability, unreliable understanding of test instructions, and eagerness to please adults by responding in the way they think the adults want them to respond (Goodwin and Driscoll 1980).

Second, formal testing procedures are not typically viewed as seriously by children as by adults. Goodwin and Driscoll (1980) believe that children do not take to heart adults' advice that the test is serious business and that they should try as hard as they can, an attitude formal testing relies on for its success. There are other criticisms leveled against the formal testing of young children. It's argued, for example, that formal testing is developmentally inappropriate for young children. Some also contend that rather than *not* taking testing seriously, as Goodwin and Driscoll claim, children in fact become severely stressed under formal testing conditions. Fortunately, observation shares none of these disadvantages with formal testing. The observer wants to see children's behavior as it occurs without adult interference. Nor does the observer want to generate anxiety or other emotions that might affect inappropriately the children's behavior.

Third, Goodwin and Driscoll believe that even when they know they are being observed, young children feel less threatened or anxious than do older children and adults. Young children presumably are also less likely than older children or adults to change their behavior in response to being observed. The assumption here is that, in the case of older children and adults, if someone knows he is being watched, it is harder for him to behave normally than if he thinks he is alone. It has been said that if we were observed behaving in what we thought were private moments, most of us would be judged insane. Observation of young children, then, supposedly yields behavior that is relatively unaffected by the process of observing it.

Aside from these reasons, there are others that give importance to the observation process. You may find yourself observing children who are in a variety of settings (e.g., in preschool classrooms, playgrounds, the home, or public school classrooms). Our knowledge of children and how they change over time ultimately depends on someone (actually, many people) studying children, observing them doing various things in various situations at various ages. Theories, which attempt to explain development, have to be tested and shown to be useful or not useful in understanding the developmental process. Such testing must ultimately involve observation. You may not be testing any theories, but theories can assist you in the observation process; at the same time, your observations can help you understand the theories. Put another way, there is a relationship between what you might learn from books, for example, and your observation experiences. On the one hand, involvement with real children can help you understand what you read and hear about them; on the other hand, what you are learning about children and their development will influence what you see as you complete the observation exercises. For example, what you know in general about language development will affect what you learn and understand about a particular child's language development. The nature of your understanding, and how you explain what you see, will depend on your knowledge, your observation skills, and the theoretical and personal perspective(s) from which you view growth, development, and even people in general. This is true in areas other than early childhood education. A Freudian therapist is very likely to see a client's problem as involving psychic conflict, whereas a behavioral therapist is more likely to see the same problem in terms of the client's reinforcement history. Each therapist, because of his professional training, sees that behavior from a different point of view and is sensitive to different aspects of the individual's behavior. If you work with children in a professional capacity, your particular training will incline *you* to see children in certain ways and to interpret their behavior in a way that agrees with your point of view or theory. This manual is designed to help you sharpen your observation skills. It also emphasizes the need for a conceptual framework from which to observe and make sense out of what is seen.

We want to emphasize, however, that this manual is *not* a source book for learning in great detail about such things as child development, early childhood education curricula and classroom practices, or procedures for intervening in the lives of children who present particular problems. Rather, this text focuses on the processes of observing and recording behavior, processes or techniques that can be applied to virtually any situation or set of circumstances in which observation and recording skills are needed. Except for the practice exercises provided in this manual, we leave it to you to find the occasions for such application and thereby also to find the specific content of your observation and recording activities.

Box 1-1 Purposes of Systematic Observing and Recording

Janice Beatty (1986) specifies eight reasons for "systematic observing and recording." She identifies these as "particular reasons" that might be adopted by "teachers and students who wish to learn more about the youngsters they work with." We give them to you here as additions to the reasons already discussed above. We would like to mention, however, that Beatty's reasons very appropriately fall under the topic of one's purposes for observing and recording behavior, which is dealt with in some detail in Chapter 3.

1. To make an initial assessment of the child's abilities.
2. To determine a child's areas of strength, and areas needing strengthening.
3. To make individual plans based on observed needs.
4. To conduct an ongoing check on the child's progress.
5. To learn more about child development in particular areas.
6. To resolve a particular problem involving the child.
7. To use in reporting to parents, or specialists in health, speech, mental health.
8. To gather information for the child's folder, for use in guidance and placement.

Source: Janice J. Beatty (1986, p. 5)

The preceding discussion has much to do with the importance of observation. There is, however, a broader aspect to the importance of observation. Observation is crucial, because so many of the sciences—social and physical—must gather data that can be seen, heard, smelled, touched, or tasted. Such data is called *empirical* data, which are data that depend on experience or observation rather than abstract theory. A psychologist must eventually leave abstract theories of human behavior and explore and measure the "real" behavior of "real" people. This exploring and measuring require observation. A psychologist interested in studying children's aggressive behavior, must at some point stop thinking about aggression in just theoretical terms, and identify what she means by aggression in empirical terms. In this example, the psychologist must observe and record visible behaviors exhibited by children—behaviors she believes indicate aggression. It is likely she will accept as aggression behaviors such as hitting, pushing, calling names, or taking a toy away from another child. But regardless of its definition, the idea of aggression must ultimately be linked to something directly observable. Based on that observable behavior, the psychologist assumes the presence or existence of aggression.

What is Observation?

In a very real sense, you will be acting as a scientist when you observe children. You will be doing what every scientist or researcher must do if she is to learn about the real world. Because of the purposes that are part of their occupations, scientists and researchers have to work with ideas that are abstract or removed from everyday life. But all of us deal with abstract ideas at some time. Examples can be found in our everyday language. We use words as symbols that stand for something else. For instance, the word 'chair' stands for a piece of furniture that one sits on (usually). In ordinary conversation, most of us can agree on what is meant by 'chair.' A problem arises, however, when we move away from casual conversation and toward descriptions of abstract ideas such as truth or beauty.

The generally acknowledged goals of science are description, explanation, prediction, and control. Being able to explain something indicates that one understands it, knows how it operates, and why it operates in that manner. Explanation first requires description. The explainer must know what he is looking at; he must be able to show the phenomenon to others, if only through a verbal description or "picture." In some instances, the explainer may have to make it clear as to why he thinks he will see what he is looking for in the specific phenomenon chosen for observation. In your case, you will be looking at children, some of whom will be a phenomenon for you to describe, explain, maybe predict and, consequently, understand.

You may decide to observe a three-year-old child for evidence of egocentrism. You will first have to define egocentrism so that you will recognize it when it occurs. You will describe those behaviors that fit your definition of egocentrism, or from which you infer its presence. It is reasonable to observe a three-year-old child because according to Piaget's theory, a child of this age is typically egocentric in some behavior and thinking.

Participation as an observer is not just a matter of watching children play, for example, and then writing down what you have seen. What you have observed must make sense and must be given meaning. There is no guarantee, however, that your meaning will be the only valid one or that you will even take notice of everything of significance in the situation. Validity (accuracy) and completeness depend on the perspective from which you observe and on your skill as an observer.

Observation includes "noting and recording facts and events" (Webster 1960) or "a taking notice or paying attention" (Webster 1981).

Unfortunately, the "facts" Webster refers to are seldom pure or self-evident. We must process them in some way. *Process* means to think about, to give a verbal label to, or to put the fact into some meaningful relationship with other facts. We seldom deal directly with the objects, events, and people in our world; rather, we deal with what is said about them. Saying something about an object, however, already involves interpretation and a perspective. Finding the appropriate words indicates knowledge of language, of the object, and the ability to place the object in a relationship with other objects or with other relevant information. Here is an illustration.

Think for a moment of what is involved in "watching children play." At the very least, you must have some idea of what play is. How do you know it is play you are observing rather than another kind of activity? If you believe that everything young children do is play, you will make no distinctions among the behaviors they exhibit. However, if your perspectives (ideas, views) on play are more sophisticated, you are likely to classify play and non-play activities according to criteria based, perhaps, on a theory. Or you may identify different types or characteristics of play, possibly using Craig's (1989) six categories or forms of play (see Chapter 17). Can you see how it is possible to view play (or anything else) in either a simple or a complex way? Let us look at one more illustration of this essential point.

Constance Kamii and Rheta DeVries (1977), two authors and researchers in early childhood education, deal with the idea of processing facts in their discussion of Piaget's ideas about the development of intelligence. They use the example of a child understanding the concept of "capital" (specifically, as represented in the statement, "Washington D.C. is the capital of the United States."). A sixth grader has some understanding of such a statement, but as Kamii and DeVries point out, with six more years of living, studying, and other maturing experiences, the statement will take on richer and more elaborate meanings. As a result, say the authors, free association to the word "Washington" might raise from the child such responses as "The White House, the Capitol, the Lincoln Memorial . . ." (1977). The adult's range of responses to Washington would be even broader than the child's (perhaps including "taxes," "an area of land 10 miles square," and "Congressional scandals"). Like the child's, the adult's response would be relevant to the particular word and its accepted set of meanings. They would not include a response such as "The price of eggs in China" or "Napoleon" (Kamii and DeVries 1977). The idea of putting one fact into a relationship with other facts (processing) is conveyed in the following passage:

> These free associations illustrate Piaget's view that since knowledge is organized in a coherent, whole structure, no concept can exist in isolation. Each concept is supported and colored by an entire network of other concepts (Kamii and DeVries 1977).

It is this organizing of concepts that makes up the processing of facts and, again, it is guided by developmental or behavioral theories and personal perspectives.

You realize by now that observing is not simply looking *at* something. Disciplined, scientific observation is looking *for* something in a particular way (or ways). These particular ways of observing children are discussed in Chapters Four—Twelve.

There is a final aspect of observation you should be familiar with. The phrase "observation process" has been used several times. That phrase has two meanings of interest to us. First, process refers to a series of related activities that require time to accomplish. Thus, to observe a child involves a number of activities and behaviors on the part of both the child and the observer. The child has to exhibit the behaviors of interest to the observer, and the observer has to do something with those behaviors. He must see them, then record and interpret them. Process also involves structure of some sort. Structure may be inherent in the situation itself, to the extent that certain activities have to follow a particular sequence or time order. For example, you have to observe a behavior *before* you can record and interpret it. Other kinds of structure can be imposed on the situation by an observer, as when she chooses a particular method of recording behaviors or a particular theoretical perspective from which to interpret and explain the behaviors.

The second use of process may be of greater personal concern to you than the first one, although both are essential to observation. Process also involves your own self. Process is "a continuing development involving many changes . . ." (Webster 1960); it's "a series of gradual changes moving toward some particular end" (Webster 1981). Change is part of observation (and vice versa), since the child will not remain the same even in the short period of time required to do an observation exercise, let alone over a period of weeks and months. You too will change. You will learn about developmental theories, norms, and research studies. You will acquire knowledge of observation techniques and skill in performing them. Your knowledge of theory and your observation experiences will interact with each other and be enhanced or improved. Your attitudes concerning children—how they grow and develop, who they are, where they "fit" in the life cycle—may also change.

I wish you success on your journey.

Summary

Observation is something we do continually, whether we are aware of it or not. We observe largely through our eyes and ears, taking in various kinds of sensory information. All observation, however, whether casual or scientifically rigorous, consists of more than the physical reception of stimuli. We truly observe or "see" when what we have received through our senses has meaning for us. We see when we can put our observations into a mental framework that has personal relevance. All of us have personal frameworks within which we describe and interpret what happens in our world. These frameworks can be called our personalities. It is also possible to have more formal frameworks to describe and interpret observed phenomena. These formal frameworks can be called theories.

Observation is important for a number of reasons. The most basic reason is that, ultimately, we learn about reality by observing it, by having contact with it through our physical senses. It follows that, at some point in the study of children, we must watch them, listen to them, and touch them, if we are to understand them.

Study Questions

1. What is the importance of seeing in a physical sense and seeing in an observational sense? How are these two kinds of seeing related?
2. Do you think observational skills are important or unimportant to being a good teacher or child care worker? Defend your position with specific reasons. Do the same regarding the importance or unimportance of observation to science and the individual. Are your three sets of reasons like or unlike each other? That is, is observation for the teacher, scientist, and the ordinary person actually three different activities, or do they share some commonalities?
3. With respect to the last part of question two above, how might observation done by a scientist in an *experimental setting* differ from observation done, say, by a preschool teacher in a *natural setting* or context? If there are any differences, what form would they likely take?
4. This chapter argues that observation is affected or determined by our personalities (i.e., our knowledge, values, attitudes, and experience). How could you show this argument to be true or false?
5. It's been said that it is *impossible not to communicate*. Is it also impossible not to observe? Take the broadest possible view of observation to answer this question.

chapter two
Overview of
Developmental Theories

Objectives

After studying this chapter, you will be able to

- define the concepts of growth and development
- discuss levels of explanation
- discuss the meaning of interpretation and its role in the observation of children
- describe various characteristics and principles of development
- discuss the different views that are held regarding certain characteristics of development
- discuss the relationship between one's views on development and what one sees when observing children

Development and Explanation: Some Preliminary Thoughts

The purpose of this chapter is to introduce you to the concepts of growth and development, as well as to the idea of explaining or interpreting behavior within the context of growth and developmental change. The nature of your involvement requires us to present more than one point of view. The important characteristics that define developmental change and the different perspectives and interpretations that are associated with various theoretical positions will be included. Be prepared for the possibility of explaining or interpreting your observational data in several ways, depending on what theoretical "filter" you are using.

Explanation, which is heavily influenced or determined by one's perspectives on development (and on people in general), is also included in this chapter.

Development and Growth

The term *development* refers to change over time—change in the structure, thought, or behavior of an individual that comes about from biological and environmental influences. This is probably the simplest sense we can get of the concept of development. Kathleen Berger (1991) offers the same uncomplicated idea when she writes that "... *the study of human development is the study of how people change over time, as well as how and why they remain the same*" (p. 2; italics original).

Sroufe and Cooper (1988) offer a slightly more sophisticated conceptualization of development. They write that "Development during childhood and adolescence refers to certain age-related changes that are orderly, cumulative, and directional" (p. 7). *Orderly* change is change that follows a predictable (Sroufe and Cooper use the term "logical") sequence, where each change paves the way for future changes and makes sense with respect to what has previously taken place. These authors define *cumulative* as meaning that any given phase of development encompasses everything that has already occurred, but the "new" or emerging phase includes something additional that was not present in the earlier phases or stages. By *directional* Sroufe and Cooper mean that "development always moves toward greater complexity" (p. 7).

These same authors identify several other aspects to development that deserve mention at this time. They call development "dramatic and predictable" (p. 9). But, they ask, how does this dramatic, predictable process occur in the first place? Three factors provide an answer to their question. First, there is a genetic/maturational factor, "a preexisting developmental plan built into the organism" (p. 9). Second, the development that has already occurred provides an ongoing and necessary foundation for all subsequent development. And third, development needs a supportive environment, what Sroufe and Cooper identify as "all of the nutrients, inputs, circumstances, and challenges the developing organism encounters" (p. 9).

The team of Mussen, Conger, Kagan, and Huston (1984) identify three basic goals of developmental psychology. These goals are related to Sroufe and Cooper's three factors discussed immediately above. They also provide a rationale by which to assess the observed behavior of children. Mussen *et al.* cite as one goal the understanding of changes that "appear to be *universal*—changes that occur in all children regardless of the culture in which they grow up or the experiences they have" (p. 7; italics original). A second goal is to explain *individual differences* in behavior. Why are some children more skillful than others in social relationships, for example, or why do children react differently to stress or changes in routine? The third goal of developmental psychology identified by Mussen and his colleagues is that of determining the influence of *context* or *situation* on a person's behavior. One child's imitation of another child's aggressive behavior might be a result of some specific contextual or situational influence, for example. Mussen *et al.* give us a useful summary of the significance of development and its various emphases or perspectives.

These three ways of examining children's behavior—searching for universal patterns, individual differences, and situational or contextual influences—are all necessary for a full understanding of development.

The emphasis placed on any one of the three depends on the theoretical orientation of the investigator and on the type of question being studied. (Mussen *et al.*, 1984, p. 8)

The last sentence in the above quotation will be particularly important later on because, among other reasons, your observations will be put into a particular theoretical perspective, which will consequently put a particular emphasis on your observational data.

Table 2-1

Sroufe and Cooper's Three Factors Explaining Development	Mussen et al's Goals of Developmental Psychology
Genetic-Maturational Factor: "A preexisting developmental plan built into the organism"	To understand *universal* developmental changes that occur in spite of individual experiences
Current level of development provides basis for future development: *Development is cumulative*	To explain *individual differences*
Development needs a *supportive environment*	To understand the effects of *context* or *situation* on a person's behavior

Development is of two general kinds: normative and individual (Sroufe and Cooper, 1988). *Normative development* consists of general behavioral changes that are shared by all children across various ages. One might consider normative development as changes that occur simply because we belong to the human species. This is comparable to the idea of universal changes touched on above. *Individual development* has two meanings. On the one hand, it consists of "variations around the average, or normative, course of development of a certain ability" (Sroufe and Cooper, 1988, p. 8). Individual development therefore occurs within a range of possible variations. On the other hand, individual development involves the element of uniqueness, the distinctiveness that every person possesses that separates him or her from every other person with respect to such things as temperament, behavioral capacities, or put most broadly, personality. Such uniqueness concerns the issue of individual differences.

Development also involves age, which most appropriately viewed, is the amount of time one has been alive (see again Sroufe and Cooper's definition of development as involving "age-related changes," page 13 above). Although time and developmental change are related, the relationship is not perfect. We cannot precisely predict any person's developmental level knowing only her age. Furthermore, the importance and relationship of age to development depends on one's point of view. *Stage theories* (such as Piaget's) see development as heavily based on maturational processes, which are processes that are primarily controlled biologically or genetically. Dworetzky (1987) defines maturation as "a genetically determined biological plan of development, one relatively independent of experience" (p. 101). Maturation, in turn, is age-related because, like age, it occurs over time. In contrast to the stage viewpoint, the environmentalist perspective does not believe age is especially relevant to development. For the environmentalist, age serves mostly as a convenient way of marking points in the life span where change has occurred.

The role of age in understanding development is like the role of a stopwatch in timing a sprinter. As the runner moves along the track, the watch can indicate how long he took to run a certain distance. There is a relationship between the speed at which he runs and how much distance he covers in a specific amount of time. This is like the relationship between a child's developmental level (where he is on the "track") and how long he has been alive ("running"). The watch cannot explain why the runner is as fast as he is; it can only mark how long it took him to get to a certain point. This is worth keeping in mind as you observe children of various ages, lest you be tempted to think that Susan behaves as she does *because* she is three. Bear in mind, however, that there are behaviors, characteristics, and developmental patterns that children of particular ages tend to share with one another. If this were not so, norms would not be possible. The point here is that age, in and of itself, does not explain development or behavior.

In spite of its limitations, age can be a useful estimator of where any given individual is likely to be with respect to various areas of development (intellectual, social, emotional, physical). This notion of average gives us what psychologists call *norms,* an important but sometimes misused concept and body of information about the growth and developmental patterns of humans. Norms are what Richard Lerner (1976) calls "statements about when in people's lives a particular behavior is typically seen. . . ." James W. Vander Zanden (1989) defines norms as "standards for evaluating a child's developmental progress relative to the average of the child's age group" (p. 176). Vander Zanden's use of "average," best allows us to think in terms of a large number of individuals, in which case age is most meaningfully viewed as an estimator of the developmental characteristics likely to be possessed by most of the persons in any given group.

Growth is easier to understand than development. This manual uses the term growth to mean changes in size or number, which are *quantitative* changes. Physical growth is the simplest kind of quantitative change to recognize and measure. A child becomes taller, heavier, and larger in circumference. These changes represent increases in the amount of bone and muscle tissue. Guy R. Lefrancois (1992) offers a good definition of growth, which, he says, "ordinarily refers to physical changes, which are primarily quantitative because they involve addition rather than *transformation*" (p. 8; italics added). The term "transformation" will be discussed in more detail later on in this chapter.

Explanation or Interpretation

The concept and study of development can be quite complex. This is especially true when one tries to explain (or interpret) development and answer questions such as, "How does development occur?" Even though explanation is not always easy, it is an essential activity and one of the major goals of the empirical sciences. Explanation is part of observation. Even the simplest descriptions involve putting information into some kind of conceptual framework. Consequently, description, pure and simple, is virtually impossible. By merely describing a behavior, one has already begun the process of interpretation, of putting new facts into a relationship with other facts already known or understood. Because of its importance, time and space will be devoted to some perspectives on interpretation and its relation to observing and understanding children.

Some Definitions and Conceptions of Explanation: *Explanation* is defined as "The act of explaining; making clear or understandable; . . . interpretation." *Explain* is defined as "To make plain or understandable; to clear of obscurity; to make clear or evident; . . . to give or show the meaning or reason for" (Webster 1981).

In addition to Webster's definition, there is a conception of explanation that is especially relevant to the basic theme of this manual. It is a conception proposed by Don Ihde (1977) who says that "explanation is any sort of theory, idea, concept . . . that attempts to go *behind* phenomena, to give the reasons for it in terms other than what appears" (italics in original).

Although it may be a bit confusing at this point, Ihde's conception of explanation gets at the heart of what is involved in observing and explaining behavior and developmental change. How is this so, and what bearing does it have on your observations?

Observation is the cornerstone of the empirical sciences, which are those that rely on the physical senses to take in relevant data and measure that data in some way. Science also goes one step further. It tries to find a relationship among the data it acquires. It is not enough simply to gather information; one must try to see how the facts science acquires fit into a broader theoretical framework. Indeed, as Brandt (1972) puts it, "Observational data possess little meaning by themselves. They allow only inferences to be made about people on the basis of their behavior." Theories provide scientists with the means to make such inferences. What a scientist (or parent or teacher) first requires are data; and data frequently are in the form of descriptions. Descriptions are a central part of your observation exercises. In addition to simply describing, you will try to interpret or explain, i.e., give a meaning to what you have seen and described. How will you do that? One way is by looking at your descriptive data through a particular theoretical perspective, which will, in a sense, "tell you" what meaning could be put on what you have observed. But, (and this is an important "but") that meaning, that explanation suggested by the theory, goes behind the phenomenon and is not itself experienced. You have supplied the meaning, but you have not experienced the meaning in the same way you have experienced the observed behavior, event or object. In fact, your observed and objectively described data are connected to your explanation by an abstract conceptual framework, possibly a theory or your own personal beliefs.

Let us look at a simple example of how Idhe's notion of explanation might work. The example is given only to illustrate Idhe's concept of explanation; in a real situation, you would want a much larger and more representative sample of behavior before drawing any final conclusions. You are observing a group of four-year-olds playing outside on a playground, and the following is an example of your objective behavioral description.

> Samuel walks over to Tommy, who is driving a truck around the sandbox on a road he's made by putting blocks of wood in the sand. "Can I play with you?" "OK," says Tommy, "but *I'm* the boss. This is *my* construction company, and you work for me!" Samuel nods affirmatively and asks, "Wha d'ye want me to do, boss?"

You have *seen* Samuel approach Tommy at the sandbox; you have *seen* Tommy playing with a truck in the sand; you have *heard* their brief verbal exchanges. You could have described more than what is given in the example; but even this extremely small amount of information raises questions: What might this behavior signify? What meaning does it have beyond its mere occurrence? Now you are faced with that "something that is not itself experienced." You might offer one of several explanations or interpretations of the two boys' behavior and interaction. Suppose you knew that Tommy's father owns a construction company. You could tentatively interpret Tommy's actions toward his play materials and toward Samuel as an indication of *imitation* or *identification* with his father. Tommy pretends to have some of his father's characteristics and behavior—he is the boss; he tells people what to do; and he behaves in an authoritative manner. In such an explanation, you would rely on a historical perspective— Tommy's family background—and would apply to it the psychological concepts of imitation and identification. You could also argue that Tommy is engaging in *anticipatory socialization,* which involves practicing some of the behaviors, values, and attitudes that are part of the adult role Tommy imagines himself filling when he grows up. You could see Samuel as a follower or as emotionally dependent on Tommy in this particular interaction. There are other ways you could explain or interpret Tommy's and Samuel's behavior. Whatever they might be, however, they would not be visible, hearable, touchable, tasteable, or smellable.

This is what is meant by an explanation giving reasons for something in terms of other than what appears. What appears are the things you saw and heard take place between Tommy and Samuel. The "other than what appears" are the abstract ideas you used to explain what occurred—the ideas of identification, imitation, anticipatory socialization, and emotional dependency. You have not, however, experienced identification. You have experienced some small portion of Tommy's behavior that, to you, indicated a particular psychological process. This general idea cannot be stressed too much. The sense we make of our world—at whatever level of sophistication—is formed through inferences that are founded on any number of factors or variables.

Each of us brings to any situation our own personalities, experiences, and even personal theories about how the world operates. What we observe is filtered or processed through our theories and beliefs, and we draw conclusions based on what gets through the filter. Each of us notices different information (stimuli, events) because each of us is sensitive to different aspects of our environment. As one writer states it, "Observation is based on attention and attention is *ipso facto* (by the fact itself) selective" (Brandt 1972, italics in original). For example, an architect is likely to notice design, style, and construction features of a building that go unnoticed by others. Furthermore, each of us may place a different meaning and value on what we have experienced or observed. The architect may see an old building with a rich and interesting history, whereas a land developer may see an old shack that has to be torn down to make room for a new shopping mall.

The very real possibility that observers will hold different perspectives justifies, if not demands, the gathering of different viewpoints before making judgments or decisions about a child. This will help to reduce the undesirable effects of bias, although bias itself cannot be eliminated.

Some biases and perspectives are personal, and none of us can completely escape or avoid them; for that reason, they are important. If you place a high value on neatness, for example, you should be alert to the presence and potential influence of this value when you observe children who do not fit your idea of how children should look when they come to school. There are other biases or perspectives that are directly related to the observation situation or are formalized as theories or philosophies.

The theory type of bias or perspective is of some concern in this manual. Our intention ultimately is to have you bring together your knowledge of developmental theories and your observation skills, so that you can look at, describe, and interpret various aspects of children's behavior in ways that suit your particular purposes. To accomplish this goal, you must be familiar with the concept of development, some of its general characteristics, and the differing ways psychologists and theories view these characteristics.

Levels of Explanation: Mussen, Conger, and Kagan (1979) identify several levels of explanation. You can explain or interpret a child's behavior in terms of immediate circumstances. For example, Johnny leaves the big block area after his playmate Billy pushes him and says, "Go 'way, I don't wanna play with you anymore!" Johnny's leaving is a response to a present stimulus that immediately preceded his leaving the block area. This level of explanation is common, because we all react to the demands the environment makes on us at any given moment.

The second level of explanation goes behind the present situation to deal with historical reasons. Another child might have responded differently to Billy's command to "go 'way," perhaps telling Billy he should go away or even striking out at him. Johnny's reaction has an explanation that lies somewhere in his past experiences. His parents may have taught him that he should respond to aggression by walking away; or maybe in his past encounters with aggressive children, Johnny lost fights or arguments, and so he avoids those situations. This level of explanation perhaps is relevant to Sroufe and Cooper's second factor required to explain developmental change, namely that present development is dependent on the development that has already occurred. In turn, future development is dependent on present development, and so on.

Mussen and his colleagues point out, however, that neither of these reasons explains the "purpose of the child's behavior." For purpose, we must look at the adaptive reason for the behavior: How does the behavior help the child to function within his physical-social setting or within the limits of his own personality and temperament? In the case of Johnny and Billy, there could be a number of adaptive reasons for Johnny's walking away. He might want to avoid the guilt he would feel if he violated his parents' or teacher's admonitions not to fight; he might want to avoid being punished by his parents or his teacher for fighting; or he might be afraid to fight, because in the past, he had been hurt by other children and wants to avoid being hurt again.

The last level of explanation offers reasons on an *evolutionary* basis. Evolutionary reasons are concerned with how we have come to be what we are, as a species, and why we exhibit some of the behaviors that we do in particular circumstances. Mussen *et al.* give the informative example of a human baby crying when punished, in contrast to monkey babies, which tend "to cower and assume a submissive posture when punished by their parents." The differences in the two species' behavior, say Mussen *et al.,* lie in genetic forces that operated during the evolution of our respective species.

Characteristics of Development

To say that development is change over time is not to say that just any old change counts. As Vimala Pillari (1988), a social worker, points out, "An accident in a house can bring about changes in people's lives, but these are nondevelopmental changes: random, unorganized, and unsystematic" (p. 3). Pillari also calls nondevelopmental changes *nonnormative life events* (p. 3), by which she apparently means those events that are not expected or for which one is not prepared. She includes such things as the death of a young child or even a "sudden financial inheritance" (p. 3) among these nonnormative life events. Psychologists believe that developmental change has certain special characteristics. The picture is made more complicated by the fact that psychologists themselves differ as to how to define or describe development or as to what characteristics or features it must possess. These disagreements result in a variety of theories and perspectives on development and behavior, as well as in a variety of opinions regarding how best to explain them. Because this manual tries to present varying points of view of the developmental process, some of the basic issues associated with the concept of development are presented now.

Development as a Continuous Phenomenon: Let us begin with the belief that developmental change takes place throughout the life cycle. Physical growth seems to stop, of course, and further change in size is more the case of putting on or taking off weight than it is the continuation of physical growth as a process. As Craig (1989) puts it, "Any single structure or capability usually has its point of optimal maturity. *Growth* usually refers to the increase in size, function, or complexity to that point of maturity" (p. 8; italics in original). Many psychologists agree, however, that we do continue to develop socially, emotionally, intellectually, and so on, until we die. This view was expressed earlier in this chapter when we cited Sroufe and Cooper's (1988) assertion that developmental theories essentially agree that there is a continuity to development, although such continuity operates against a background of ongoing developmental change. This agreement regarding the continuous aspect of development occurs despite the fact that various theories take different perspectives or approaches. Some focus on innate or inherited characteristics, whereas others focus on environmental experiences. Still others argue for the interaction between heredity and environment.

Whatever view you take, continuity explains why it is that certain characteristics possessed at one stage in life are likely to be present at later stages, even though developmental changes have occurred that in other respects make the individual different from what she was before. Shyness, for instance, is a characteristic that tends to show continuity from one developmental period to another, perhaps even persisting through adulthood.

Qualitative vs. Quantitative Change: "Qualitative" and "quantitative change" are important concepts. As Lawrence Schiamberg claims (1985) "the study of human development emphasizes two types of change in human beings over time: *quantitative* change and *qualitative* change" (p. 5; italics original). The term "quantitative" is often used when talking about physical growth, where it is the quantity or amount of something measurable—such as height or weight—that changes with maturation. Growth changes can also include such other things as "number of years of education and size of family" (Schiamberg, 1985, p. 5). Qualitative change, on the other hand, often refers to changes in psychological functions, such as speech, emotions, and intelligence. Here, there is not the adding on process that characterizes quantitative change. In qualitative change, the basic nature or organization of the child's behaviors and behavior patterns changes. For instance, speaking in three- to four-word sentences is not just more of the child's earlier cooing or babbling; nor is solving relatively complex arithmetic problems simply more of the earlier ability to match up one set of objects with another set to get the same number. In attaining these higher-level skills or capacities, it is believed that some kind of reorganization or basic modification has occurred in the way the child thinks, the way she perceives and reasons about the world. Piaget called such a reorganization a change in the child's cognitive structure. Lefrancois (1992), you will recall (see pages 15-16 above), defined growth as a process of addition rather than a process of transformation. Transformation is here equivalent to the idea of reorganization. Addition and transformation, therefore, address respectively the difference between quantitative and qualitative change. Jerome Kagan (1971) described quantitative and qualitative change like this: "The phenomena of growth fall into two patterns: enlargement and change. The leaf expands as it grows, but it does not alter its essential form. The butterfly, on the other hand, passes through dramatically different stages en route to adulthood." The leaf exemplifies quantitative change; the butterfly, qualitative change.

The Cumulative and Directional Aspects of Developmental Change: Although some psychologists believe that development leads to behaviors that are qualitatively different from earlier behaviors, they do not say that later behavior patterns have no connection with earlier ones. Some believe quite the opposite: Every stage or behavior within a stage builds on what has gone before, and it forms the foundation for what is yet to come. In more technical language, development is said to be cumulative. This characteristic is one of the three factors that Sroufe and Cooper (1988) say are needed to explain how development takes place (see page 13 above). In this view, all developmental change contributes to the essentially forward direction of the developmental process. The idea of a "forward direction" to development apparently can involve at least two ideas or approaches: One can ask whether development leads to some "ideal goal" or "most mature level of functioning" (Mussen, Conger, and Kagan, 1974, p. 34). Or one can more simply define "directional" as meaning that "development can always move toward greater complexity" (Sroufe and Cooper, 1988, p. 7), a concept we shall discuss below (see p. 17).

Not all psychologists believe that development moves toward some ideal goal. As Mussen, *et al.* (1974) point out, "Learning theorists do not assume that the child is necessarily traveling in any special direction, even though his behavior is changing every day." In this context, behavior and development lead to the ability to survive in an environment—to adapt to the demands of a particular physical and psychological environment. Piaget, on the other hand, thought of the individual as progressing toward a state of developmental maturity characterized by certain mental abilities such as the ability to reason and deduce logical conclusions. What is relevant to your observations is the question of how you will interpret differences among children of various ages, as well as differences that a given child will exhibit in his behavior. Will differences and changes be most meaningfully explained as quantitative or as qualitative ones? Will you see the child as progressing toward some optimum goal or end state of development in which all behav-

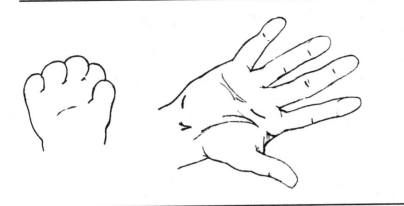

Figure 2-1 The change from this fetal hand to a fully-formed hand is an example of differentiation.

iors build onto one another and ultimately contribute to the child's reaching that optimum goal? Or will you see the child as changing because of the continual learning of responses, but which do not necessarily lead to any particular goal or developmental objective?

Complexity, Differentiation, and Hierarchical Integration: There is another characteristic of development that most psychologists would agree on regardless of their theoretical orientations: Development, as a reflection or manifestation of its "directional" aspect, results in increasing complexity in organization and functioning. As a child gets older and more mature, his behavior, emotions, motives, abilities, and language become more sophisticated and refined, not less so. This increase in complexity is partly the result of the child's learning how to do more things, but there is something else. The child's knowledge and abilities increasingly form a unified, integrated whole. Psychologists speak of differentiation and hierarchic integration when referring to this movement toward complexity. *Differentiation* means that behaviors that initially are expressed in a diffuse way, eventually separate out and become more skilled, more specific, and more independent of one another. "More specific" means that previously unspecialized body parts and responses become specialized; they take on particular functions or play particular roles. For example, the very young infant exhibits seemingly random muscle movements; she moves almost her entire body when responding to even a specific, focused stimulus such as a pin prick to the foot. Later on, however, she is able to move just her foot, thus indicating that body movements and muscle groups have become differentiated and capable of responding more precisely to specific stimuli.

    Hierarchic integration takes place when the child can combine various skills, behaviors or movements and have them work together as a harmonious unit. Thus, finger movements become differentiated from larger arm movements, and although each type of movement can serve a different purpose and be brought into play independently of the other, the arms and fingers can also work together as an integrated unit. This coordination permits the child to reach for and grasp an object. Reaching and grasping generally also involve visual functioning, which illustrates even greater integration. As another example, the child initially differentiates single words as she acquires a speaking and listening vocabulary; eventually, she combines those words into complex, grammatically correct sentences. With this integration, he can express increasingly more complex thoughts and ideas.

Developmental change is also thought by some to occur sequentially and in an orderly, lawful fashion. It is not haphazard or random in its course. Stage theory best depicts development as a sequential, orderly movement. Development is seen as occurring in a stair-like manner; the general timing, rate, and order of the stages are determined by genetic or maturational factors. Piaget's theory, for example, maintains that there are four such steps: (1) the sensorimotor, (2) the preoperational, (3) the concrete operational, and (4) the formal operational stages, in that order. Freud and Erikson also proposed stage theories, but with different content. The sequential nature of development also imposes several restrictions on how change can occur:

a. The various stages or steps cannot be skipped—the child cannot go from the sensorimotor stage to the concrete operational stage, for instance.
b. Their essential order cannot be disturbed—the child cannot go from the sensorimotor stage to the concrete operational stage, and then go back to "pick up" the preoperational stage.
c. The order of the stages as well as their content are universal—they are found in children everywhere regardless of their social or cultural backgrounds.

These restrictions, by the way, appropriately fall under the universal aspect of development as proposed by Sroufe and Cooper (1988) and Mussen et al. (1984).

The limitation on the order that stages must follow does not account for the fact that not all children progress equally far through all the stages. Not everyone reaches Piaget's final stage of formal operations, for example, which could be the result of individual differences, a particular gentic inheritance, or we suppose, situational factors.

One important feature of stage theories is that they allow us to recognize certain principles or laws by which change can be described, explained, and predicted. It is the orderliness and predictability of change—within certain limits—that help make possible the scientific study of children.

Perhaps the most evident sequences that take place in a child over time are those that describe physical-motor development. The sequences in which motor abilities emerge have been designated as *principles,* which means that they operate predictably in all children in all cultures. The *cephalocaudal principle* (head-to-tail) of motor development says that the child first gains control over the movements of his head and neck (lifting

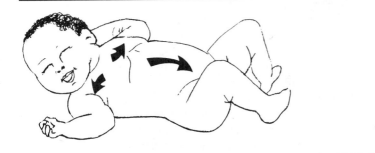

Figure 2-2 Physical-motor development occurs along cephalocaudal (head to tail) and proximodistal (center-to-edge) principles.

the head up off the mattress, for example), whereas control over foot movements comes last. A second principle, the *proximodistal principle,* says that the child first gains control over those body parts closest to the body's midline—the shoulders, upper arms, and chest; then he gains control over the more distant parts such as the fingers. These sequences also describe a pattern that progresses from gross (large) muscle control to fine (small) muscle control. This genetically preprogrammed sequence of motor skills can be observed as the child accomplishes the milestones in motor development depicted in Table 2-1.

Heredity-Environment Controversy (Nature vs. Nurture Issue): The nature-nurture debate centers around the question of what is the primary source or cause of developmental change. There are typically three answers or perspectives to this question:

1. Developmental change comes from genetically determined processes of *maturation,* which are those changes that are "built into" the individual and unfold naturally and sequentially with the passage of time. This view, representing the *nature* side, is Arnold Gesell's maturationist theory of development;
2. Developmental change is caused by experiences (stimuli) that come from the external environment; the child responds to these stimuli, and he learns according to the principles of reinforcement. This view is represented by learning theory, or what is also referred to as the environmentalist or behaviorist view. This is the *nurture* side of the issue.
3. That the source of developmental change comes from the *interaction* between the environment and the forces of maturation. This view is represented by Piaget's, Freud's and Erikson's theories.

These perspectives, by the way, are parts of much broader *philosophies* of human development: the maturational model, the mechanistic model, and the organismic model. Other models such as the psychoanalytic and the humanistic are available as perspectives of human development.

Table 2-2   Milestones in Motor Development

AGE	MOTOR	EYE-HAND
Three months	Lifts head and chest while lying on stomach. Sits with support.	Grasps objects, briefly holds them, brings to mouth.
Six months	Holds head steady while sitting; combination of sitting with some support and short periods without support.	Uses thumb with skill.
Nine months	Complete head control. Good trunk control; sits alone. Crawling motions appear (early as 7 months).	Shows some handedness; hand activities coordinated with each other.
Twelve months	Sits from standing position. Creeps (9-10 months) on hands and knees. Stands while holding on, walks when held; pulls self up to standing position.	Handedness distinct. Holds crayon, makes lines.
Fifteen months	Stands alone and starts walking alone.	
Eighteen months	Starts to run.	

Adapted from Travers (1982, p. 125)

As Berger (1991) so aptly points out, "whether it is nature or nurture that yields the greater impact, the implications [of the answer] are significant" (p. 11). She goes on to describe some of the potential consequences of taking one or the other side of this issue. For instance, math aptitude appears to be roughly equal in boys and girls in elementary school, but at about eighth grade, boys on average, begin to perform at higher levels than girls. Berger asks whether this discrepancy is the result of maturation or of differences in experience. She argues that if the seeming difference in math performance is the result of genetically related differences in fundamental ability, then it would be foolish and frustrating to push young women to do as well in math as men. On the other hand, if such differences are the result of learning or socialization, then "precious mathematical talent" would be wasted "by not encouraging girls to develop their full math potential" (Berger, 1991, p. 11).

Development as Sequential in Nature—The Continuity vs. Discontinuity Issue: We have already discussed the term "continuity" as one of the characteristics of development. In that discussion, however, continuity meant *stability over time;* the persistence of certain traits from one stage or period of developmental change to another; or the fact that development is considered to occur throughout the entire life span, with any given level of development being dependent on, or partly a function of, whatever development has occurred up to the present moment.

In the continuity vs. discontinuity issue, a different meaning is needed. Here, continuity refers to a more or less gradual growth or developmental progression, where what seems to be an abrupt change—a baby's first step—is actually not abrupt at all, but is, as Berger (1991) puts it, "the final event in weeks of growth and practice" (p. 12). Incidentally, continuity is frequently associated with the concept of quantitative change, which again, is change characterized by gradual increments or additions to some trait, ability, or physical structure. Continuous (and quantitative) change is sometimes represented by a line such as that in Figure 2-1.

Discontinuity, in contrast, proposes the emergence of identifiable stages, with each stage showing qualitative differences from all previous stages. Thus, discontinuity is linked with qualitative change in a manner parallel with the link between continuity and quantitative change mentioned above. "Milestone" events, such as taking a first step or learning to talk, are considered the beginning of a new stage. It's critical to understand that in the discontinuity view of development, walking and talking are *not* just more of the earlier crawling or creeping and cooing and babbling stages. Instead, these new capacities are the result of the transformation, reorganization, or restructuring brought about by the interaction of maturation and experience. Furthermore, new potentials for behavior are opened up as a consequence of such reorganization. The discontinuity view of development, which is a stage-oriented view, is often represented by Figure 2-2.

In an earlier publication, Stone and Church (1979) also dealt with this issue, but within the context of the question "How does one describe behavioral changes—what terms does one use—and how detailed are those descriptions?" Although the term 'development' seems to imply that all individuals undergo the same changes, there are individual differences in the way change occurs and expresses itself. Everyone changes, and some aspects of change are shared by all human beings. Stone and Church (1979) refer to development as "changes in the structure and properties of behavior which take place in the course of a lifetime." Changes in the "structure and properties of behavior" involve some common and basic occurrences. For example, all "normal" children eventually walk, talk, control their bodily functions, learn to solve problems and make decisions, acquire a self-concept, and so on. As Stone and Church (1979) point out, however, ". . . no two people's lives follow the same course, even though there are some common features to be found in the life histories of almost everybody."

Development is the result of such factors as each person's unique personal characteristics (intelligence, attitudes, personality traits, health, temperament), family characteristics (size, parental discipline and rearing techniques, socioeconomic status), and the events that take place in her life. As Stone and Church indicate, each individual reaches maturity partly in his own way; what we all have in common is our humanity, and it is our humanity that provides developmental change with the common characteristics it possesses.

There are some variations in the viewpoints regarding description and individual differences. For the behaviorist (mechanistic or environmentalist model), change is described as the acquisition of a new association, a new connection between a stimulus, a response, and the consequences of that response. For example, if six-month-old Roberta smiles at her mother during meal time, and if that smile brings a pleasant reaction from her mother, Roberta is more likely to smile again during meal time. Roberta will have acquired what is called a *stimulus-response bond.* At some point, Roberta may smile at other persons and in other situations; if smiling again leads to positive reinforcement another link will have been added to the learning chain. Those who believe the learning theory point of view believe that learning, and therefore development, is a matter of accumulating more and more of these new connections or stimulus-response bonds. According to the learning theory perspective, individual differences are quite easy to account for: different children have different experiences, different sets of associations, and different learning histories.

Those who support the interactionist (Piagetian, cognitive) perspective claim that one must describe development and its accompanying behavior "in great detail," and must "demonstrate how it (the behavior) differs from what was present before, and try to infer the change in mental mechanisms leading to the change in behavior" (Mussen *et al.,* 1979). "Change in mental mechanisms" involves qualitative change. From the stage theory or interactionist perspective, differences between individuals are accounted for in several ways. "The Piagetian view, insofar as it addresses the issue, can only explain individual differences in terms of exposure or nonexposure to the conditions that will permit maturational possibilities to fulfill themselves" (Mussen, *et al.*). According to Piaget, cognitive development depends on the biological process of maturation together with the amount and kinds of stimulation and experiences needed to grow intellectually and cognitively. A deprived environment may stifle cognitive development; but inadequate genetic potential can have the same effect. A somewhat different position is reported by Richard Lerner (1976), who states that according to stage theory, people may differ from one another in only two ways: (1) in the *rate* or speed at which they progress through the various developmental stages, or (2) in the final level of development attained. Thus, individuals can differ in how fast they develop or in how far they develop. Not all children take two years to get through Piaget's sensorimotor stage, for example; nor does everyone reach the period of formal operations, Piaget's final stage of cognitive development.

The above discussion can put individual differences and universal patterns of development into something of an adversarial relationship, although it is not one that will unduly concern us. We bring it to your attention so that you can at least observe children and possibly draw conclusions based on the assumption of individual differences within the broader framework of universal patterns.

Activity vs. Passivity in Development—Which Role Does the Child Play?: Are children active or passive during their development? Is the child an active participant in her own development, or does she, sponge-like, simply "soak up" stimulation and experiences from the external environment? The distinction is crucial, especially when one is considering the education and socialization of children. The environmentalist point of view sees the child as essentially passive. According to this theory, it is the environment, and how it is arranged with regard to reinforcements, that produces learning and, therefore, development. Put another way, the child (and adult) is a reactor to environmental stimuli and depends a great deal on the consequences of those reactions.

In contrast, for stage theorists such as Piaget, ". . . humans spontaneously initiate their actions; they play a constructive role in their own psychological experience and development" (Langer, 1969). Humans are therefore actors who seek stimulation. Again, it is the contributions of both heredity and environment that result in developmental change. One of the contributions of heredity is to preprogram humans to initiate interactions with their surroundings.

Deficit or Difference?: Kathleen Berger's (1991) "deficit or difference" issue is an interesting one. She asks "Is there one pattern of human development that is the usual or normal one? Or are there as many paths of development as there are individuals" (p. 13). She notes that the idea of "one universal pattern [of development] was held by many of the first scientists interested in development" (p. 13). The concept of norms came out of the early studies that were based on this belief in universal development.

But Berger (1991) points out that the idea of universality is being questioned by another perspective. She writes that

> differences have increasingly come to be seen as alternative paths of development rather than inferior ones . . . Contemporary developmentalists are much more likely to recognize the unique characteristics of each child, each family, each culture, than they are to stress the universal generalities that apply to all of them. (p. 13)

Stone and Church (1984) said much the same thing as Berger in this regard. Following a discussion of continuity and regularity in development, they state that

Figure 2-3 Children need stimulation to grow intellectually and cognitively. (Reprinted from Machado, Early Childhood Experiences in Language Arts, figure 9-3)

> What we are saying is that our account of development must acknowledge the common path of human development, yet still recognize that there are many different ways of becoming human. (p. 6)

This is evidenced by the different beliefs psychologists hold about development. Even the developmental changes we observe in real children are not always readily understood or unambiguous, particularly when we compare children with one another and find sometimes marked, and sometimes subtle, differences among them.

This is not to say that there are no predictable aspects to developmental change. Psychology has discovered principles and regularities that govern and define growth and development in particular areas of functioning (recall, for example, the discussion of the principles of motor development). [But] such regularities notwithstanding, what you observe, and the sense you make out of your observations, are influenced by the various issues that have been discussed. For example, do you believe children are active participants in their own development, or passive reactors to environmental stimuli? Do you conceive of change as the adding on of more and more stimulus-response associations, or as the progressive acquisition of qualitatively different abilities? You can supply additional questions.

An important point here is that these differences in beliefs have a strong influence on what you "see." But perhaps even more important, they have an influence on what you do to, with, or for children.

Egocentrism and Autonomy: Salkind (1981) notes that development and maturation result in a lessening of *egocentrism*. This is an important concept in Piaget's theory. Egocentrism is the young child's inability to view the world from perspectives other than her own. As Papalia and Olds (1993) put it, egocentrism "*is a form of centration: these children are so centered on their own points of view that they cannot take another's view at the same time*" (p. 303). Childhood egocentrism, as proposed by Piaget, is not the same as egotism or selfishness. It is often applied to adults who are unwilling (rather than unable) to take another person's point of view. Instead, egocentrism is a "limitation of thought, something preventing children from imaginatively stepping outside themselves and seeing from a different viewpoint" (Papalia and Olds, 1987, p. 281). Egocentrism can be demonstrated in many ways. A three-year-old, for example, begins to tell you about what happened to her before she came to school that morning. In her story, she mentions names of people you do not know and have never heard of. The child does not realize that "Billy" has no meaning for you; she does not bother to explain who Billy is so you can follow her tale of adventure. As the child matures, she becomes less egocentric and more *sociocentric* or capable of seeing the world from different points of view. You should note here that childhood egocentrism, as proposed by Piaget, is not the same as egotism, which is often applied to adults who are unwilling (rather than unable) to take another person's point of view.

The second trend noted by Salkind is the *development of social autonomy.* This refers to the child's increasing independence and ability to rely on himself for the satisfaction of various needs and desires. In short, the child becomes more self-sufficient. This aspect of change and of children's behavior will certainly be a noticeable one, especially as you observe children through various periods in the life span.

Three Controversies or Recurring Themes

Discussion of the remaining characteristics of development will take a slightly different track from that taken with the preceding material. Following such writers as Berger (1991) and Lefrancois (1986, 1987), among others, we shall identify the developmental characteristics to be presented as basic issues or themes in developmental psychology. Berger (1986) deals with two traditional issues and adds a third that perhaps is not as well known as the other two. She phrases these issues as questions: Nature or Nurture?, Continuity or Discontinuity?, and Deficit or Difference? (pp. 10-16). Lefrancois (1992) refers to "recurring questions" (pp. 24-25), which he

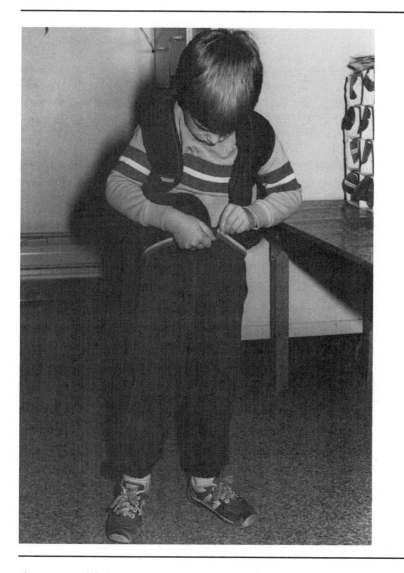

Figure 2-4 Self-help behavior (Photo by Karen Norton)

identifies as the "nature-nurture controversy"; the question ". . . is development a continuous, relatively uninterrupted process or does it consists of separate stages"; and "is it best to view children as an active, exploring organism . . . [or as] a more passive recipient" (pp. 24-25).

Some of the following discussion should be familiar to you. We have already touched on such topics as stage theory, the environmentalist perspective, and maturation. Now, we re-present some of these issues within the broader context of "controversy" or "recurring questions."

Summary

In this chapter, we have discussed some of the conceptual and theoretical characteristics of development; characteristics that vary, depending on which theory or viewpoint one is using. Development is not a simple, straightforward concept with consistent, uniform properties. This is evidenced by the different beliefs psychologists hold about development. Even the developmental changes we observe in real children are not always readily understood or unambiguous, particularly when we compare children with one another and find sometimes marked, and sometimes subtle, differences among them.

This is not to say that there are no predictable aspects to developmental change. Psychology has discovered principles and regularities that govern and define growth and development in particular areas of functioning (recall the discussion of the principles of motor development, for example). Such regularities notwithstanding, what you observe, and the sense you make out of your observations, are influenced by the various issues that have been discussed. For example, do you believe children are active participants in their own development, or passive reactors to environmental stimuli? Do you conceive of change as the adding on of more and more stimulus-response associations, or as the progressive acquisition of qualitatively different abilities? You can supply additional questions.

An important point here is that these differences in beliefs have a strong influence on what you "see." Perhaps even more important, they have an influence on what you do to, with, or for children.

Study Questions

1. What is a major difference between growth and development? Do you think the difference is an important one with regard to observing and understanding children? Why or why not?
2. Mussen and his colleagues identified four levels of explanation: immediate, historical, adaptive, and evolutionary. Describe three imaginary observation situations where the first three levels of explanation might be used to understand or explain a child's behavior.
3. Describe in your own words what is meant by the statement that explanation attempts to go *behind* a phenomenon. What does this statement have to do with observing and interpreting children's behavior?
4. A teacher believes that children are passive with respect to their development; another teacher believes they are active. What differences might you observe in the respective classrooms of these two teachers? What kinds of interactions might take place in the two contexts?
5. Of the two concepts, individual differences and universal patterns of development, which one do you think would be easier to base conclusions on after observing some children's behavior?

chapter three
General Guidelines
for Observing Children

Objectives

After studying this chapter, you will be able to

- discuss the steps that must be taken to prepare to observe
- discuss the role of inconspicuousness in observing children
- analyze the role of professional ethics in observation
- identify factors that affect observation
- discuss the three categories of errors in observation
- discuss the three aspects that affect the accuracy and reliability of observation
- analyze the potential dangers of evaluating the worth of children's behavior
- distinguish several kinds of groups
- discuss several approaches to group observation

The following guidelines provide a framework within which you can formulate your own thinking and behavior for various observation situations.

Preparation for Observing

Preparation involves several organizational steps that must be taken before you enter the observation setting.

What Are Your Purposes?: There are many reasons to observe children. You should have yours clearly in mind as you approach your exercises. Identifying your objectives is a central task, because everything else depends on it. Objectives must be defined precisely enough to bring the observational activity down to a manageable size. Brandt (1972) confirms the importance of this issue when he points out that the sheer complexity of behavior in naturalistic settings "makes it virtually impossible to study all significant factors at one time." He goes on to note that the task of the observer ("investigator") is not one of studying the total "complex of activity" in a given setting, but rather "one of isolating and then studying the most important components of that complex." Brandt's advice relates to the statement made in Chapter One—scientific observation is not merely looking *at* something; it is looking *for* something.

Figure 3-1 Teachers observe for various reasons. What might this teacher's observational goals be?

Observational objectives are numerous. An objective might be to gain experience in observing children of various ages. Gaining experience in observing children, on the other hand, ultimately can serve further purposes that are more specific and sharply defined. Learning how children behave in particular situations, and why they behave as they do, is such a purpose. Such information could be used to change the equipment and materials in a classroom, or to change the arrangement of the equipment and materials. Modification of seating patterns during story time might be made because of a teacher's observation that certain children, when together, seem to foster arguments or inattentiveness to the teacher. Or, a teacher and her staff may want to assess the effectiveness of their efforts to bring a shy four-year-old out of his "shell" and to encourage him to interact more with the other children. Some observational objectives are not specifically identified beforehand. Nonetheless, as in the above example of children's disruptive behavior during story time, certain behaviors and events are noticed, because a teacher and staff are alert to the general objective of using observation to promote the well-being of the children in their care.

In relation to the exercises in this manual, you have to know why you are in a particular observational setting. What are you supposed to see there? The success of your efforts to see what you are looking for, depends only partly on your knowledge, values, experiences, and skill. Objectives have to be matched with resources, settings, and recording methods. For example, if an exercise calls for observing an infant's reflexes, it would be inappropriate to observe preschoolers. If you are to observe behaviors that occur infrequently, time sampling should not be the method you choose, because time sampling is best used with behaviors that occur often (see Chapter Seven).

Other questions must also be answered before you begin to observe. What developmental area or behaviors are the focus of the observation (social, physical/motor, language)? How much time are you to spend observing those behaviors (an hour, several minutes, for as long as they occur)? Whom are you to observe (individual children, a group, a particular child, several particular children)? How are you to record your observations (check list, duration record, specimen description, time sampling)? What kind of interpretations are you to make (based on a given theory, on what has taken place in the setting)?

Some of these questions are directly related to the specific recording technique you use. Let us look at the question of how long to observe. On the one hand, a time sampling procedure requires observing and recording for intermittent but uniform and relatively short time periods of several seconds or minutes. On the other hand, event sampling calls for observation over longer time periods, the length of which depends on how long the child exhibits the selected behavior.

Where Are You Going to Observe?:   The site of your observations is related to your objectives, and as they change, the site may have to change. If a

Figure 3-2   Observation can take place inside the classroom. (Reprinted from Machado and Meyer, Early Childhood Practicum Guide, figure 12-1)

limited number of facilities is available, the observations, or certain aspects of the observations, will also be limited. Under those conditions, your observations will have to fit the possibilities afforded by the setting. For example, if the only structured environment in which to observe children is one local day-care center that provides care to children from three through five years of age, then you will not be able to observe two-year-olds. Your observation exercises are limited to the children accessible to you and to the characteristics and abilities typical of those age groups. In other cases, you might have access to a number of facilities and opportunities, such as day-care centers, nursery schools, Kindergartens, elementary schools, and public playgrounds, which offer a wide range of ages and environments. Under those conditions, you will have more flexibility. You will need to carefully match observation exercises and purposes with specific settings.

What May You Do in the Setting?:   Knowing why you are in the observation setting includes knowing what you may or may not do there. Some settings may give you considerable leeway to do what is necessary to accomplish your objectives. Others may be more formal and not allow certain behaviors. For example, some preschool teachers may not allow you to sit out of the way just observing and recording; instead, you may be asked to help the children during toilet time, snack time, or when they dress to go out. Some teachers may require you to step outside the classroom to take notes. In those cases, you will have to rely on your memory until you can get to your notebook and record your data. What you may do can be affected by the recording technique you choose. A checklist, for example, would not prevent some participation on your part. A teacher might have fewer objections to in-classroom recording with a brief checklist than with a more elaborate specimen description. You need to learn what is allowed and expected of you as an observer *before* you take on that role. This is made doubly important by the fact that school directors and classroom teachers differ widely in their expectations regarding acceptable behavior.

It is possible that you may experience difficulties in completing some observations because of limitations imposed by the setting. Therefore, if there are other options open to you, you may want to select a more compatible observation setting.

Inconspicuous Observation

Why Be Inconspicuous?:   There is a principle that says that observing a phenomenon changes it. Observing people *can* change their behavior. Their awareness of the observer's presence can distract them or motivate them to behave in ways they believe will please the observer. Behavioral changes brought about by the act of observing are of deep concern to researchers who want to study groups such as gangs, families, or nonindustrialized societies. Such researchers—anthropologists and sociologists, for example —sometimes attempt to minimize these unwanted effects by engaging in what is called *participant observation*. This means that the observer becomes

Figure 3-3 Some schools have observation rooms with one-way windows and counter top desks. (Reprinted from Machado and Meyer, Early Childhood Practicum Guide, figure 18-4)

part of the group and participates in as many of its activities as is appropriate for the circumstances. Teachers are participant observers as a matter of course, and there is little doubt that they are accepted by the children and can observe them without unduly influencing their behavior. It can be quite different in the case of an observer who is not perceived as part of the group or setting, particularly someone who comes and goes. Some believe that eventually, the observer will blend into the group and be accepted, which reduces the impact of being watched by an outsider. One can argue that it is virtually impossible for an observer to mask her reasons for being in the group well enough for the group to forget those reasons. In short, the argument goes, those being watched will always "perform" for the person doing the watching.

There may be some exceptions to this influence. Thorndike and Hagan (1977) write that "the young child has not developed the covers and camouflages to conceal himself from public view as completely as has his older brother and sister, so there is more to be found out by watching him." Inconspicuous observation tries to prevent or minimize unwanted influence on behavior. It remains a debatable point whether being observed continues to have an influence on behavior after the observer has become an accepted member of the group. Anecdotal reports on the issue do indicate that young children adapt well to the presence of strangers.

The Difficulty of Remaining Inconspicuous: Being inconspicuous is not always easy. Any unfamiliar person in the classroom will capture the attention of the children until the novelty has worn off. Sometimes observation booths are available, which allow you to observe without being seen (through the use of two-way mirrors). Their use is based on the assumption that the children do not know there is anyone behind those mirrors, or that if they do know, an unseen observer interferes less with normal behavior than one who is visible. The author's experience has been that children learn all too quickly about the existence of observation booths, as well as whether anyone is inside watching them.

There are additional problems when observation objectives call for recording behaviors that cannot be observed from a distance. Language behavior, for instance, requires you to be close enough to a speaker to hear him. Naturally, getting that close, as well as having to be there with notebook (or if permissible, tape recorder) in hand, brings with it the possibility of calling attention to yourself. Problems can also arise when there is uncertainty concerning whether you should intrude into a situation. This question brings us to another aspect of inconspicuousness.

How and When to be Inconspicuous: In spite of the difficulties mentioned above, reliable and inconspicuous observation is possible within the requirements and limitations of the given situation. In this writer's view, an extremely important part of being inconspicuous is remaining as detached as possible or necessary from the children and their activities. This does not mean you should be cold and aloof, but only that you not try to influence behavior beyond what is required by the observation objectives or beyond what you are permitted to do in the setting. This advice should be followed according to its intent and within its appropriate context. For example, naturalistic (or informal) observation depends on the subjects of study exhibiting behavior spontaneously, and not at the prompting of the observer. There are occasions, however, when children are asked to behave in particular ways, such as in testing situations or formal research studies. In those contexts, the observer has to intrude into the children's environment in a way dictated by the purposes of the study or test. More generally, however, nearly every environment demands some particular behaviors from the individuals in it. Most environments, for example, require individuals to behave in a socially conforming manner. Other kinds of demands are made, too, depending on the purpose and characteristics of the setting. In other words, our actions are almost always structured in some way; they occur within some set of acceptable boundaries. Inconspicuousness can be achieved by not further structuring or affecting children's behavior beyond what is already part of the setting and situation. Consider a brief example.

Suppose you want to observe a child's language behavior. This could require writing down word for word what the child says, to whom she speaks, and any other important circumstances surrounding her use of language. Language is a complex phenomenon, however. One can study just the language itself, that is, such things as vocabulary, sentence structure, and sentence length. One can also examine the conditions under which the child uses language and for what purposes—to ask for help, to give commands, to ask questions, to self-regulate behavior, or to persuade others. All of these are part of language development and usage.

If you are interested, for example, in seeing how Jenine uses speech under naturalistic or non-test conditions, you would have to allow her language to occur on its own. Thus, Jenine might speak very infrequently and not say very much when she does speak. If so, you may be unable to tell much about her language proficiency, but a great deal more about the social and psychological aspects of her speech—the circumstances under which she tends to talk, to whom, to what ends, and so on. What do you do in such a case?

You could remain inconspicuous by accepting Jenine's speech behavior as it naturally occurred. But, if the circumstances warrant it, you could also "test" Jenine by engaging her in a conversation and trying to draw out of her more speech than she had demonstrated up to that point. In such an instance, you would be trying to determine her level of language ability, the level at which she is able to communicate with speech. Here a distinction is made between learning (ability, skill, proficiency) and performance. The distinction is important and useful, for it points out that a child may know how to do something, but may not necessarily exhibit his ability. Most of us know how to hit, for example, but we do not go around hitting; we do not ordinarily demonstrate this skill.

If you test the child in any way, but your objectives do not justify testing, then you have unnecessarily sacrificed inconspicuousness. You have entered into the setting and changed what occurred there. Again, however, merely being present in an observation setting sacrifices some inconspicuousness. Of equal concern is how much freedom you will have to test or interfere in any way with what is going on. In a preschool, for instance, the teacher may not allow you to interact with the children; you may have to be a nonparticipant observer. The freedom issue is directly related to the process of prior preparation. Consequently, how much you are allowed to participate, or how much influence you are allowed to exert, should not take you by surprise. Participation is an aspect of observation that you should always discuss with the person in charge of the setting before you begin to observe.

In summary, think of inconspicuous observation as observation that imposes or introduces nothing into the observation setting, or on the persons and objects in the setting, beyond what is necessary to achieve legitimate objectives. Your objectives must never conflict with the objectives, philosophy or procedures of the preschool, school, or any other location in which you are doing the observing. Nor must your objectives and procedures violate the rights or privileges of any individual or group. There will be some contexts where the restrictions are fewer than those in private facilities. Public places, such as government buildings, playgrounds, and parks, are governed by laws, regulations, and even a philosophy. But these are different from the regulations and philosophies governing child-care facilities, if only because the latter have the specific goals of caring for and fostering the growth, development, physical safety, and psychological security of children.

Figure 3-4 This observer is engaging in "participant observation." By becoming part of the group he has become inconspicuous as an observer.

Some of the above concerns and issues also apply to professional ethics and confidentiality.

Professional Ethics and Confidentiality

Professional ethics and confidentiality are concerns that are inseparable from all observation activities. When you go into a particular place, you are, in some cases, a guest, (such as in a private preschool or a public elementary school). In all cases, you are a representative of your school or institution. Your behavior therefore reflects not only on yourself, but on your school and your department. If you are not a student, you still have obligations to those whom you are observing. You also have obligations to others who might have come before you and laid the groundwork and good will so necessary for observation and research activity. You also have an obligation to anyone who might come after you. One person's improper behavior can spoil it for everyone else.

The Need for Professional Ethics: Research using human subjects is open to intensive scrutiny today. Gone are the times when a researcher is at liberty to do almost anything he wants in the name of science. The rights, safety (physical and psychological), and privacy of the individual are now of extreme importance when conducting research. These restrictions sometimes make the study of human behavior difficult; nonetheless, protection of rights and safety justifies that difficulty and must be preserved. Your observations are, strictly speaking, a form of research; they provide the methods and data for answering research questions. You are trying to learn about children, to understand their behaviors and how they change over time. In doing this, you will ask yourself questions; you will construct a written record of what certain children do in various situations; you will make interpretations, and might even evaluate their behaviors. In short, you are getting information about people, which must always be done with care and sensitivity. Sometimes this information will be potentially embarrassing or could be misused to characterize an individual or group unfavorably, a situation unacceptable under any circumstances. Even positive or seemingly harmless information, however, places the child and her behavior at the focus of attention, and that can cause some parents and teachers discomfort or even alarm. This concern can be partly alleviated by not using the children's real names, thus assuring parents and teachers that your observation reports will not reveal the real identity of any child. This is an assurance that is required by the ethical concern for privacy and confidentiality.

There are other concerns that involve ethics. Parents may feel distressed at the possibility of an outside observer discovering any deficiencies in their child. Parents often compare their child with other children: Does Aletha talk as well as her age mates, her family might ask? Carl's father may ask if he is as coordinated physically as the other children in the preschool—especially the other boys. Renee's mother may express concern about whether

Renee is socially popular, a leader, bright, and so forth. Parents might be touchy about anyone other than the school staff observing and recording their child's behavior and developmental progress. This is especially true if the child has any characteristics that set him apart from others in a way the parents view as unfavorable. Such sensitivity on the parents' part must be matched by your own equal, if not greater, sensitivity. You must protect the child's and the parents' privacy, and you must give careful consideration to their feelings.

There is one guiding principle that is worth mentioning, perhaps because it is so easily and so frequently violated, and because it seems to cover so many situations in which ethics play a part. The principle is this: Do not communicate (talk, write, use nonverbal gestures) about any child to anyone other than the person who gave you permission to observe. ("Anyone" here includes your roommate, your best friend, your parents . . .). Furthermore, if you do discuss a child with some appropriate individual, be certain that the child in question, any of the other children, or any other adult, do not overhear what you say. Remember, when it comes to children, "Little pitchers have big ears."

This principle does not rule out discussing a child privately with an instructor or in a formal classroom setting, when the purpose is to aid your understanding of the child or the observation process, or to solve problems you may be encountering in doing the observations. Such discussions can still be carried on without violating the child's and the parents' rights to privacy and confidentiality.

Privacy, confidentiality, and rights also include the right of parents not to have their child be a subject of observation. Therefore, if any parents do not want their child observed and information about him recorded, you are obligated not to do so. It may be less obvious, but if a child does not want to be observed, the same ethical constraints apply as when parents refuse their child's participation. This leads us to the issue of permission.

Permission extends beyond just the specific target of observation and study. You should not—indeed may not—walk unannounced and uninvited into a classroom to do your exercises. Prior permission is always necessary; at the very least, it is a sign of courtesy and respect for the teachers, staff, and children. In some instances, it can also be a matter of trespassing on private property. Gander and Gardiner (1981) suggest that written permission be obtained when observing in schools. The district supervisor or principal and the teacher can grant such permission. Gander and Gardiner also point out that school officials act in what is called *in loco parentis* ("in place of the parents"), and additional permission from the parents is therefore not necessary.

In situations where adult roles are less clearly defined than they are in the schools (e.g., in clubs, Sunday schools, and similar organizations), Gander and Gardiner recommend that permission (written is safest) be obtained from those in charge and from the parents. If you observe in a public place, such as a park, swimming pool or playground, permission is not necessary. Nonetheless, even public settings require that you be unobtrusive; you are not permitted to disturb others, to try to get children to perform for you, or in any way to violate the rights of others in the setting. It is further suggested that, in a public place, if you are going to record the behaviors of children whose parents are present, you explain what you are doing and ask their permission (Gander and Gardiner, 1981). Asking is a gesture of courtesy, and it may help avoid suspicion.

Professional Behavior: Professional ethics demand that you behave at all times in a professional manner. This is a significant and weighty obligation, for it requires that, when necessary, you set aside your own personal preferences and wishes. Always act in accordance with the legitimate requirements and expectations (1) of the observation setting, (2) of those individuals in that setting and, in the case of minors, of those persons responsible for them, (3) of the faculty and institution whom you represent, and (4) of the observation exercises themselves. This last item refers to being intellectually honest in the performance of your exercises. In other words, be faithful to the discipline and subject matter of which your observations are a part.

Factors That Affect Observation

Observation consists of seeing certain things and recording what you have seen in a way that can be used for a particular puspose. Making meaningful, useful observations is not an easy task. There are a number of factors that can affect your observations.

Sensitivity and Awareness: Earlier, we discussed how sensitivity to children changes with experience and training, which are long-term influences. There are, however, more immediate influences that can limit your sensitivity and awareness and possibly bias your observational data and interpretations. At this very moment, you possess a particular understanding or, as Lay and Dopyera (1977) put it, a "set of understandings or discriminations that you are capable of making about any child you encounter" (p. 70). Whatever your level of skill or understanding, there will be times and conditions when you will not observe at the level of which you are capable. Certain things will interfere with how you see the subject of your observations.

Fatigue, Illness, and Discomfort: Fatigue is an obviously limiting condition, as are illness, physical discomfort, and psychological disturbances. These conditions can distract you and take your attention away from the task at hand. You can also be distracted by psychological disturbances such as personal problems, anxieties and fears, or trying to do too much at once. Sometimes disturbances will come from the external environment and can limit your perception—noise, temperature extremes, poor lighting or crowded conditions. Many of these variables will be beyond your personal control, but your ability to recognize the effects they have on you can be invaluable. At the very least, you will be able to identify potential sources of distraction and other types of error and, if possible, offset them in some way.

The Influence of Self or Personality: Perhaps one of the most difficult factors influencing observations is your own self or personality, a problem Lay and Dopyera (1977) refer to as "sorting out 'you' from what you view" (p. 72). Our individual experience, attitudes, needs, desires, and fears tend to act as "filters" through which we not only process what we observe, but which also affect what we notice in the first place. An observer may, for example, have a tendency to project his own feelings onto a child; he may believe that the child feels what he thinks he felt as a child or would feel in the present situation. Or, a teacher may tend to dislike or like someone who has certain characteristics or exhibits certain kinds of behaviors. These biases can influence the teacher or observer to pay either too little or too much attention to certain aspects of the child's behavior or personality, and obstruct perception of other equally important features. This seems to be especially true when the behaviors or characteristics are disliked or considered taboo by the observer. In such a case, there is an inclination to be turned off by a child who displays these traits. Such a negative reaction can be a powerful determinant of how you see and interpret that child's behavior. This becomes important again during the evaluation process.

Controlling our Biases: We all have biases, and although they cannot be completely eliminated, we can be conscious of them and take steps to control them. It is very important that the traits or characteristics that we like or dislike, easily accept or do not easily accept, do not cause us to lose our objectivity. It is particularly important not to pass judgment on children or make evaluative statements that reflect poorly on their character or worth.

To say, as an example, that a child is aggressive or dependent, meaning that he is to be thought of forever thereafter as having an aggressive or dependent personality, is not part of your observation exercises. You may, however, describe aggressive or dependent *behavior* when a child displays it. The focus on behavior can be illustrated by the now well-known advice to parents on how to respond to a child's misbehavior: Do not tell the child that she is a bad girl. Tell her that what she did is wrong. The behavior is the focus of criticism, not the basic worth and character of the individual. Positive self-esteem should always be reinforced in the child's mind, despite lapses into behavior that adults find undesirable.

Influence of the Setting or Situation: Other factors that could influence your observations are those imposed on you by the setting and the individuals in it. These include such things as the size and arrangement of the physical space; the equipment and materials available to the children and, in some cases, to you; and the characteristics, skills, and personalities of the children. The size and arrangement of the space can limit your observations by making it difficult to stay close to a given child or to be inconspicuous. Equipment and materials have an influence by providing children the means of exercising their skills and pursuing their interests. Characteristics of the children affect what you can do in the setting, because they help determine the kinds of behaviors that will be exhibited. Some children may be active physically, others passive and inactive; some may talk a lot, others little; some may interact a great deal with their peers, others hardly at all. The presence of various behaviors can provide you with examples of what you want to observe. Whether the absence of certain behaviors is to your disadvantage depends on your objectives. For example, if Tasha typically avoids her classmates, that avoidance might give you valuable information about her self-concept, her social skills, or her status among her peers. If, however, your aim is to observe "normal" or more extensive social behaviors and interactions, you may have to select another child.

Categories of Errors in Recording Observations

There are three categories of errors you can make in recording your observational data: (1) errors of omission; (2) errors of commission; and (3) errors of transmission (Richarz, 1980).

Errors of Ommission: Errors of omission occur when you leave out information that is helpful or necessary to understanding a child's behavior. If your objectives call for it, you should include enough information to provide a complete picture of what happens during a behavioral episode. Such a picture helps you form broader and more generalized conceptions of a particular child than would otherwise be possible. Consider the following example.

Millard, a four-year-old preschooler, is playing by himself in the sandbox with a small dumptruck. While he is playing, Kent comes over and without saying a word, grabs the truck out of Millard's hand. You happen to look over toward the sandbox just as Millard hits Kent and grabs the truck. How might you describe and interpret this episode? You could decide that Millard had behaved aggressively toward Kent, and you might continue to observe the behaviors of the two children. The point here is that something important would be missing if you had accepted the incident as it appeared. Your interpretation of Millard's behavior as aggressive would be premature and not quite correct. You would have left out the critical incident of Kent initiating the aggressive action. Some would call Millard's response assertiveness. Missing part of a behavioral sequence or interaction may not make your objective description invalid; you could record very accurately the behaviors and events you did happen to observe. But remember it is not just the descriptions that are important; they must acquire a meaning that will help you understand the child and his behavior. In the above case of Millard, the meaning of his actions toward Kent would have been significantly altered, if not distorted, by leaving out that critical segment of behavior. You will describe for a purpose, and part of that purpose will be to understand the broader context of the behavior.

There are many reasons why errors of omission are made: various distractions, simply missing behaviors that have already occurred (as in the above example), or poor note-taking. Note-taking is heavily influenced by the passing of time. You may not be able to take a lot of (or any) notes during the observation session and may therefore have to rely on memory. The longer you wait to record your observations, the more you are likely to forget. Naturally, this argues for writing up your notes as quickly as possible. A very important factor is the particular way you see what you are observing: what and how much you perceive; whether what you notice is meaningful to you and, in your opinion, worth writing down; and the relationship between what you see and the purpose of your observations at the time.

Errors of Commission: In contrast, errors of commission occur when you include more information than is actually present in the situation. This involves such things as reporting that behaviors, speech, or interactions took place when in fact they did not; or reporting that certain persons were in the sitting/situation when again, in fact, they were not present at all. These errors are also made for a number of reasons, including inattention, relying on a faulty memory, and those factors that contribute to errors of omission. It is not always easy to catch these errors, particularly when they stem from your individual way of seeing. We all have gaps in our perception and understanding; at least they may be thought of as gaps by someone who sees things differently from the way we do.

Errors of Transmission: The third category is called errors of transmission. In this case, the fault lies in recording the behaviors you observe in improper sequence. This can be a serious mistake, for it is frequently the order of events that gives them meaning: What happens at 9:20 A.M. can influence what happens at 9:35 A.M., and so on. The chances of making this type of error can be reduced if you record the time at which you observe a particular behavior. Under some circumstances, you can record the times at which a given behavior begins and ends, or the time at which you start and stop observing and recording a behavior. This can be done for each behavior, event, and interaction that you observe throughout the entire period. Besides reducing errors of transmission, timing behaviors gives you information about such aspects as the length of the child's attention span and the proportion of time the child spends on particular activities.

Three Aspects of the Observation Process

If you are careful to avoid these errors, accurate and reliable observation is possible. There are three aspects to the observation process, which, if you keep them clearly in mind, will increase your accuracy and reliability. These aspects are (1) objective description, (2) interpretation (inference or explanation), and (3) evaluation.

Objective Description: This is the foundation of observation, since so much else depends on it. Objective description, sometimes referred to as reporting, consists of recording what you see as precisely and completely as possible. The term 'completely' must, however, be considered in relation to your specific purposes. There are occasions when you will want a great deal of information, which will therefore require a great deal of recording. On other occasions, your purpose may be satisfied by just recording whether a specific response has occurred, as in the case of recording how often children act "aggressively." The key word here is objective, which means "without bias or prejudice; detached; impersonal" (Webster 1960). Objective reporting leaves out your interpretations, evaluations, impressions, and speculations, and the descriptions of what you see and hear would be agreed to by anyone observing the same scene. For instance, the statement "Carlita climbed on a tricycle and rode across the room for about ten feet. The trike tipped over, Carlita fell off and began to cry" is an objective description. Another observer would describe the events much the same way. It is important to remember that absolute objectivity is not possible. Each of us views the world from a bias or perspective that differs from someone else's. In the case of the above example, just being able to describe Carlita as "riding a trike across the room" requires knowledge of tricycles and of what is meant by "riding." An acceptable level of objectivity is possible, however, in part because we in this culture share common language, values, norms, and experiences; therefore, most of us understand riding trikes.

Interpretation/Explanation: Interpretation means going beyond your objective descriptions and trying to explain or give them some meaning. If, in the above example, you were to add "because she was hurt," that would be an interpretation, especially if Carlita herself had not indicated that she was hurt. The "because she was hurt" is an interpretation (possibly an accurate one) because it goes further than simple description. You and your roommate, for example, might disagree about whether Carlita was hurt; your roommate could interpret her crying as resulting from fear or frustration rather than pain or injury.

Interpretation or explanation, then, involves attempts to identify the cause of some behavior or event; to assign motives to an individual; to determine the objectives of a behavior; in short, to provide any additional information that might make your objective descriptions more meaningful than they would otherwise be.

Evaluation: This third aspect of observation is possibly the most dangerous part of the observation process, for it is at this point that you apply your values and attitudes to the child's behavior, characteristics, and personality. Evaluation refers to placing a value on, or judging the worth of, something. Unfortunately, it is all too easy to make hasty judgments or to form stereotypes about someone. Once we have the stereotype, there seems to be no need to learn more about the individual and possibly to modify our opinion of him based on further contacts and interactions.

The groundwork for evaluation is already laid during the observation and recording process, for it is there that terms such as "dependent," "aggressive," and "anxious" are used to describe and explain behavior. What is critical here is that terms such as these are often used in careless ways. They can be legitimate concepts, but they should always be strongly linked with observable behavior. Moreover, labeling a child as "lazy," for example, does not explain the child or his behavior. "Lazy" is a convenient way of summarizing one's views or attitudes about a child. What has to be described are the behaviors that led to the decision to call him lazy. What has to be explained are the reasons for those behaviors.

Derogatory labels such as lazy, dull, and unattractive should not be in the observer's written vocabulary. Any conclusions concerning a child's general characteristics or traits should be based on frequent, representative, and objectively described samples of behavior. This advice applies to both positive and negative attributes.

Group or Individual Observation

The distinction between individual and group observation is an important one. It represents a distinction between data that are useful for one purpose and data which are useful for quite a different purpose.

Limitations of Group Observation

First it is virtually impossible to observe a group and gain significant information about specific individuals. Meaningful observation of specific individuals is similar to having a meaningful conversation. You can listen only to one person at a time, and only one person can speak at a time, otherwise the conversation becomes incomprehensible. If you wish to observe even as few as two children simultaneously, you must watch first one child, then the other, shifting your attention back and forth between them.

Observing more than one individual at a time makes sense when there is an interaction going on. When two individuals are influencing or responding to each another, the interaction and its context also become important. There is an inseparable relationship between behavior and the setting in which it occurs. Behavior is influenced and governed by the characteristics of the setting, which include the nature, purpose, and location of the interaction, and the specific persons involved. Your comments in a conversation are governed in part by the other person's comments, by where you are, and by the topic of conversation.

Keep in mind that if you observe a group, you will be unable to obtain much information about individuals. You can study the behavior of groups as well as the behavior of individuals in groups, but it is necessary to consider the differences.

What is a Group? Perspective One: A group is sometimes defined as a collection of individuals who are assembled in a particular place. This simplest of groups has no purpose around which it is formally structured; it merely consists of a number of persons who happen to be in the same place at the same time. You will recognize, however, that they could gather together for common reasons, such as to shop or watch a sporting event. Of much greater interest is the true group, which is a collection of individuals who are organized around a common purpose and who have an identifiable social structure.

Figure 3-5 A peer group.

Some groups are formed by an outside authority or agency. A school system establishes kindergartens, elementary and high schools; a community agency, church, or parents' group sets up a nursery school, and so on. Such groups can be referred to as *institutional groups* (Brandt 1972). This kind of formal group can contain subgroups that are spontaneously formed by the members themselves. Membership is often determined by mutual interests and common characteristics. This kind of group is referred to as a *peer group,* which can be defined as "friends and associates who are usually of similar age and social standing" (Federico 1979). But peer groups can be much more limited than this definition suggests. For the purpose of observing and studying children, a peer group is any group of children whose members interact with one another.

A preschool class, for example, could be an institutional group; a public kindergarten and elementary school class are clearly institutional groups because of their connection to the larger educational system. The third grade classes of two city schools could comprise peer groups. But, three children who play together in Mrs. Martin's preschool are also a peer group. This kind of group can be the focus of your observations.

What is a Group? Perspective Two: There is another way of defining or looking at the concept of group that is worth a little bit of discussion. Patricia Yancey Martin and Gerald G. O'Connor (1989), who take a systems perspective on social phenomena, identify the characteristics of small groups based on what they define as a group's four *components*. These are of interest because they can provide a framework within which to put your observations of children's group behavior. We shall adapt these authors' broad and somewhat theoretical views on groups to fit the case of children.

Component One: Member Characteristics

"*Member characteristics* are the properties, or qualities, of individuals who belong to groups" (Martin and O'Connor 1989, p. 165; italics original). The authors cite a number of individual characteristics that are of significance to observers of young children.

There are the demographic characteristics of age, gender, race, ethnic and cultural heritage, and religious commitment. They also cite the extremely important factors of "unique family and developmental biography and a distinctive psychological makeup and style" (p. 165). Also included in member characteristics are "feelings of self-concept or self-esteem . . ." (p. 165). These feelings translate into differences in assertiveness, in how loudly or persistently a child will talk, and so on. The length of time a child has belonged to a specific group is also important and can have a bearing on how that child behaves in the group.

The premise here is that these member characteristics affect how a group will engage in various activities, as well as the outcomes of those processes. Think of this "premise" as essentially meaning that all stimuli to which the group responds; all behaviors displayed by the group, as a group, fundamentally depend upon the characteristics, abilities, personalities, and so on, of its individual members. They are the filters through which all inputs come into the group and outputs leave the group. Think of it this way: there can be no track team if the persons who are to make up that team cannot run. A group of preschoolers cannot be a goal-striving group if the individul members don't have the wherewithal to accomplish the necessary tasks leading to the final goal.

Component Two: Member Behaviors

Member behaviors are defined very simply by Martin and O'Connor (1989) as "the actions of individuals in a group," although they add "during group meetings" (p. 165). We can replace this last phrase by "during group activities" or "during group interactions." Martin and O'Connor emphasize that member behaviors will differ according to the basic purpose of the group—a task group, for instance, as opposed to a play group. It's essential to note that, according to the authors, "member behavior is necessary for group development" and that "without member behaviors, individuals remain isolated and a group never forms" (p. 165).

Member behaviors appear so basic a requirement that you might wonder why Martin and O'Connor even mention it. For our purposes, we would only ask you to keep in mind that it's not just any collecton of individuals that constitutes a group. There must be some consistent behaviors that "connect" members in some meaningful way. Furthermore, as we shall discuss below, an essential characteristic of a group is the relationships, or relationship patterns, that eventually form and distinguish not only one group from another, but also distinguish a group from a "non-group."

Component Three: Group Contextual Characteristics

"*Group contextual characteristics* are the properties of a group as a system that are relatively constant or enduring" (p. 167; italics original). These characteristics "include the social, relationship, and procedural phenomena that *emerge* through members' individual and interpersonal behaviors" (p. 167; italics original).

Group contextual characteristics depend upon the interactions among group members, which lead to the development of such things as "group goals, rules, procedures, a common identity, shared standards for assessing both each other's and the group's actions and progress, and so on" (p. 167). Martin and O'Connor (1989) identify three contextual characteristics of small groups: group norms, group climate, and "a group's normal round of procedures" (p. 167). These deserve some discussion.

Group norms are shared standards for appropriate behavior. As Martin and O'Connor put it, "norms have a *should* quality to them" (p. 167; italics original). It's important to point out that norms are often associated with *roles*, which are recurring patterns of behavior that are in turn associated with a position in a social group. (For example, the social position of *teacher* requires such role behaviors as giving instructions, handing out assignments, and giving grades.) Of potential interest to the observer of young children is Martin and O'Connor's claim that "certain aspects of the *role of group member* are normative, that is, they are required because of shared expectations for members' behavior, whereas others are not" (p. 167; italics original). For example, a preschool group may have the (adult-generated) expectation that there be no behaviors such as pushing or other forms of aggression, but there may be no particular expectation regarding the kind of games or activities the group should engage in.

Group climate is very close if not identical in meaning to our concepts of setting, situation, and context. Martin and O'Connor (1989) define group climate as "the shared socioemotional atmosphere or mood of a group" (p. 168). You should recognize that a group's climate can remain relatively stable or it can change. Changes can be the result of things that happen within the group as such, or that affect the group in relation to its environment (Martin and O'Connor, 1989, p. 168). For example, an especially dominant child might leave a group, which could leave the group without an effective leader. The effects of that situation depend, of course, on a number of factors; but the broad effects could be a dramatic change in how the group behaves, the goals or tasks it undertakes, and even whether the group stays together at all.

Moving the group to another environment (climate) can also change the dynamics and relationship patterns for the better or for the worse. Different equipment and materials in the new setting, for instance, might change the group's behavior and possibly even its leadership. In a former setting, one child may have been the leader because of his or her skill with a particular piece of equipment. In a new setting, a different child may be especially competent with yet a different piece of equipment, thus gaining the group's deference with respect to its use and role in the group's functioning. The possibilities are great indeed.

A *group's normal round of procedures* is, according to Martin and O'Connor, "the agenda of typical or routine activities that a group follows to accomplish its goals" (p. 168). Preschool groups may establish such rounds of activities if they exist long enough for the members to reach this kind of agreement and settled routine. Of course, it's also possible that the simple addition of a new but dominant member might change the "round" for as long as that individual is present in the group. That is to say, a group's normal round of procedures depends on the group's purposes as well as on all of the components being discussed.

Component Four: Group Episodes

Group episodes, say Martin and O'Connor (1989), are "shared, system-level events, incidents, or happenings that occur in groups that are characterized by continuous activity" (p. 168). The authors present an informative analogy for thinking about group episodes. They write that "Episodes are like scenes in a play; each has distinctive content and meaning but can be understood fully only in relation to the total 'drama' or group context" (p. 168). The concept of episode reflects the extreme importance of context in understanding behavior. Indeed, it can be said that an individual's behavior ultimately has meaning *only* in some social context or other. This is so because human beings can seldom, if ever, totally remove themselves from the social environment or from the already existing influences of such an environment.

It's assumed here that as "a series of shared events," episodes "are more than the discrete acts and behaviors of individual members" (Martin and O'Connor, p. 168). Essentially, this means that episodes depend for their meaning or significance on the *relationships among the group members*, rather than on the actions of any particular person or persons in the group. Martin and O'Connor (1989) give episodes the very important role of giving "meaning to members' behavior and help[ing] them interpret and make sense of what is said and done" (p. 168).

Use will be made of the episode concept in your observation exercises. According to the concept, children's behavior, *as individuals*, can make sense only when viewed from the perspective of the larger group and its influence on each individual member. Each member's behavior "connects" with someone else's behavior, which is how relationships are established. Ultimately, a network is constructed, in which the behavior of a number of individuals combines or interacts to produce what we call a group. Sarah's behavior while in the group is affected by, say, Mark's behavior. Staying with Martin and O'Connor's analogy, Sarah and Mark are actors in a play. One does or says something as a result of what the other has done or said. It's like following the directions of a script. Most importantly, Sarah's behavior, as a individual, makes the most sense when it is considered *in relation to Mark's behavior*. This relationship is the group episode, or it forms part of a larger group episode. Relationships also make behavior social; their absence effectively leaves behavior *asocial* (or nonsocial).

Some Approaches to Group Observation: Almy and Genishi (1979) point out that "Teachers have always known that every group of children has its own distinctive qualities. Like individuals, each group or class is unique." Each group also has distinctive influences on its members; therefore, the group is part of the setting. Here is an example.

> Julie, Erica, and Floyd often form a small play group. Their activities are varied, ranging from dramatic play, where Floyd nearly always plays the "daddy" and Julie and Erica take turns being the "mommy," to building with big blocks, where there is no set or consistent pattern of interaction among the three children. They seldom quarrel, and any disagreements tend to be short-lived. None of the three children seems to emerge as a leader.

> From time to time, Erica also participates as a member of another group, this one consisting of herself, Roger, and Tanya. These three children, however, seem more restricted in their activities. They seldom play house because arguments usually break out between Erica and Tanya over who will play the mother. Roger does not like to build with blocks, and the girls do not press for that activity. Tanya seems more of a leader than a follower, although Erica will occasionally challenge her attempts to lead. This second group does not play together for the relatively long periods of time that characterize the play of the first group.

How could you approach these two different situations?

One way would be to concentrate on the behaviors of each child as an individual. You would notice the different responses, play patterns, and peer relationships, but they would be put solely in the context of the individual. Thus, you could describe Erica's behavior in each of the two groups: what she said and how she said it, her gross and fine muscle activities, her social and emotional responses, and so on.

A second approach would be to observe individual behaviors, as before, but place them within the larger framework of the three-person groups in which they occurred. Now Erica's behavior is seen in light of its group context. You might notice, for instance, that her language usage differs, depending on which group she is in at the time. You might try to describe the relationship between her language and the characteristics of the group and its members. It would also be of interest to examine other interaction patterns and attempt to explain them, perhaps on the basis of the children's differing personalities or the different way the teacher treats the two groups.

A third approach would be to look primarily at the group itself, taking less account of the behaviors of each single member and more account of how the three children are acting as a single unit. You could describe the group as though it were an individual, even attributing to it characteristics or traits—a friendly group, a hostile group, or a hard-working group.

Behavior can be significantly influenced by the larger group, although such influence is not always dramatic. Some children take very little part in the group life of their peers, seemingly preferring to focus their attention and energy on trying to please adults (e.g., see Almy and Genishi 1979). Groups, in turn, react differently to different individuals. Some children are not readily accepted into a group, while others are not only accepted but quickly become the leader. As illustrated in the previous example, children behave differently in different groups and situations. We have all known someone who acted so differently from what we are accustomed to, that we tried to explain the unusual behavior by saying it was her companions that caused the change in her personality.

Your Goals in Observing Groups: The above discussion emphasizes the need to observe children in context and to determine how their actions might change in various settings. All of us belong to a number of groups—a family, school, work organization, and social organizations—and our positions and behaviors vary from one group to another.

Your goals in observing groups will vary, depending on what you want to learn. A goal could be to determine how a child's behavior differs in various groups. Leadership and follower patterns in various groups are also worthy topics for observation. How do leaders emerge in different groups? How does the leadership change in a given group? How does a particular child express her leadership? Is a particular child a leader in all situations, or only in some?

Sometimes group patterns of behavior might be of interest. These can be discerned through a frequency checklist that records how many children use a particular space or engage in a particular activity (e.g., see Table A in the Appendix). A checklist will not tell you about the dynamics of group interaction, but it will tell you which classroom areas or activities are the most popular and draw the heaviest traffic. This information is important in planning future activities or arranging the physical environment. Very useful information can also be obtained by keeping a record of the particular areas and activities that are used by specific children. A teacher may notice, for instance, that Jonathan usually spends his free play time in the big block area. Repeated observations reveal that Jonathan's fine motor coordination is poor. He therefore feels uncomfortable in activities that require skilled hand-eye coordination. As a result, he plays with equipment and materials that involve large muscle groups. Here you have an example of a child matching his abilities with the opportunities provided by a given environment. This data would be relevant to a group observation if the teacher concluded prematurely that Jonathan plays in the big block area because of the other children who play there. In other words, Jonathan's play and social behavior might erroneously be interpreted in terms of group membership, rather than in terms of his difficulty in performing fine motor tasks.

Groups and individual behaviors within groups are important aspects of understanding children. Your overall objectives for observing will determine where and how groups fit into your specific observation activity.

Summary

There are a number of steps that must be taken before entering the observation setting. The most important step is determining the purpose of your observation; this will affect everything else you do. Selecting the site of the observation and knowing what you may do in the observation setting are also steps in the preparation process.

Being inconspicuous when observing is very important. Naturalistic observation requires as little interference with children's behavior as possible. There are times, however, when children are asked to behave in particular ways, such as in testing or formal research studies. Your overall observation objectives will determine whether you remain completely separated from the children's ongoing behavior or intervene in some way.

The need for professional ethics cannot be too heavily stressed. Ethics and confidentiality protect the rights and well-being of everyone associated with your observations. Professional ethics was discussed under the general notion of professional behavior.

Making meaningful, useful observations is not easy, and several factors that affect observation were discussed. Your sensitivity to children, fatigue, illness, and discomfort all contribute to what you see when you look at children. The most difficult factor influencing observations, however, is your personality—your values, attitudes, experiences, knowledge, and so on. These attributes act as filters through which you process what you see and that affect what you notice in the first place.

The influence of the setting and situation was also discussed. Space size, equipment, materials, and people in the space, and how they are arranged will affect your observations.

Three categories of errors were covered in the chapter. There are errors of omission, commission, and transmission. These errors affect the accuracy and reliability of your observational data. In spite of the possibility of error, however, accuracy and reliability can be achieved, and three aspects of observation were discussed in this regard: objective description, interpretation, and evaluation. Evaluation was characterized as possibly the most "dangerous" part of the observation process. It is in evaluating a child that you attach a value to her behavior, character, and even her worth as an individual. Extreme caution was advised, and even positive evaluations must be supported by frequent, representative, and objectively described samples of behavior. In any case, derogatory labels and descriptions must never be part of a child's observation record.

Distinctions were made between individual and group observations. The limitations of observing groups of children were presented, with a significant limitation being the loss of information about specific individuals. It was pointed out that one can study the behavior of groups and the behavior of individuals in groups, but the differences should be borne in mind. Several kinds of groups were defined, but peer groups are the most likely focus of your observations. Several approaches to observing groups were discussed. Some goals of group observation include issues such as documenting changes in children's behavior as they functioned in different groups, leadership and follower behavior patterns in various groups, and assessing the effect of a group on a particular child's behavior.

The concept of group was also discussed by way of viewing a group as characterized by four components: (1) member characteristics, (2) member behaviors, (3) group contextual characteristics, and (4) group episodes. Three specific contextual characteristics of small groups were also discussed, namely (1) group norms, (2) group climate, and (3) a group's normal round of procedures.

Study Questions

1. Your overall purpose for observing is a key element to success. Identify and discuss some of the problems an observer might encounter if she did not have her objective clearly in mind before entering the observation setting.
2. List some questions concerning professional behavior that *you* think should be answered before starting to observe in a preschool. How would you answer them?
3. How are interpretation and evaluation related? Which one has to be done first, and why?
4. Why is objective description important to the accuracy and reliability of observation?
5. Give some examples of when group observation is more valuable than individual observation. How would you actually do the observing?

Part 2

The Elements of Observation

As a real, practical activity, observation is "all of a piece": it possesses its own integrity or unity, especially when it's done with skill. But like any process, observation consists of parts or elements, each of which must fit well with all of the other parts if it is to be successful.

The eleven chapters in Part 2 discuss what we have chosen to call the elements of observation. The distinction between Parts 1 and 2 is somewhat arbitrary, for, in fact, developmental theories and the general guidelines for observing children (Chapters 2 and 3) are every bit as much the elements of observation as are the various methods of recording behavior. The term 'elements,' however, is particularly appropriate in this case, because it describes those special components of observation that make possible the *objective* recording of behavior and the keeping of more or less permanent records. Without such "elements," observation remains merely casual watching similar to what one does while sitting on a park bench or in a restaurant. Unfortunately, this kind of "observation" is subject to all of the adverse effects of no predetermined observation plan and a fallible memory.

The intent of Part 2 is to provide you with at least seven ways of recording behavior in virtually any setting or situation. We must stress, however, that none of the methods is of much use without careful prior preparation—preparation that ranges from knowing where you are going to observe, to having some understanding of how children develop, to familiarity with your method of choice and how to use it properly and effectively.

Given all of the above, we believe that these elements of observation, judiciously studied and reasonably mastered, will, with persistent application, help to make you a skilled and astute observer of the behavior of young children.

chapter four
Methods, Behavior, Plans, and Context

Objectives

After studying this chapter, you will be able to

- relate the concept of method to observation
- identify the role of behavior in observation
- interpret the relationship of a plan to observation
- analyze the relationship between observation and the context in which it occurs

How To Do It:
Some Preliminary Thoughts and Cautions

This chapter discusses the concept of methods of observing and recording children's behavior. Methods are the "how-to-do-it" aspects of the observation process.

We go through our lives using methods of one kind or another to accomplish tasks. Any method is in some ways similar to observation—it depends for its success on an individual's skills, knowledge, experience, and other factors that go into making that person who he is. Just as there is more to observation than what meets the eye, there is more to a method than what one reads in a book or hears from a teacher.

A method is a way of doing something. "A manner of procedure, esp. a systematic or clearly defined way of accomplishing an end; plan; system or order in thought or action . . ." (Webster, 1981). A method specifies a procedure by which one can accomplish a goal. In this manual, a *method* is considered a set of instructions with two major characteristics: (1) it must specify what one has to do to achieve some objective, and (2) it may also describe how to do what one needs to do to achieve the objective. "What" provides the objective of the instructions, "how" describes the actions or steps that lead to the accomplishment of the objective. Methods then, are designed to give one the skill, understanding, and knowledge necessary to achieve some end.

Suppose, for example, you were asked to intervene in a preschool classroom situation. It's your first day on the job in a local preschool, and some of four-year-old Margaret's behavior is disruptive and possibly harmful to the other children. Suppose further that this particular preschool uses behavior modification principles and techniques to change undesirable behavior as well as to establish desirable behavior in the children in its care. The head teacher tells you first to determine a frequency baseline for Margaret's target behavior. Then she instructs you to weaken or eliminate the target behavior through the use of non-reinforcement. Finally she tells you to establish a new behavior, initially on the basis of a continuous reinforcement schedule and gradually going to a variable ratio schedule of reinforcement. Could you do this? Again, it would depend on your understanding such concepts as *baseline frequency, nonreinforcement,* and *continuous* and *variable ratio schedules of reinforcement.* It would depend further on your ability to implement or apply these principles, to translate them into actual practice.

Consequently, the directions on how to observe and record behavior will be useful only if, first, you understand what the directions mean and how to use them, and second, you know something about the subject to which the method is being applied. You must already have knowledge to acquire more knowledge, skill to acquire more skill. Descriptions of methods will not provide an unerring path to successful observation; none of the techniques is self-evident or self-explanatory, not even to observation experts. Instructions are potentially a means of developing the skill and knowledge needed to use a particular observation and recording method. If that use becomes a "natural" part of you, your reading about observation methods will have been successful.

Again, critical relationships exist between you and what you see, and between you and any "how-to-do-it" approach to an activity.

Behavior: A Central Element of Observation and Recording

Behavior is the major object of everything you will do in observing and recording. Behavior, according to the *New Webster's Dictionary of the English Language* (1981), is "the aggregate of observable actions or activities of the individual as matter for psychological study." Pillari (1988) defines behavior as "everything that is potentially observable about a person or event" (p. 2). For our purposes, behavior will be considered anything an individual does that can be directly seen, heard, smelled, tasted, or touched. The word directly means that the behavior you are observing is right there or immediate. Walking, running, eating, and speaking are examples of directly observable behaviors. They involve visible or hearable muscular actions or responses. It is behavior then, that one observes: a child walking around the room, talking to a friend, or painting at an easel.

Behavior Sampling and Observation Plans: Behavior has an important characteristic: It occurs continuously, without ceasing, for as long as one is alive. Even sleeping is a behavior, although it is not as exciting as a hockey game. If one is alive, one is behaving. Herbert F. Wright captured the continuous quality of behavior when he referred to it as a "stream." He wrote: "The behavior of a person is a lifelong continuum. It is in the nature of a stream that it can never be seen in its entirety" (Wright 1960).

Wright's behavior-as-a-stream metaphor is a useful one. Observation can be thought of as entering that stream at some point and taking a sample of the behaviors that are flowing by. However, entering the stream and taking a sample is somewhat like going shopping. You need a plan to do it successfully. Deciding what to buy and where to buy it is analogous to deciding what behaviors to observe in children (aggression, dependency, language), and where you might find those kinds of behaviors—in a preschool classroom or a public playground. Deciding how much you are going to buy is like deciding how much of the behavior stream you are going to try to observe on a given occasion. Finally, you must decide how to get to the store and bring home your purchased goods. This is comparable to choosing an observation method, a way to enter the child's stream and take a sample of the behavior you want.

The method you choose will determine some of the other details required by your plan, such as how much of the behavior stream is to be observed, and the form the observational data will take. A specimen record, for example, covers a large portion of the child's behavior stream, and the data are in narrative, or raw form. Time sampling deals with smaller portions of the behavior stream, and the final data can be just a checkmark indicating whether a given behavior or category of behaviors has occurred.

Your overall plan must always come first. All other decisions will follow from that plan.

Settings and Situations

Setting and situation can have different meanings. Setting, for some (Wright 1960) covers tangible factors such as physical space, the objects in that space, and opportunities and resources that permit individuals to behave in certain ways. A preschool classroom is a setting because it has observable and measureable physical dimensions located in a specific place. A classroom setting contains equipment and materials the children can use to behave in particular ways, such as blocks to build with, tricycles to ride, and books to read.

In contrast to setting, situation is mainly concerned with the social and psychological conditions in the setting. What is the nature of the children's play—active and cooperative, or active and individualized? What kinds of activities are being encouraged by the teacher (or by the children themselves)? What unexpected event may temporarily capture the children's attention, and thereby change the ongoing stream of behaviors?

Settings and situations are related to one another in a special way—situations occur within settings. Settings have physical and social-psychological characteristics. Physical spaces generate feelings in us. We do not

Figure 4-1   The observation setting—a preschool in action. (Photo by Karen Norton)

respond the same way to every environment. Different people also create different atmospheres.

Wright (1960) made three assumptions concerning the relationship of setting to situation. First, he assumed that some settings are more conducive to certain situations than to others. Some settings, for example, promote certain social interactions better than others. Something as simple as seating arrangements can work for or against children talking to one another.

Second, he assumed that the relationship is not fixed. He noted that although the same setting can support different situations, identical situations can occur in different settings. As an example, two groups of children could use the same setting at different times and both groups could be active, outgoing, and cooperative. Or, in contrast, one group could be subdued and withdrawn, showing little interaction with materials or among themselves.

The idea of identical situations occurring in different settings is illustrated by the following example. Think of two Head Start classrooms. Each is conducted in a different setting, and yet many of the same activities can take place, and much the same warm, supportive atmosphere may characterize both situations.

Finally, Wright assumed that "the behavior of the child at a particular time does indeed depend more directly upon the situation than upon the setting in which it takes place." Wright's third assumption has the most implications for us as observers.

Context: The word context is more suitable than setting or situation, because context includes setting and situation. Context involves place, time, circumstances, other people, and even psychological and physical condition. Places, times, and people determine or influence how we behave and feel. Places allow some behaviors, but not others. Compare what you may do on the beach with what you may do in an office. Physical space permits some activities, while excluding others. (Can you swim in a bowling alley, for example?) Personal interactions are also affected by context. Individuals occupy *statuses* within social groups, and those statuses require certain behaviors or *roles*. These statuses and roles regulate individuals' behavior toward one another. Think of the relationship between a teacher and a student. The status of teacher requires certain kinds of role behaviors, such as teaching, grading, and counseling students. Student is a different status, with different role behaviors, such as attending class and doing homework. The nature of the student-teacher interaction is largely determined by these statuses and roles.

If you observe children in a preschool classroom, the classroom is the broad context for the children's behavior. But there are smaller settings and situations within the overall classroom context, and these smaller settings may occupy some of your attention during observations. Snack time, story time, free play time, nap time, and the block, art, and sandbox areas are examples of these smaller physical and social environments. These smaller contexts can determine what the children are allowed to do and the behaviors they exhibit.

Summary

This chapter discussed the idea of method, which was defined as a set of instructions that tell us what to do to accomplish some task or objective. It was pointed out, however, that methods do not guarantee success. The effectiveness of any method depends on the skills and knowledge of the individual using it. Thus, to acquire knowledge and skill, one must already have knowledge and skill.

Behavior is the central element in all observation of children. Behavior is anything a person does that can be directly seen, heard, smelled, tasted, or touched. Behavior was also discussed in metaphorical terms as a stream that never stops as long as one is alive. Sampling involves entering the child's behavior stream and catching a portion of the behavior flowing by. Plans are the prearranged steps one takes to enter the stream and sample the desired behavior.

Setting and situation were also covered in the chapter. Setting is the physical aspects of the child's environment; situation is the social and psychological characteristics of the environment. Both of these terms were combined into the general term context, which includes all the factors that pertain to setting and situation.

Study Questions

1. Describe a method you use in a common daily activity. What skills and knowledge are required to use this method? How is the method you have described similar to an observation method. Do they share any characteristics?
2. Why is visible behavior a central part of observation, rather than such things as thoughts or feelings?
3. What is the relationship between plans and methods? Are they similar or dissimilar? How?
4. Describe an imaginary context. How might the characteristics of that context affect the observation of behavior?
5. If you wanted to observe and record such things as thoughts or feelings, how would you have to go about it? What would you have to do to make such observation and recording possible?

chapter five
An Introduction to Observation and Recording Methods

Objectives

After studying this chapter, you will be able to

- discuss the differences between formal and informal methods of observation
- compare open versus closed methods of recording behavior
- describe the relationship between the degree of selectivity and the type of method used for recording behavior
- identify the role of inference or interpretation in the observation process

Methods of Observing and Recording Behavior: Some General Characterisitcs

Seven methods for observing and recording behavior are covered in this manual: (1) specimen description, (2) time sampling, (3) event sampling, (4) anecdotal records, (5) diary records, (6) frequency counts, and (7) checklists. Each of these procedures has its own characteristics, uses, advantages and disadvantages; each is best used under certain conditions for certain objectives. Before learning about each method, it is useful to consider several general characteristics of observation methods.

Goodwin and Driscoll (1980), among others, distinguish between the broad categories of formal and informal observation methods. These authors also describe several distinctions among formal methods, which they label (1) open vs. closed, (2) degree of selectivity, and (3) degree of observer inference required.

Because of their importance in understanding the different methods, the general features of formal and informal methods and of the distinctions among formal methods will be discussed.

Formal and Informal Observation

Formal and informal methods of observation differ mainly in how strict the conditions are for using them. Formal methods are conducted in a highly structured manner, which is why they are usually chosen for research studies. Goodwin and Driscoll (1980) outline some of the factors involved in using formal observation methods within a research context.

It typically involves defining categories carefully, constructing elaborate data forms, training observers and establishing their interreliability, and recording, analyzing, and interpreting data using relatively sophisticated procedures.

This statement emphasizes the careful way in which formal observation is carried out and data are analyzed and used.

The relationship between formal observation and research studies is conveyed by the term controlled, which is an alternative to the term formal. Research is a highly controlled activity, and when observation is used in research studies, it is also controlled.

Informal methods, in contrast, involve a "less structured and less elaborate" approach to observation (Goodwin and Driscoll 1982). The strict research format is missing in informal observation; informal methods are therefore more suited to "instructional planning and day-to-day program operation. . . ." They are also more suited to an immediate, intuitive use than formal methods. This does not mean that attributes such as accuracy and dependability may be sacrificed when using informal methods. But, compared to formal methods, informal ones may be easier and more appropriate to use under some circumstances. Informal observation is also called "naturalistic observation," a name that captures the ideas of ease of use and lack of tight control.

Open vs. Closed

Recording techniques can be classified according to whether they are open or closed (see Wright 1960, Goodwin and Driscoll 1980). Open and closed methods differ in whether they preserve the *raw data* for later analysis. A distinction is appropriate here. Raw data are descriptions of behavior and events as they originally occurred. Pillari (1988), citing Coombs (1964), describes raw data as "the bits of information that are selected and constructed by the investigator as empirical facts for further analysis" (p. 2). *Data*, on the other hand, are described as "a body of facts that have already undergone interpretation according to the investigator's chosen method" (Pillari 1988, p. 2). So, for example, a narrative description of two children playing together in the big block area is raw data. But, if that description is reduced to a checkmark on an observation sheet, the raw data are lost even though, by Pillari's definition, you have preserved data. In short, then, open methods preserve raw data, closed ones do not.

Please note the important connection between *data, method,* and *interpretation.* It should be clear that preservation of *raw data* can be significant, inasmuch as different interpretations can be made of the raw data, thereby yielding different sets of data. Loss of raw data, however, results in the loss of any data other than that provided by the investigator or observer through interpretation according to some method.

The contrast between open and closed methods can be illustrated by an analogy to two books. Imagine a book containing information about children. Imagine further that, although you are permitted to look in this book to learn its contents, you have been given a limited time to do so. The best you can do, therefore, is summarize some of the information using a coding scheme. Furthermore, once you leave the book, it is closed and locked up; there is no going back to read more. Later, you look at your notes and you see that the book talked about aggressive behavior thirteen times, dependency behavior eight times, and not at all about language behavior. Your summary record might mention children's names, but there is no description of how the aggressions were expressed. You cannot go back to the book and figure out how you came to the decision to note Melinda's hitting Johnny as an aggressive event. Indeed, you have no record of Melinda hitting Johnny at all; you have only a checkmark to indicate that aggression occurred. There is no information on the circumstances surrounding behavior. This is a description of a closed method. The raw data are still in the book, out of your reach.

Imagine a second book that, like the first, contains information about children. You are again permitted to use the book, but this time you are given longer to read. Rather than summarize, you record what you read in as much detail as you can. Now, instead of noting how many times one child behaved aggressively toward another, you describe those aggressive behaviors—who aggressed against whom, in what specific setting and situation, the consequences of the behavior, and so on.

When you leave this second book, it remains open to you. You brought with you so much of the second book that you can examine and reexamine your records and notes. You may come to conclusions about the children and their behaviors that would not have been possible from your summary of the first book. The second book is like an open method—the raw data are in your hands, to use as you wish.

Degree of Selectivity

Degree of selectivity, which is closely related to openness and closedness, determines how many behaviors are targeted for observation and recording. Some methods are very unselective; no specific behaviors are chosen ahead of time, and almost everything that occurs is acceptable for observing and recording. Other methods are the opposite; the observer records only specific behaviors that she has chosen before entering the observation setting. For example, only instances of dependency behavior or of interpersonal exchanges between a child and an adult might be recorded in a closed method. Instances of motor behavior would be disregarded.

Degree of selectivity is comparable to the size of the holes in a fishing net. If the holes are small, you can catch fish of all sizes and kinds.

If the holes are large, only the bigger fish will be caught, and the smaller ones will escape through any hole larger than they are. Similarly, if an observation method's degree of selectivity is low, it is like fishing with a small-holed net. You will catch the small details of behavior, context, and sequence. If the degree of selectivity is high, of course, the holes in the observation net are large and will capture only certain behaviors.

This analogy also points up the close relationship between selectivity and the characteristics of openness and closedness. The number of details that can be recorded with a particular method is comparable to the number of fish that can be caught with a particular net. The bigger the holes in the net, the fewer the number of fish; the smaller the holes, the larger the number of fish since the net is capable of catching big fish as well as small ones.

Degree of Observer Inference Required

Inference means drawing a conclusion based on data, premises or evidence. For our purposes, inference means the same thing as interpretation or setting out the meaning of something. Inferences or interpretations are essentially conclusions based on directly observable data, but are not themselves directly observable. The conclusion is reached through a mental process; a connection is made between information we can perceive directly through our physical senses, and some other condition that we cannot learn of in that way.

You say "hello" to a friend, and she makes no response. You might infer—interpret her behavior to mean—that she is (1) angry with you, (2) angry with someone else, (3) preoccupied, (4) ill, or (5) teasing you, among a number of other possibilities. Whatever the case, your friend's anger, preoccupation, illness, or teasing is not what you observe. You can only observe the fact that she walked by without speaking to you. The rest is inference.

Various methods require different degrees of inference. Methods also differ as to when in the observation process inferences must be made. Some methods require no initial inference, since they involve no preselection of the behaviors to be recorded. Considerable inference may be involved if one wants to give meaning to the behaviors after they are recorded. In a case like this, inference takes place after the fact. It is not involved in decisions regarding behaviors to record, or categories a behavior should be in, at the time of the observation. Some methods do require inferences at the time of initial observing and recording. Making inferences during the recording phase of observation does not rule out making inferences later on. The inferences made during and after observing and recording serve different purposes.

If you do not care what kinds of fish you catch, you will use a net that will get you all kinds of fish, and there is no need to be choosy while you are fishing. Once you have hauled in your net, however, you might be interested in examining your catch. What kinds of fish are they? What does it mean to have caught them in these particular waters, under these particular conditions? Of what significance is it to have found this species of fish in the same area as this other species?

Suppose, though, that you do care what kind of fish you catch; you want a fish of one particular species. In this case, you have to know something about that fish; you have to be able to recognize it when you see it. Consequently, you throw out your net when that particular fish swims by, and not at any other time. Can you see the similarity to observation methods, and degree of inference required? With an open, unselective method, you do not worry over what behaviors are being caught in your net; indeed, you trap or record as many of them as you can. If you wish, you can examine your data and make inferences after the fishing is done. But, with a closed and selective method, you make an on-the-spot decision or inference as to whether Betsy's taking a toy away from Susan is an example of aggressive behavior. Is it the kind of "fish" you are looking for? If it is, then you record it; furthermore, once you have it and many others like it in your net, you can analyze and use the data. For example, the number of times various children exhibit aggression can form the basis for a behavior modification program in the classroom. Frequent aggression by a child, as documented by observation records (frequency counts, for example), can give the teacher a measurable basis for judging whether her efforts to eliminate the behavior have been successful.

The issue of when during the observation process inferences are made, is covered in the discussion of the methods themselves.

Summary

This chapter covered some important characteristics of methods of observing and recording behavior. Two types of methods were discussed: formal and informal. These types differ primarily in the strictness of the conditions that govern their use. Formal methods are characterized by careful prior preparation and strict control of all aspects and phases of the observation and recording process. Informal methods involve a less structured and less elaborate approach to observation, and for this reason, they are often used by teachers in the classroom.

Formal methods can be described along the dimensions of openness versus closedness, degree of selectivity, and degree of inference required. Openness versus closedness refers to whether or not the method preserves the original (raw) observational data. An open method was compared to a book that one is allowed to read and take extensive notes on, which can then can be used at a later time. The notes preserve much of the original book (the raw data). A closed method was compared to a book that one is given only limited time to read, thus requiring brief note-taking in the form of a code. These notes omit the details of the book's content, thus failing to preserve the raw data. Degree of selectivity refers to whether the observer may record anything that occurs during the observation session or is restricted to certain predesignated behaviors and events. Selectivity was presented as analogous to a fish net with holes of varying sizes: the larger the holes, the greater the degree of selectivity; the smaller the holes, the less selective a method is. Degree of inference required was discussed in terms of whether inferences are made at the time of initial observing and recording or at a later time. Some methods require immediate inference at the time of recording; others use inference when the observing and recording are completed.

Study Questions

1. What do the terms "formal" and "informal" mean with regard to observation? What do they mean with regard to a social gathering, for example? Are the meanings similar or different in the two situations?
2. To what, other than observation and recording methods, might the characteristics of openness and closedness be applied? Do the essential meanings of openness and closedness change or remain the same in the different applications?
3. How are openness and closedness related to degree of selectivity? Could they be independent of each other; that is, could a method be closed without also being selective, or open without also being unselective?
4. What is the difference between observation and interpretation?
5. Why is the distinction between "raw data" and "data" an important one? What is the significance for you, an observer, of the difference between these two kinds of information? What role do the two kinds of data play in your own observation activities?

chapter six
Specimen Records

Objectives

After studying this chapter, you will be able to

- define the role of specimen records in the observation process
- identify the relationship between the recording technique and the selectivity of the specimen record
- determine the limitations of specimen recording
- explain the role of inference in specimen recording
- identify the advantages and disadvantages of specimen recording

General Description

The specimen record, which is a formal method of observation, goes by several names. Goodwin and Driscoll (1980) mention "running behavior records," and Lay-Dopyera and Dopyera (1982) discuss the specimen record under the name "descriptive narrative." This last name is the best one, for it implies the most about the specimen record's characteristics.

We would point out that Irwin and Bushnell (1980), following Cohen and Stern (1958, 1978), make a distinction between the specimen record and the running record. The running record is described by Cohen and Stern as "a classroom observational technique for teachers, and it involves "taking on-the-spot records of behavior as it is occurring" (1958, p. 7; cited in Irwin and Bushnell 1980, p. 100). Janice Beatty (1986) defines the running record as "a detailed narrative of behavior, recorded in a sequential manner as it happens" (p. 9). Specimen records, according to Irwin and Bushnell, "are the researchers' counterpart to running records" (p. 102). Like running records, they describe behavior in narrative form, but they differ from running records in that they "require more rigorous detail and predetermined criteria" (p. 103). The distinction seems to rest on the degree of formality required of the two techniques, with the running record used "by teachers in a more informal way" and in situations where "the observer is definitely not a part of classroom activities" (Beatty, 1986, p. 11). We shall not struggle to preserve or emphasize the distinction. Instead, whether you will actually use a running or a specimen record technique will be determined by the circumstances under which you do your observations, as well as by your own personal skills. For practical purposes, however, we shall recommend the format and intent of the specimen record technique, especially in order to stay in keeping with Irwin and Bushnell's assertion that specimen record descriptions are usually based on predetermined criteria such as the time of day, the person, and the setting. We believe that the observation exercises impose criteria such as these, and, therefore, it is technically more correct to speak of the specimen record than of the running record.

In any case, in the specimen record technique, you continuously record in as much detail as possible what the child does and says, by herself and in interaction with other persons or objects. The chief goal of specimen recording is to obtain a detailed, objective account of behavior without inferences, interpretations, or evaluations. It is an important feature of the specimen record in that it details not only behaviors, but also the context (setting and situation) of the behaviors and the sequence in which they occur. It is also essential that the behaviors be *described* and not simply referred to in broad terms. A good description should enable the reader to close his eyes and get a mental picture of the scene. To say, "John played with the big blocks for 20 minutes" tells very little about John, the big blocks, played, or where all of these events took place. The potential completeness and inclusiveness of the specimen record is seen in Goodwin and Driscoll's note that "the permanent record itself might consist of just movies, videotapes, or audiotapes, if mechanical observation means have been used, or some combination of mechanical recording and observer's notes." Although the written specimen record is not as capable as movies and videotapes of "mirroring" the original raw data of the observation, it is capable of yielding rich, detailed information. Specimen records "provide a comprehensive, descriptive, objective, and permanent record of behavior as it occurs" (Goodwin and Driscoll 1980).

The specimen record in theory has no time limits. But practical considerations such as fatigue do impose limits on any single observer. In practice, therefore, the specimen record uses limited observation periods of approximately an hour. The observing and recording are continuous during that period. Longer records can be obtained by several observers recording on a rotating basis.

Open vs. Closed

The specimen record is the most open of all the observation methods. Its openness is a result of its unselectiveness and the amount of information it enables you to gather. The record preserves the description of behaviors, chronological sequences, and contexts. Consequently, those data are available in their original, unprocessed form for further examination and analysis.

Degree of Selectivity

The specimen record is not selective at all. Everything that occurs within an observation period is fair game for the recorder's pen. One observes and records with a small-holed net, being perfectly willing to haul in any kind of behavior that happens by.

We should emphasize, however, that strictly speaking, *selectivity is inherent in all recording methods.* This is because an observer can't see everything and must decide from among any number of persons and events exactly who and what to watch. Degree of selectivity, therefore, is relative and depends upon the specific recording method you are using. When we say that the specimen record "is not selective at all," we mean only that selectivity operates minimally compared with other methods.

Degree of Inference Required

At the time you are observing and recording, little inference is required, because everything that takes place is targeted for recording. When observing with the specimen record, therefore, you do not have to consider whether the behavior or the context is the "right one," just as when fishing with a small-holed net, there is no concern about whether you have trapped a carp or a minnow. One is as good as the other. Again, however, interpretations may be attempted after the fact. If you want to give to the original data any meaning that goes beyond that provided solely by objective description, inferences become necessary. In other words, you may want to examine your fish once you have brought them into the boat. You may wonder why carp and minnows got trapped in the net at the same time. You may wonder why Beth Ann is friendly toward Jane, while in the same context she is hostile toward Mark.

Advantages

Some of the advantages of the specimen record stem precisely from its openness and lack of selectivity. Because of these characteristics, the method can provide a complete account of what has occurred during the time you were in a child's behavior stream. Furthermore, the specimen record has the important advantage of capturing context (setting and situation) along with behavior. Wright (1960) placed considerable importance on this combination. "Everyone knows, at least intuitively, that the meaning and significance of an action and even its occurrence depend directly . . . upon the coexisting situation." Information concerning what and where can be especially useful when trying to understand individual children and how they behave in various contexts. As is well known, every child has his own unique style, attitudes, fears, and abilities. The specimen record, like a fishing net with small holes, catches these differences, these nuances in children's behavior, and permanently preserves them. Furthermore, it catches all of these behaviors, contexts, and styles under naturalistic conditions, without the artificial influences of experiments in a laboratory.

The permanence of the specimen record is also an advantage. Such records get more valuable as they get older. It is useful to compare specimen records obtained at an earlier time with more recent records. This comparison helps us learn about changes in children's behavior and development across time and place (see Wright 1960; Gaver and Richards 1979).

Specimen records are usable under many circumstances. They require no prepared observation sheets or coding schemes, nor any special language or jargon. The richness and subtlety of plain language is a major strength of the specimen record, although it is a strength that depends on the observer's language skills.

The specimen record allows considerable variations in the amount of time spent in the behavior stream. Narratives may describe behaviors ranging from several seconds to twelve hours or more (see, e.g., Barker and Wright 1951). The extended record usually involves several observers taking turns recording.

Disadvantages

The specimen record can cost a great deal in staff energy and time. The method can be inefficient for obtaining representative samples of behavior quickly. Part of the inefficiency comes from the failure to quantify behavioral data ahead of time through a predetermined coding scheme. For example, you cannot record the frequency of a behavior at the time you observe it. Specimen records can be analyzed for such things as frequency counts, but these analyses would have to be done after the observation session. They would also be time consuming.

Skill and effort are needed to notice and get down on paper the numerous details that are the goal of narrative description. Lay-Dopyera and Dopyera (1982) comment that because "the writing load is intense, many observers restrict themselves to a brief episode," which suggests the method of time sampling.

Summary

The specimen record is a formal method of observation that also goes by such names as running behavior record and descriptive narrative. In this technique, you record in as much detail as you can everything that occurs in the way of behavior and its context. The record is objective, without any evaluations or interpretations in the narrative description itself. The specimen record is the most open of all the observation methods. It is not at all selective, and it involves no inferences at the time of initial recording.

There are a number of advantages to the specimen record. It provides a rich, detailed account of a child's behavior and the circumstances in which it occurred. The record is permanent and can be used for a later comparison with more recent records. The method is costly in time and effort, however, and is not very efficient for quickly gathering representative samples of behavior. The technique also requires skill because of the many details that are the targets of narrative description.

Table 6-1 Specimen Record

Child Observed   *Melissa*
Child's Age   *4 years*
Setting   *Preschool classroom*
Time   *9:20 to 9:30*
Activity   *Free play*

Objective Behavioral Description	**Interpretations**
9:20-9:22 Melissa arrives about 35 minutes late; puts her coat in her cubby. She stands in the doorway of main classroom and looks around; remains motionless for ½ minute, moving only her eyes as she glances briefly at other children and their activities.	Melissa seems shy, almost withdrawn. From moment of arrival, she seemed reluctant to enter into things. May be because she didn't want to come in first place.
9:22-9:24 M. finally walks toward reading area on far side of room from cubbies. Moves slowly at first, scraping the toe of her right foot at each step, for about 5 feet. She passes by the puzzle table where 2 children are seated; no communication exchanged. She now walks more briskly to a table with some books lying on it. Tina, Ralph, and Morton are seated at the table; Ralph and Morton are sharing a book, Tina is watching them "read." Melissa says nothing to the three children as she sits down.	Melissa still seems uncertain; even her motor behaviors seem restricted; she walks slowly, shuffling, as though unsure of herself and of her relationship with the other children or her environment. Seems to have trouble deciding what to do. Not at all communicative; makes no overtures to any of the children who were "available" for such.
9:24-9:29 Ralph and Morton don't look up or acknowledge Melissa in any way. Tina says, "Hi, Melissa, wanna read a book with me?" M. cocks her head to one side and says softly, "I don't know how to read." T. replies "We can look at the pictures." M. looks over toward the big block area and without looking at T., says "OK." Tina smiles broadly and goes to a shelf containing a number of books. M. picks up one of the books and flips slowly through the pages.	Tina is outgoing and friendly as Melissa approaches; M. is still uncommunicative; still seems shy and uncertain; speaks softly as though afraid of being heard. Tina persists in spite of M's lack of enthusiasm. M. also seems distractable or inattentive. She shies away from T's efforts to get close physically. Tina moves at a quick pace—much more energetic than M.

T. returns with a book and says "I like this one, let's look at this one." M. merely nods; T. sits down close to M, but M. moves slightly, keeping a distance of about 6-8 inches between her and T.

9:29-9:30   Ralph looks up and says "Hey, you two, wha'cha doin'?" T. tilts her head upward, thrusts out her chin slightly and says "Never mind, we're busy." M. says nothing, but gets up from the table and walks slowly toward big block area. Morton still reads.

Tina is much more outgoing and sure of herself than M. T. didn't interact too much w/Ralph and Morton; may have felt left out of their activity. T. definitely seemed pleased to see M.; displayed no unfavorable response to M's "unsocial" behavior. T's response to Ralph quite assertive, but in a friendly way; almost like she claimed Melissa as *her* playmate, maybe in retaliation for the two boys ignoring her earlier. M. still seems uninterested, even uncertain of what to do.

Study Questions

1. What is a distinguishing characteristic of the specimen record? What are some advantages and disadvantages of this characteristic?
2. How does the specimen record's degree of selectivity affect the way one specifically records observational data?
3. Under what conditions would you probably not want to use the specimen record? Under what conditions would you probably want to use the method?
4. What is the role of interpretation in the specimen record? When is interpretation most likely to be used or needed?
5. When would what you intended to be a specimen record actually turns out to be a running record? Would the data differ significantly between the two reports?

chapter seven
Time Sampling

Objectives

After studying this chapter, you will be able to

- relate the importance of the representativeness of behavior to the time sampling method.
- determine the most appropriate coding system to use in a particular time sampling observation
- identify the characteristics of time sampling in relation to the dimensions of open versus closed, degree of selectivity, and degree of inference required
- analyze the advantages and disadvantages of the time sampling method of observation

General Description

The name *time sampling* identifies one of this method's distinguishing features; the observer watches and records selected behaviors during preset uniform time periods and at regularly recurring or randomly selected intervals. Behaviors and events that occur outside of these time periods are not recorded. The length and distribution of the observing and recording periods can vary widely depending upon your purposes, the total amount of time you are in the setting, and the typical frequency with which certain behaviors occur. You could decide to observe a child for one minute every five minutes, beginning on the hour over a total period of one hour; this is a regularly recurring interval. Or you could randomly select one-minute intervals from within a one-hour period, observe during those and end up with the same total number of individual recordings as with the systematic approach (Brandt 1972).

Representativeness of the time sample is extremely important. "The length, spacing, and number of intervals are intended to secure representative *time samples* of the target phenomena" (Wright 1960, italics in original). Brandt (1972) also notes that behavior samples are chosen . . . "in order to be representative of a population of behavioral units larger than that of those observed." Brandt points out, however, that representativeness is only possible for those behaviors that occur frequently.

A time sampling session might be structured in the following manner. The observer spends three minutes on each of 15 children in a preschool classroom. She observes the first child for three minutes. Using a previously coded observation sheet, she records each instance of dependency or cooperative behavior exhibited during that period. The observer then moves on to the second child and repeats the process, until she has observed and recorded the dependency and cooperative behaviors of all 15 children.

Variations on the time sampling procedure are numerous. Variations are possible not only in the length and distribution of time intervals, but also in recording techniques. For instance, an observer might decide to spend six minutes on each child, but follow an on-off, observe-record procedure. This is especially appropriate when using a combination of coding scheme and narrative description. Here, he could observe the child for one minute, indicating only whether the target behavior(s) occurred. The second minute could be used to write a brief narrative description of the behavior and its context. The remaining one-minute intervals would be used in the same on-off fashion until the six minutes of observation were completed. The time periods could be divided in some other way—for example, observe for 10 seconds and record for 50 seconds. The variations possible are revealed by Goodwin and Driscoll's (1980) report of studies in which observation and recording took place as frequently as every three or six seconds.

Certain behaviors are always preselected as targets for observation—for example, the children's dependency, speech utterances, or attentiveness to assigned tasks might be chosen. Coding schemes are often used with the time sampling method. These schemes require making an appropriate mark on an observation sheet whenever the child displays the behavior of interest. There are two kinds of coding systems: category and sign systems (Irwin and Bushnell 1980; Goodwin and Driscoll 1982). A sign system, say Irwin and Bushnell, "requires that the categories of behavior be mutually exclusive. . . ." This means that no given behavior can be placed in more than one category, for each category chosen excludes all others. The category system also requires "mutually exclusive categories of behavior but, in addition, the categories must be *exhaustive*. They must include the total range of behaviors so that anything the child does can be tallied" (Irwin and Bushnell 1980). Let us look quickly at a coding scheme that uses a sign system.

Examine Table 7-1. In this example, several facets of a child's behavior are defined for notice and recording. The categories are Task Orientation, Cognitive, Motility, and Interpersonal Behavior. These broad categories are further divided into specific behavioral characteristics. Thus, if you observe what you interpret as interpersonal behavior (broad category 4), you would then determine the direction or pattern of the behavior—Child to Teacher, Child to Other Child, or Other Child to Child. From there, you would have to make yet another decision as to the nature of the interpersonal behavior using the descriptions provided in the checksheet: Complies, Ignores, Resists, and so on. Table 7-1 gives you enough space to record the behaviors of ten children, or of one child over ten time intervals, whichever best suits your purpose. It also provides space for brief descriptions of the context of the recorded behaviors. A good example of a category system is Parten's (1932) six categories of social participation, which are frequently referred to as play classifications (see Table 7-2).

Much simpler coding schemes are available. Gander and Gardiner (1982), for instance, note a procedure where each minute is divided into fifteen-second intervals that are represented in some kind of graphic form. During each fifteen seconds of observation, if the selected behavior occurs, an "X" is placed in the appropriate spot on the form; if the behavior does not occur, an "O" is recorded. Over a period of three minutes, the record could look something like the following, where each / marks off a fifteen-second interval and each I marks the end of one minute (adapted from Gander and Gardiner):

X / O / O / X I X / O / O / O I X / X / X / O I

Figure 7-1

Table 7-1 Sign System of Time Samplings

	Recording Interval or Children Observed
1. *Task Orientation:* A. Attentive to T; B. Intent Indiv. Work; C. Disinterest; D. Attentive to other children; E. Social work; F. Intent non-teacher prescribed work; G. Aimless wandering; H. Verbal disruptive; I. Physical disruptive	_____
2. *Cognitive:* A. Seeking information; B. Offering information; C. Curiosity and experimentation; D. None	_____
3. *Motility:* A. Expansive; B. Average; C. Constricted	_____
4. *Interpersonal Behavior:*	_____
4.1 *Child to Teacher:* A. Absent; B. Present Response to Teacher Initiation: A. Complies; B. Ignores;I C. Resists; D. None	_____

Seeks help, support, approval: A. Absent; B. Present   _____

Verbalization to Teacher: A. Confident; B. Hesitant; C. Whine; D. None   _____

4.2. *Child to other child:* A. Absent; B. Present   _____

Type: A. Active interchange; B. Approach tentatively; C. Passive watching; D. Imitates; E. Avoids   _____

Tone: A. Friendly; B. Neutral; C. Hostile Control: A. Dominates; B. Neutral; C. Passive   _____

Cooperation: A. Shares; B. Resists sharing; C. None   _____

4.3 *Other Child to observation child:* A. Present; B. Absent   _____

Type: A. Active interchange; B. Approach tentatively; C. Acceptance; D. Reject   _____

Tone: A. Friendly; B. Neutral; C. Hostile   _____

Brief Description of Situation

1. _____
2. _____
3. _____
4. _____
5. _____
6. _____
7. _____
8. _____
9. _____
10. _____

Reprinted, with permission from Dr. Donald S. Peters

This could be repeated any number of times for any number of children.

It may be helpful if you can think of time sampling in relation to the concept of a behavior stream. A person's life consists of a continuous stream of behavior that flows through time. The time sampling method looks for samples of certain kinds of behavior in a child's behavior stream; but, it looks for those behaviors only in specific parts of the stream identified by intervals of time. So, an observer using the time sampling method might reason along the following lines:

Table 7-2 Parten's Six Classifications of Play or Social Interaction

1. *Unoccupied Behavior:* Here the child is not engaging in any obvious play activity or social interaction. Rather, she watches anything that is of interest at the moment. When there is nothing of interest to watch, the child will play with her own body, move around from place to place, follow the teacher, or stay in one spot looking around the room.

2. *Onlooker Behavior:* Here the child spends most of her time watching other children play. The child may talk to the playing children, may ask questions or give suggestions, but does not enter into play. The child remains within speaking distance so that what goes on can be seen and heard; this indicates a definite interest in a group(s) of children, unlike the unoccupied child, who shows no interest in any particular group of children but only a shifting interest in what happens to be exciting at the moment.

3. *Solitary Play:* This is play activity that is conducted independently of what anyone else is doing. The child plays with toys that differ from those used by other children in the immediate area—within speaking distance—and she makes no effort to get closer to them or to speak to them. The child is focused entirely on her own activity and is uninfluenced by what the others are doing.

4. *Parallel Play:* Here the child is playing close to other children but is still independent of them. The child uses toys that are like the toys being used by the others, but he uses them as he sees fit and is neither influenced by nor tries to influence the others. The child thus plays *beside* rather than with the other children.

5. *Associative Play:* Here the child plays with other children. There is a sharing of play material and equipment; the children may follow each other around; there may be attempts to control who may or may not play in a group, although such control efforts are not strongly asserted. The children engage in similar but not necessarily identical activity, and there is no division of labor, or organization of activity, or of individuals. Each child does what he or she essentially wants to do, without putting the interests of the group first.

6. *Cooperative or Organized Supplementary Play:* The key word in this category is "organized." The child plays in a group that is established for a particular purpose—making some material product, gaining some competitive goal, playing formal games. There is a sense of "we-ness," whereby one definitely belongs or does not belong to the group. There is also some leadership present—one or two members who direct the activity of the others. This therefore requires some division of labor, a taking of different roles by the group members, and the support of one child's efforts by those of the others.

Adapted from Parten (1932)

I am going to look for aggressive behavior in this group of children; but I want to observe all of the children, and I'm interested in how often aggression is displayed among the group. Therefore, between the hours of 9:00 and 10:30 A.M., a one and one-half hour segment of these children's behavior streams will flow by. I want to enter into that one and one-half hour part of their lives and see what is happening. To do this, I'm going to divide up the total 90 minutes among all 15 children, which gives me six minutes for each child. In order to get a reasonably representative sample of behavior, however, I'll probably repeat this entire process several times over the course of a week so that I'll end up with, say, three six-minute recorded samples of behavior for each child.

Open vs. Closed

Both Wright (1960) and Goodwin and Driscoll (1980) classify time sampling as a closed method. They consider it closed because of its use of coding schemes or "at the point of initial data collection" (Goodwin and Driscoll 1980). A coding scheme applied at the time of observation loses raw data; it is that loss that defines a closed method.

Time sampling methods are not always closed, nor need they be completely closed. We have considered the possibility of combining a closed coding scheme and an open specimen record or event sampling method. But even the use of only narrative descriptions is acceptable. Lay-Dopyera and Dopyera (1982), for example, describes the "on-off" sequence we discussed earlier as "... observation, note-taking, and note expansion." Although time sampling often uses a coding scheme to record behaviors, the terms "note-taking" and "note expansion" indicate that a form of narrative record can also be used. The principal feature of time sampling is the use of precisely and uniformly defined time intervals, and not the specific recording technique used. Consequently, we will consider time sampling an open method to the extent that it preserves the raw data.

Degree of Selectivity

The time sampling method is very selective; it "fishes" with a large-holed net, and the net is cast only when the preselected behavior appears in the child's behavior stream. It is not like the specimen record, which, you will recall, fishes with a small-holed net that stays in the stream throughout the observation period.

Degree of Inference Required

Time sampling does require initial inferences or interpretations. This is so because the method requires you to make an immediate decision concerning whether to record a behavior. That decision is based on whether you see the behavior as falling under a particular descriptive category, as an example of aggression, cooperative play, or what have you.

As with the specimen record or any of the other methods to be discussed, time sampling can require inferences at other points in the observation process. Once you have collected your data, you may want to use them to draw conclusions about such things as the relationship between the observed behaviors and certain characteristics of their context. For example, you may discover that Billy seems to behave aggressively when he is in the big block area during free play. Drawing conclusions about such relationships, however, requires information on context and behaviors that is not ordinarily obtained with coding schemes. Therefore, some narrative description may have to be a part of your recording technique. In any case, such inferences would be made after the observations were completed; so, they are not an inherent part of the method, but part of the use made of the recorded data.

Advantages

Time sampling has many advantages. There are no restrictions on the kinds of behaviors that can be studied with this method. Wright (1960) cites the range of behaviors that have been time sampled as early as the 1930s. He refers to behaviors ranging from "imaginative behavior" to "friendships and quarrels" to "tics or 'nervous habits'." The method has a long history, which attests to its reliability and usefulness.

The method is economical in terms of required time and energy. Time sampling is efficient because it regulates precisely the content of the observation and the amount of time one observes (Wright 1960; Irwin and Bushnell 1980). Efficiency is also achieved by using preestablished coding schemes, which reduces variability in observer judgments and inferences. This potential elimination of differing judgments contributes to an agreement among several observers, thereby increasing *inter-observer reliability*.

Time sampling also provides representative and reliable data, if one gathers a large number of observations related to a particular research problem. Large numbers of recordings are possible because of the method's efficiency and the ease with which data can be recorded using coding schemes.

Yet another advantage of the time sampling method is its ability to combine several different techniques for recording—coding and narrative description, for example. This allows the observer to use two different nets; one net catches limited kinds of data (whether the behavior has occurred at all), the other net catches the details of context and behavior. One can also use event sampling or some other form of narrative description by itself.

Disadvantages

This last advantage is an important one, for it also points up a significant disadvantage of a time sampling format that uses only coding schemes.

Coding schemes do not capture the details of context, what the behaviors look like, how the behavior sequence turns out, how the behaviors change over time, or how the behaviors are related to each other (Wright 1960; Irwin and Bushnell 1980). Brandt (1972) points out these same weaknesses when he writes that "Time samples lack the continuity, contextual completeness, and perhaps naturalness of event samples. . . ." From this perspective, then, time sampling is chiefly used to measure the frequency of behaviors.

Frequency of occurrence of a given behavior is a limiting factor, however. Behaviors are not displayed equally often, nor do all behaviors occur with great frequency. It makes no sense to record every 15 seconds whether a particular behavior took place, when that behavior occurs every 28 minutes on the average. Gander and Gardiner (1982) address this problem when they relate behavior frequency with decisions concerning the length of the observation periods and the length of the recording intervals. If a behavior can be expected to occur fairly often, it may make sense to set aside several segments of time for observing and recording and to specify recording intervals that are relatively frequent and short. Gander and Gardiner use the example of a child's social interaction and suggest that "you might decide to observe for three five-minute sessions at five-minute intervals, and note whether your target behavior is occurring every fifteen seconds." This procedure assumes that social interactions take place frequently enough to justify dividing your recording intervals into such small segments. It therefore follows that longer recording intervals should be adopted when the behavior of interest occurs less frequently. But as Gander and Gardiner point out, these decisions take "a little experience." These decisions may also depend on the observer doing some preliminary observations to determine the frequency of the behaviors. Irwin and Bushnell (1980) indicate that for time sampling to be an effective method, a behavior should occur at least once every 15 minutes on the average.

Time sampling does not treat behavior as it naturally occurs. When using predefined and restricted units of time, it is inevitable that the natural length of the behaviors will not correspond exactly to the somewhat arbitrary length of the observing and recording intervals. It is as though you throw your net into an entire school of fish, but you haul in only a very small number of them. From that very small number you will be able to tell almost nothing about the ones that got away. This has been referred to as "the observation of action fragments" (Wright 1960). A problem arises if these fragments do not accurately represent what is going on in the larger behavior stream. Here is an illustration.

You are observing a classroom, and you watch each child for five-second intervals and record on a precoded sheet any occurrences of aggressive behavior. After each interval, you move on to another child, repeating this procedure until every child has been observed. The process is then repeated, until you have obtained some predetermined total number of observations. Suppose that while you are giving your five seconds of attention to Jean, she screams at Harold, "Get out of here, you bad boy!" You decide this is an example of verbal aggression, and you appropriately mark it as such on your recording sheet. You then shift your attention to the next child. What you may have missed from this sequence were the preceding dramatic play behaviors, in which Jean was the "mommy" and Harold was her "son." "Mommy" was simply scolding her "son" for misbehaving, symbolically speaking. You may also have missed Harold's response: "I'm sorry mommy, please don't spank me." In this illustration, Jean's remarks taken out of context, misrepresented the larger sequence of which they were a part. This example argues for gathering a number of time samples to ensure the representativeness and validity of your data.

Irwin and Bushnell (1980) also report that the use of predetermined categories might bias what the observer sees. As they put it, "you look for things to fit the categories rather than describe what is occurring, and [use of predetermined categories] can cause you to overlook behaviors that might be important in helping understand the behavior or pattern under study." This weakness of time sampling is found in any method that is highly selective and closed.

A final comment on time sampling may have to do with either advantages or disadvantages, depending on your point of view. Coding schemes impose certain problems and obligations on the observer. Look again at Table 7-1. The categories (actually signs) in Table 7-1 may appear straightforward, but their simplicity is deceptive. Before you could use Table 7-1 as a time sampling technique, every one of those signs would have to be defined. How would you recognize "curiosity and experimentation" if you saw them? How would you know whether a child's verbalizations to her teacher were confident, hesitant, or whining? These decisions require inferences; moreover, they require consistent inferences. It is improper to accept a set of behaviors as verbally disruptive at one time, then a few minutes later put similar behaviors into a different category. Defining such descriptive categories as precisely as you can is a strength of the time sampling method; but at the same time, such definition requires a lot of prior preparation.

Summary

The time sampling method has two distinguishing features. It observes and records selected samples of a child's behavior, and it does so only during predetermined intervals of time. Time sampling aims at representative samples of behavior. To achieve this requires you to observe over a large enough number of intervals to capture the typical quality of the stream from which the sample is taken.

The variations on the time sampling method are numerous. Although coding schemes are usually used with time sampling, narrative description can be combined with such schemes. There are two general types of coding schemes: category and sign systems. A sign system of coding requires mutually exclusive categories of behavior. No given behavior can be included in more than one category. A category system requires mutually exclusive categories and exhaustive categories. The categories must include the total range of behaviors.

Time sampling varies on the dimension of open versus closedness. If only coding schemes are used, the method is closed; if combined with narrative description, it is open to that degree. The method is very selective and records only specific behaviors. Time sampling requires inferences at the time of initial recording; a decision must be made as to whether to record a particular behavior. Inferences may also be needed after the data are collected, depending on your purposes.

Time sampling is economical of time and effort. It regulates precisely the content of the observation and the amount of time you observe. An important disadvantage of time sampling is that it does not capture the details of behavior and context. It also is not a useful method for recording infrequent behaviors. The amount of preparation needed to define the behavioral categories used in the coding scheme can be an advantage or a disadvantage, depending on your point of view.

Using the same specimen record data, let us see what a time sample might look like. This format uses a sign system, and the data are restricted just to Melissa, Tina, Ralph, and Morton. Because this time sampling data is obtained from the previous specimen record description (focusing primarily on Melissa), there will be no information recorded for Tina, Ralph, and Morton until the recording interval matches the time in the specimen record when their behaviors would actually have been observed. In a real time sampling session, of course, the observer would have recorded Melissa's behavior (if appropriate), then he would have observed Tina, then Ralph, then Morton, and so on, for the entire class. The present illustration merely simplifies the description.

The numbers in the cells (boxes) refer to the behaviors that define the major categories. The procedure for this example would have been the following: Procedure—Observe a child for 5 seconds, record for 5 seconds; wait 50 seconds, then repeat the process with the next child until all children have been observed.

Table 7-3 Time Sampling—Interactions with Others and with Environment

Children Involved   *Melissa, Tina, Ralph, Morton*
Children's Age   *Four Years*
Observation Setting   *Preschool Classroom*
Time Began   *9:20 to 9:30*
Activity   *Free Play*

Behavior Category

General Response to Setting

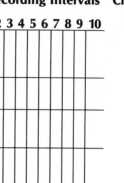

Recording Intervals   Child

1 2 3 4 5 6 7 8 9 10

1. Enters setting willingly (specify which area involved—big block area (BBA), reading area (RA), etc.)
2. Enters setting reluctantly
3. Refuses to enter setting

General Response to Equipment/Materials

4. Uses equipment/materials freely
5. Limited or sporadic use of equipment/materials
6. No use of equipment/materials

Study Questions

1. What does it mean to say that a sample of behavior is representative? Why is representativeness a potential problem in time sampling? How can this problem be solved or at least minimized?
2. What is a coding system? When is a coding system necessary in time sampling?
3. Describe an example of a coding system. What are its characteristics?
4. What makes time sampling a closed and highly selective method? When might time sampling not be closed?
5. Why is inference necessary in time sampling? When does it occur?

chapter eight
Event Sampling

Objectives

After studying this chapter, you will be able to

- examine the differences and similarities between time sampling and event sampling
- identify behaviors that could constitute an event
- identify procedures to record an event
- identify the characteristics of event sampling in relation to the dimensions of open versus closed, degree of selectivity, and degree of inference required
- analyze the advantages and disadvantages of event sampling

General Description

Event sampling is the last formal method of observation to be discussed. Just as the word "time" is central to time sampling, so the word "event" is central to event sampling. Although both methods use the word "sampling," their procedures and results can be quite different.

Recall that in time sampling, preselected behaviors are the targets of observation and recording. Whether you come away with any recorded instances of these behaviors, however, depends not only on whether they occur, but also on whether they occur within specified intervals of time. So, you can see that time sampling methods take two different samples out of the child's behavior stream: (1) specifically defined segments of time, and (2) specifically defined behaviors. The limiting condition here is that these two samples must occur at the same time. The designated behavior must be displayed sometime during the designated time interval, otherwise, the behavior either escapes notice or it is not recorded because it did not occur at the proper time.

Event sampling differs from time sampling in that it takes only one sample from the child's behavior stream, namely, specifically defined behaviors or events. *Events* are behaviors that can be placed into particular categories. For example, quarrels can be an event; but quarrels are made up of specific observable behaviors such as loud speech, certain kinds of facial expressions, or arguing over possession of a toy. You observe two children exhibiting certain behaviors, and you must decide whether these behaviors belong in the category labeled quarrels. The event must have certain characteristics if it is to be labeled a quarrel.

Event sampling seems simple. You select an event for observing, whether it be quarrels, social interactions, or dependency behavior. Again, you define the event in terms of the *behaviors* you will accept as examples of that event. You position yourself in the observation setting where the children can be seen, and you wait for the event to occur. When it does, you can do one of three things. Goodwin and Driscoll (1982) summarize the recording technique used with event sampling as immediate coding of the occurrence of certain events. Lay-Dopyera and Dopyera (1982), and Gander and Gardiner (1981), however, write of describing the event in detail. Gander and Gardiner say ". . . you should record the entire sequence of behavior from beginning to end in as much detail as possible to provide a rich body of information to use in drawing inferences." Therefore, you can choose (1) a coding scheme, (2) a narrative description, or (3) a combination of these two. The previous discussion of coding schemes in time sampling also applies to event sampling. When using narrative description, you will observe and record for as long as the event lasts. (Note how this differs from time sampling, where observing and recording are limited to predetermined amounts of time.)

Open vs. Closed

Both Wright (1960) and Goodwin and Driscoll (1982) classify event sampling as a closed method. For our purposes, though, it can be open or closed. Detailed narrative description preserves the raw data, thus fulfilling the requirements of openness. If only coding schemes are used, the method is closed.

Degree of Selectivity

There is a high degree of selectivity, since only specific events chosen beforehand are observed and recorded.

Degree of Inference Required

The degree of initial inference is high, just as in the time sampling method. Remember that an inference is any decision as to whether a behavior or set of behaviors belongs to a particular category. Does Ralph's clinging to the teacher's hand belong in the category "emotional dependency?" Also remember that even the simplest of these inferences is not self-evident. One must recognize clinging behavior and must know or decide whether clinging is an accurate or appropriate element of emotional dependency.

Advantages

Event sampling shares some of the advantages of both the specimen record and time sampling. The potential for rich, detailed descriptions of behavior and its context is an advantage, just as it is in the specimen record. Event sampling can also be very practical; it is a very suitable method to use with behaviors that do not occur frequently. Of course, the infrequent observer may not find this an advantage; the odds are against infrequent behaviors occurring at the same time as infrequent periods of observation. Thus, teachers or others who are in the observation setting often and for relatively long periods of time may find event sampling a useful method.

Wright (1960) points out that event sampling "structures the field of observation into natural units of behavior and situation." These "natural units" allow you to study the relationships between behavior and its context. The specimen record does the same thing, but it captures "everything" in the behavior stream. Therefore, specific behavior episodes—the natural units of behavior—have to be got from the larger body of information. Even though event sampling deals with natural behavior units, it is limited because it still breaks up the continuity of behavior. As a result, the inability of event sampling to preserve large segments of the behavior stream may be regarded as a disadvantage.

A final advantage of event sampling is that it can combine narrative description and coding schemes, thus gaining the efficiency of immediate coding and the completeness of the specimen record. Because events are predefined patterns of behaviors, you can use a coding scheme such as a check list to record features of the context that are predictably related to the event. For example, in a preschool setting, various locations within the room (e.g., big block area, dramatic play area), kinds of equipment and materials (paints, crayons, puzzles, trikes, etc.), official activity at the time the event occurs, and the children and adults present at the time, can be listed for easy checking and coding. The narrative description can be structured around questions that relate directly to the particular event. Positive social interchanges, for instance, have certain behaviors associated with them. Therefore, you can be prepared to record information concerning what the children said during the social episode; what physical actions the child performed (hugging, smiling, giving a toy); what immediately preceded the social behavior; or the outcome of the event (adapted from Wright 1960).

Disadvantages

Some of the disadvantages of event sampling have already been mentioned. The most notable disadvantage is its unsuitability for studying infrequently occurring behaviors. This limitation, however, also applies to time sampling. Also, if full details of behavior and context are desirable or necessary, event sampling may not be the appropriate method.

Table 8-1   Event Sampling—Social Behavior

Child Observed   *Melissa*
Child's Age   *Four Years*
Observation Setting   *Preschool Classroom*
Activity   *Free Play*
Behavioral Event   *Social Interactions*
Time   *9:20 to 9:35*

Event Description	Interpretations
9:24-9:29 Melissa slowly approaches the reading table where Tina, Ralph and Morton are seated. M. sits down, but says nothing to the others. Tina responds immediately to M's presence; greets her with "Hi, wanna read a book with me?" M. replies that she (M.) can't read. T. replies that they can look at the pictures. M. agrees with a softly spoken "ok." Tina smiles and goes for a book. M. does not look at or speak to Ralph and Morton, nor they to her. T. comes back and tries to sit close to M., who resists by moving away slightly keeping about 6-8 inches between them. Ralph speaks to the two girls, asking them what they're doing. T. responds, "Never mind, we're busy." M. says nothing but gets up from the table and moves slowly toward the cubby area.	Melissa seems shy, withdrawn, apathetic. She doesn't respond to Tina's greeting, barely even looks at her; seems not even to notice Ralph and Morton, who also ignore her. M. avoids close contact with Tina; seems to reject physical or psychological proximity. M. is easily distracted, does not focus well socially, as evidenced by her lack of eye contact with Tina and by her looking around the room as T. tries to engage her in a social exchange. M's actions don't appear to stem from any dislike of Tina; no evidence of hostility—indeed, M. is emotionally bland. Appears to have no interest in the company of others.
9:29-9:30 M. breaks contact with Tina and Ralph and walks toward big block area.	Melissa still seems withdrawn and uninterested; she makes no response to Ralph's friendly overture.

Summary

Event sampling differs from time sampling in that it takes specifically defined behaviors or events from the child's behavior stream, but is not concerned with when the behaviors occur or with the length of the recording period. Events were defined as behaviors that can be placed into certain categories; for example, loud speech and certain facial expressions could be put into the category of quarrels, which constitutes an event. The event must be carefully defined before beginning the observation.

Event sampling was discussed as being either open or closed, depending on whether you use narrative description or coding schemes. A combination of both is also possible. This method is highly selective, and the degree of initial inference is high.

Event sampling shares some of the advantages of both the specimen record and time sampling. There is the potential for detailed behavioral descriptions and the use of efficient coding schemes. Infrequently occurring behaviors can be suitable targets for event sampling, if you are in the setting often or for relatively long periods of time. There is the disadvantage that although event sampling records details of behavior and context, it still breaks up the overall continuity that characterizes all behavior.

Study Questions

1. How are time sampling and event sampling similar? What are some important differences?
2. What is an event? Give two examples of events and identify some of the behaviors that make up each event.
3. Describe how you might prepare for and carry out an observation session using the event sampling method.
4. Compare the specimen record and the event sampling methods. How are they alike and how do they differ?
5. Under what circumstances would you want to use event sampling rather than another method?

chapter nine
Diary Description

Objectives

After studying this chapter, you will be able to

- describe the characteristics of the diary description method of observation
- discuss the characteristics of the diary description in relation to the dimensions of open versus closed, degree of selectivity, and degree of inference required
- describe the advantages and disadvantages of the diary description

General Description

Diary description is an informal method of observation, and it is considered the oldest method in child development (Wright 1960). Traditionally, it is used over extended periods of a child's life (*longitudinally*). In this technique, daily records are made of selected aspects of the child's growth and development. It is not as inclusive as the specimen record, because continuous contacts with the child over a period of weeks, months, or years, prohibit the intense writing load required by the specimen record.

The diary record has the objective of "recording in sequence *new* behavioral events in the behavior continuum of one subject, usually an infant or a child of preschool age" (Wright 1960; italics in original). Goodwin and Driscoll (1982) confirm this use of the diary, indicating that "Emphasis is on recording new behaviors demonstrated by one child." These new behaviors are often part of a particular developmental area such as intellectual functioning, language behavior, and social-emotional behavior. This type of diary description has been referred to as a *topical diary.* (Wright 1960). Piaget's records of his own children's cognitive development are a classic example of a topical diary. A broader focus is maintained by what Wright called a *comprehensive diary,* which "records in order as much of everything new as it can. . . ." The general intent of the diary description is to chart a child's step by step progress over a period of time.

The diary description demands a close and almost continuous contact between the child and the observer. Such closeness is rarely achieved except by a parent or guardian.

Open vs. Closed

Diary description is classified as an open method, because it captures the details of the child's behaviors, behavioral changes, and their context. It preserves those details as raw data that can be examined, analyzed, or compared later with other records.

Degree of Selectivity

Although the comprehensive diary as described by Wright appears to be unselective, it does limit itself to new behaviors that add to the recorder's understanding of the developing child. It is therefore not as undiscriminating as the specimen record. The topical diary is even more selective than the comprehensive diary; it limits itself to new behaviors that occur only within specific areas of growth and development.

Degree of Inference Required

The inference required in the diary record is much like that required in the time sampling and event sampling methods. At the least, the observer must make judgments as to whether a particular behavior is indeed new and whether it legitimately belongs in the topical area that is the focus of study. For example, is the smile displayed by two-month-old Rebecca a true indication of social behavior or is it merely gas pains? Any later use of the completed record can require further inference.

Advantages

The diary description shares with the specimen record a richness of detail, breadth of coverage, and the permanency of the written record (Wright 1960). The breadth of its coverage includes the context of the behaviors as they occur at a given time, and their sequence. Thus, rather than isolated incidents, behaviors become connected to one another within an unfolding developmental framework. This connectedness is part of the longitudinal character of the diary description.

Permanency of the record allows future comparisons with other forms of observational data, including developmental norms.

Disadvantages

The obvious disadvantage of the diary description is its limited usefulness to most observers. The need for continuous and close contact with the child rules out almost everyone but parents or other members of the child's family. Even teachers seldom have such an extensive relationship with a particular child (Goodwin and Driscoll 1982).

Summary

The diary description is an informal method of observing and recording. It is considered the oldest method in child development. Historically, the diary description has been used over relatively long periods of a child's life to record selected aspects of her growth and development. Two types of diary descriptions were discussed: the topical diary, and the comprehensive diary. The first type emphasizes new behaviors demonstrated by the child; these new behaviors are often part of a developmental area such as intellectual functioning or language behavior. The comprehensive diary is broader in scope than the topical diary, and it records "as much of everything new as it can" (Wright 1960).

The diary description is considered an open method; it preserves the details of the child's behaviors and their context. The diary is limited to new behaviors that add to the observer's understanding of some aspects of the developing child, and so it is somewhat selective. The diary description requires inferences regarding whether a given behavior is new and belongs in the topical area being studied.

The diary shares with the specimen record the advantage of providing rich, detailed descriptions of behavior, breadth of coverage, and the permanency of the written record. Its major disadvantage is that not everyone can use it because it requires close, continuous contact with the child.

Sample Diary Description: Case Study Use

January 12, 1993. Jon L., male, age 3 years, 4 months.
Area of Observation: Social Development

Today, Jon initiated play in the big block area with Marion, a three-year-old girl. This is very unusual for Jon; in the three months (since September 1992) he's been attending the preschool, he has typically been shy and rather aloof. He is smaller than most of the other boys in the class, and the staff suspects that he is intimidated by their greater physical size. We have not, however, witnessed any bullying by the other boys.

Jon has an older, bigger brother, who may be contributing at home to Jon's apparent fearfulness or shyness in the company of the larger, stronger children. This is a possibility we should check out in our next parent conference.

Mrs. Owens (teacher) also witnessed Jon's behavior with Marion. She showed her pleasure with his actions by commenting on how nicely the two of them played together. Jon reacted positively to her remarks; he smiled and appeared to increase his efforts to interact with both Marion and the blocks. They played together for about 7 minutes, when Adrian, one of the bigger boys in the class, tried to join them.

Jon almost immediately left the big block area and sat down with a book at one of the reading tables. No further interactions between Jon and any of the other children occurred for the remainder of the morning.

January 18, 1993.

A real breakthrough seems to be taking place in Jon's social behavior. Since the observation of Jan. 12, the staff and I have been seeing what we think are glimmerings of a desire on Jon's part to be with at least a few of the other children. Today, about 10:00 A.M., Jon "timidly" asked Michael K., who is not much bigger than Jon, if he would play in the sandbox with him. Michael agreed. The two boys played amicably with two trucks, driving them on "roads" they constructed with wooden blocks. Play lasted for about 9 minutes; it ended when time came for snacks.

It must be noted that during their play, Jon was not assertive. Michael pretty much dictated or directed what was to happen, who was to "drive" which truck, and where the "roads" were to be placed in the sand. Nonetheless, Jon didn't appear to be especially anxious or intimidated by Michael's leadership role. He must be observed again to see whether he attempts to be more forceful in expressing his own desires or goals.

Study Questions

1. When are diary descriptions typically used?
2. How does the selectivity of the diary description compare with that of the specimen record and event sampling methods? To which of the latter two methods is the diary description most similar? Why?
3. How is inference involved in the diary description? In which other method or methods is inference involved in the same way as in the diary description?
4. Why is the diary description not a likely method for most observers?
5. The above example of a diary description most appropriately illustrates the diary's use as a *case study* (see Irwin and Bushnell, 1980, p. 85). First, find out about some of the purposes for which a case study is used. How do the purposes of the case study conform to the characteristics of the diary description? What specific criterion of the diary description method is met in the above example?

chapter ten
Anecdotal Records

Objectives

After studying this chapter, you will be able to

- discuss the characteristics of the anecdotal record method of observation
- discuss the characteristics of the anecdotal record in relation to the dimensions of open versus closed, degree of selectivity, and degree of inference required
- describe the advantages and disadvantages of the anecdotal record

General Description

The anecdotal record is another method of informal observation. It is a method often used by teachers, and the record may follow a child from grade to grade and teacher to teacher. It is a record that teachers make for future reference and as an aid to understanding some aspect of the child's personality or behavior.

Goodwin and Driscoll (1982) list five characteristics of the anecdotal record. First, the record is the result of direct observation of a child. This is important, for it legitimately rules out records based on rumors. Second, the record is a prompt, accurate, and specific descriptive account of a particular event. This confirms the necessity of direct observation. Third, the anecdotal record supplies the context of the child's behavior; it identifies setting and situation so that the behavior is not separated from the events that influenced or caused it. This context includes accurate accounts of what is said by the child or other appropriate participants. Fourth, if any inferences or interpretations are made by the observer, they are kept separate from the objective description and are clearly identified as inferences or interpretations. Finally, the anecdotal record concerns itself with behavior that is either typical or unusual for the child being observed. If the behavior is unusual, it should be so indicated. Irwin and Bushnell (1980), however, note that anecdotal records "are not limited to highlighting new behaviors" and that such records "report whatever seems noteworthy to the observer, whenever that behavior occurs."

Arguments have been made for recording only "events highlighting personality characteristics or adjustment rather than those bearing on achievement, creativity, intelligence, or problem solving" (Goodwin and Driscoll 1982). The reason for this selectivity is that there are other more effective ways of documenting behaviors such as achievement. These authors, however, go on to recommend that even cognitive areas should be documented in the case of very young children.

Open vs. Closed

The anecdotal record is an open method, assuming it preserves the raw data provided by detailed description.

Degree of Selectivity

The anecdotal record can be highly selective, especially if the observer records only, as Goodwin and Driscoll phrase it, "strikingly unusual behavior." If one follows other criteria for the anecdotal record, however, selectivity decreases, and whatever is of interest can be the target for observation and recording.

Degree of Inference Required

Inferences or interpretations can be made in an effort to explain an event or behavior, especially if the behavior is not typical for the child. Again, determining whether a behavior is ordinary or unusual requires a decision that goes beyond immediate sensory information.

Advantages

An important advantage of the anecdotal record is that it gives the teacher a running account that helps him understand a child's behavior in particular situations and settings. It also allows continuing comparisons of a child's behavior, which then provides a way of documenting changes— for example, changes in the way a child handles stressful conditions or in his social interaction patterns with children or adults. Irwin and Bushnell (1980) say that the anecdotal record is the easiest to do of the recording methods, since it needs no special setting, codes or categories, or time frame. This claim has also been made for the specimen record.

Disadvantages

Despite their common use, anecdotal records are not necessarily easy to write. They have been criticized because of the relative ease with which bias can affect the selection of events to be recorded (bias that could creep in because the observer likes or does not like certain characteristics); the vulnerability of the record to improper wording, thereby leading to misinterpretation or negative value judgments about the child by the reader; and the obligation to use the record productively, which is not always easy.

Summary

The anecdotal record is often used by teachers to help them understand some aspect of a child's personality or behavior. Five characteristics of the anecdotal record are: (1) it is the result of direct observation; (2) it is a prompt, accurate, and specific description of a particular event; (3) it gives the context of the child's behavior; (4) inferences and interpretations are kept separate from the objective description; and (5) it records behavior that is either typical or unusual for the child being observed. Some writers maintain, however, that anecdotal records may report anything of interest to the observer.

The anecdotal record is an open method. Its selectivity varies somewhat, depending on whether you record everything of interest or only unusual behaviors. Inferences are required if you try to explain the meaning of a particular behavior or event. The method's important advantage is that it gives the teacher a running record to help him understand a child's behavior in particular situations and settings. It also allows ongoing comparisons of behaviors, which provide a way of documenting changes in the child's behavior. An important disadvantage is that they are not easy to write, and some critics argue it is easy for bias to enter into the selection of events and behaviors to be recorded.

Table 10-1   Anecdotal Record

Child Observed   *Melissa*
Observation Setting   *Preschool classroom, during free play*
Observer   *Mrs. Thompson*
Date   *1/23/93*

Melissa came to school late today. She stood in the doorway to the main classroom and just looked around for about half a minute at the other children involved in various activities. She finally walked across the room toward the reading table, scraping the toe of her right foot for about 6 steps or so. She then picked up her pace a bit and, on reaching the table, sat down. Tina, Ralph, and Morton were already seated at the table. Tina had been watching the two boys "read" a book together; she greeted Melissa with a bright "Hi, Melissa, wanna read a book with me?" The boys neither looked up nor said anything. Melissa told Tina that she (Melissa) couldn't read, but Tina replied that they could look at the pictures. Melissa agreed with a softly spoken "ok"; she made no eye contact with Tina—in fact, she looked over toward the block area as she spoke her consent. As Tina went to get a book from the shelf, Melissa began idly flipping through some pages of a book that was lying on the table. Tina returned with a book, saying "I like this one; let's look at this one." She tries to sit close to Melissa, but she moves away slightly, putting 6-8 inches distance between them. Ralph asks, "Hey, you two, wha'cha doin'?" Tina responds with "never mind, we're busy." As she says this, she tilts her head upward and sticks out her chin slightly. Melissa makes no response; she gets up from the table and walks slowly toward the big block area. Mrs. Johnson announces clean-up time, but Melissa again does not make any relevant response; she doesn't participate in clean-up.

Comments

This is the second time in three days Melissa has been late for school. As I recall, on the other occasion, she also seemed different from her "usual self."

Melissa stood in the doorway as though reluctant to leave her position there. I sensed that, momentarily at least, she would have rather been somewhere else.

M's response to Tina's suggestion to look at pictures uncharacteristically lacked enthusiasm. She usually likes to look at books.

I can't understand M's reaction to Tina's trying to sit close to her. It's almost as though M. is rejecting Tina. The contrast between Melissa's and Tina's behavior seems especially marked.

Note: I'll have to do some follow-up observations of Melissa. Her seemingly apathetic, unsocial behavior needs to be checked—it may just be a bad day for her. Must check with some of my staff; they may have noticed she's become somewhat withdrawn over the past several days. Bring this up at next staff meeting.

Study Questions

1. Why is the anecdotal record popular with teachers? How are such records used by teachers?
2. If the anecdotal record is used to record unusual behavior, how might records of such behavior be useful to a teacher? How might records of typical behavior be useful to a teacher?
3. On what does the degree of selectivity depend in the anecdotal record?
4. What makes the anecdotal record easy to use? Another method also claims to be easy to use for the same reasons? What method makes the same claim as the anecdotal record, and at the same time, how are these two methods different?

chapter eleven
Frequency Counts
or Duration Records

Objectives

After studying this chapter, you will be able to

- determine the relationship between frequency records and duration records
- examine the uses of frequency counts and duration records
- identify the relationships between frequency counts or duration records and event or time sampling
- determine the method of observation, degree of selectivity, and degree of inference required in using frequency counts or duration records
- explore the advantages and disadvantages of frequency counts and duration records

General Description

The term frequency immediately identifies this method's primary characteristic. The observer simply makes a mark on an observation sheet every time a particular behavior occurs. A variation of the frequency count is the *duration record*. As Goodwin and Driscoll (1982) indicate, there are occasions when the length of a behavior is more useful to know than just its frequency.

One use of frequency counts is in the establishment of *baselines* in behavior modification. Baselines are simply frequency counts of a behavior that the teacher, experimenter, or therapist wants to modify. The effectiveness of the particular modification procedure is measured by whether the frequency of the behavior after the procedure is less than or greater than the baseline frequency. (Less than or greater than, depending on whether an undesirable behavior is to be reduced or eliminated, or a desirable behavior is to be increased.)

Both frequency counts and duration records require you to define, in advance, the behaviors you want to observe and record. The specific behaviors of interest are often dealt with as categories; for example, cooperative behavior, dependency behavior, aggression, or perhaps the various play classifications (parallel play, associative play, and so on). Frequency counts and duration records are similar to event sampling because the behavior or category must occur before it can be recorded. However, as verified by Goodwin and Driscoll's account, the frequency count can also follow a time sampling procedure, where one or more observers watch a child for designated periods and lengths of time. This affords the most economical use of time, as well as an opportunity to gather a representative sample of a given behavior. Of course, when you use a time or event sampling format, you also take on the advantages and disadvantages of those methods.

Open vs. Closed

Frequency counts and duration records are decidedly closed. Neither preserves any raw data.

Degree of Selectivity

Both methods are highly selective. If you are going to count something, you first have to specify what that something is. The same is true for measuring how long something lasts. Nevertheless, it is conceivable that frequency counts and duration records can be incorporated into some of the other methods already discussed. It can be very useful to time the duration of behaviors when using event sampling, for example. As discussed in Chapter 3, this can help prevent errors of transmission and give you relevant information about the child's attention span, level of interest in an activity, and so forth. Specimen recording can also make use of frequency counts, although it is likely that they would be made after the recording was completed.

Degree of Inference Required

Inferences and definitions are required in these methods since you must define ahead of time what specific behaviors are included in the category you want to observe and record. Such definitions are a form of inference; you are interpreting specific behaviors as indicating a category (cooperation, social interaction, and so on). Further inference is required as you observe a child doing various things. Do you see specific actions and responses as cooperation, dependency, aggression, or do you see something quite different? Furthermore, it happens that even with the most carefully defined categories, children will display behaviors that do not exactly fit a category, or the behavior happens too quickly to be seen in its entirety. These conditions will call for a judgment from the observer.

Advantages

The most obvious advantage of the frequency count or duration record is its simplicity. Nothing seems easier than making a tally mark every time a particular behavior or event occurs. The recording technique itself is simple to use and entails very little effort from the observer. The duration record is more complicated than the frequency count, since it involves using a watch to time the behavior. This is not in itself difficult, but it is an extra step that requires you to watch the behavior carefully to know when it begins and ends. This careful notice is also necessary in event sampling, but unlike event sampling, duration records do not involve the writing of narrative descriptions.

Frequency counts have the advantage of giving almost immediate quantifiable data, which can in turn be used or represented in a number of ways. Goodwin and Driscoll (1982) mention representing the frequency of the behavior by bar graphs and using the data to calculate rates of behavior per some unit of time (such as the number of instances of aggression per minute), or to calculate the percentage of time a child spent in a particular behavior. For example, you could determine that of the total time observed, a child spent 30 percent of her time in cooperative play and 20 percent in solitary activity. Frequency counts and duration records are also useful in noting changes in behavior over time. Duration records are appropriately used when the extent of the child's involvement is most important. The fact that a child exhibits a behavior may be less significant than how long she exhibits it. Social participation, for example, might be better evaluated in terms of the length of the interactions a child has than in terms of how often she has them. Frequent but very short social contacts might indicate an inability to sustain social behaviors. In this case, a simple frequency count could mislead the observer to the conclusion that the child is highly social.

Disadvantages

The primary disadvantages of frequency counts and duration records lies in their closedness. They reveal nothing about the details of the behavior or its context. Again, one might be recording action fragments that are not descriptive or indicative of the larger behavior stream.

Summary

The frequency count tallies the occurrences of a particular behavior. The duration record, a variation of the frequency count, measures the length of a behavior. The duration record is used when the extent of a child's behavior is more important than just its frequency.

Frequency counts and duration records are closed and highly selective; if you are going to count something, you have to know what that something is. Inferences are required in these methods, because you must define beforehand what behaviors will fit the category you want to observe and record—for example, cooperation, social exchanges, and so on. Frequency counts have such advantages as simplicity of use, provision of immediate quantifiable data, and usefulness in noting changes in behavior over repeated observations. The chief disadvantage lies in their closedness; they reveal virtually nothing about the details of behavior and its context.

A Sample Frequency Count Format
for Four Categories of Behavior

Name/Time	Aggression	Cooperation	Dependency	Autonomy
Barbara K.	I I I I I I /	I I I I I I /	I I I I I I /	I I I I I I
Jason P.	I I I I I I /	I I I I I I /	I I I I I I /	I I I I I I
Brian L.	I I I I I I /	I I I I I I /	I I I I I I /	I I I I I I
Alice W.	I I I I I I /	I I I I I I /	I I I I I I /	I I I I I I
Darius H.	I I I I I I /	I I I I I I /	I I I I I I /	I I I I I I

This sample frequency count format is only one of many possible formats. You will see that you could record only five instances of each of the four behaviors designated for study. Five might be sufficient, however, if you were observing and recording for brief periods of time. It would probably be unlikely, for instance, that Brian would exhibit more than five aggressive behaviors within the span of one minute.

But, the form is merely a concept, and it is as flexible as you need it to be. Indeed, you can record frequencies on a blank sheet of paper. The spaces indicated above are simply to give you a visual reference as a guide to what is involved in recording how often a specific behavior occurs. A simple mark is recorded (IXI) whenever the child exhibits the behavior of interest. Perhaps the most difficult task is to keep accurate track of the time periods within which you want to record the behavior. For example, if you are watching Barbara K. for one minute between 9:00 and 9:01 A.M., and you want to move on to Jason P. for the minute between 9:02 and 9:03, you must make certain that you do observe for precisely that period of time. If, in fact, you devote a minute and a half to Barbara and only forty five seconds to Jason, any differences in behavior frequency between the two children could be attributed to the differences in the amount of time you observed each child.

The above sample also limits you to five "slots" to record the oc-currence of a behavior. But if you wanted to record behavior frequencies over a long period of time (an hour, or a morning, for instance) in order to establish a baseline on a particular child, an open-ended form would be appropriate. You would simply make a mark every time the behavior occurred. If the frequency of the behavior was greater or less than desired, steps could be undertaken to modify the behavior's frequency upwards or downwards.

A duration record is really quite simple. It has the qualities of a frequency count but also records the length of time the behavior lasts.

The sample form given above can easily be modified into a duration record by providing spaces for recording time spans. In fact, you may eliminate the spaces for frequency checks, since every time record also indicates the occurrence of the target behavior.

Study Questions

1. When might a duration record give more important information than a frequency count? Will a duration record lose information about frequency?
2. For what purpose might a frequency count be the most useful method of recording? the least useful method?
3. What do time sampling and frequency counts have in common?
4. What advantages and disadvantages does the frequency count share with time sampling?

chapter twelve
Checklists

Objectives

After studying this chapter, you will be able to

- determine appropriate uses of checklists
- examine the characteristics of checklists
- discuss the characteristics of checklists in relation to the dimensions of open versus closedness, degree of selectivity, and degree of inference required
- discuss the advantages and disadvantages of checklists

General Description

Checklists have many uses and are very simple to use. A checklist is any record that denotes the presence or absence of something. A shopping list and a class attendance sheet are simple checklists. When observing children, checklists are used to record the occurrence of specific behaviors in a given context.

Brandt (1972) notes two types of this recording method. One important class of items recordable by a checklist is what he calls *static descriptors*. Static descriptors are "a set of descriptive items pertaining to highly stable characteristics of research subjects or settings that are to be checked or filled out, thus ensuring systematic notation of the data." Age, sex, race, socioeconomic status, characteristics of the physical environment, and time of day are examples of common static descriptors.

A second class of items for checklist recording is *actions* (action checklists, Brandt 1972). Actions are behaviors and are therefore of prime concern to observers of children. A typical action checklist records occurrences of specific behaviors during an observation period. A list of behaviors is made up for each child, and the observer marks the behaviors that the child exhibits anytime during the observation period. A checklist can also be used to record whether the child can demonstrate certain behaviors on request. In this case, the checklist becomes a form of test.

Examine Tables 12-1 and 12-2. These particular examples are checklists used in a local Head Start program known to the author (courtesy of Helen Chauvin, Director). As you can see from Table 12-1, behaviors can be checked off at any time; but the checker must be certain that the child can perform the behaviors, or that the characteristics in question are true of the child. What is important and useful about this checklist is that the teacher or observer is not bound by time or context. He can record the information at any time. (This list, incidentally, is only partial; the original contains 166 items.) Table 12-2 combines a straightforward list of motor and self-help skills with normative data that indicate the age at which children typically acquire various skills. For example, the part of the Inventory called the "Blueprint" indicates that by three to four years of age on the average, children acquire the large motor skills described by items 24 through 32.

There are so many kinds of checklists that they may not be easily recognized as such. Consider the following example. The *Denver Developmental Screening Test,* although called a *test,* is also a checklist. The *Denver Test* provides norms for various behaviors within four developmental areas. It also provides the examiner with a series of questions, directions, and actions to elicit particular verbal, cognitive, or motor responses from the child. The examiner checks whether the child can answer the questions and demonstrate the desired behaviors. The child's performance is also matched against the norms for his age. Similarly, a preschool teacher might want to determine what specific skills the children in her class have: Who can hop on one foot, bounce a ball at least five times, count to ten? Such a checklist can be used to measure a child's skills when she first enters the preschool program, and again at a later time (see Table 12-3). Brandt (1972) says that checklists "are especially appropriate when the behavior alternatives with respect to a given problem are somewhat limited, mutually exclusive, and readily discernible to observers."

Table 12-1 Children's Behavior Checklist

Name _____ School or Agency _____

Age _____ Grade _____ Sex _____ Time of Day _____

Birthdate _____ Checker _____

Directions: Check only those statements which you feel are really true of the child. Do not guess if you are not certain.

1. (   ) Vigorous and energetic in his attack on a project
2. (   ) Overcautious, not venturesome, afraid to attempt the untried
3. (   ) Nearly always accomplishes tasks in spite of difficulties
4. (   ) Voice animated, alive
5. (   ) Does not become fatigued easily
6. (   ) Poor in concentration

7. (   ) Merely copies other children's reactions, not original
8. (   ) Concentrates well at his task
9. (   ) Original and inventive reactions
10. (   ) Curious and questioning
11. (   ) Expresses himself well for his age
12. (   ) Resourceful in dealing with difficult situations
13. (   ) Poor use of language for his age
14. (   ) Patient
15. (   ) Absorbed; self-sufficient in his activity
16. (   ) Restless; a certain dissatisfaction with his own activity
17. (   ) Retiring; wishes to be in the background
18. (   ) Even-tempered
19. (   ) Frequently disturbed; easily upset by the disagreeable or the exciting
20. (   ) Seldom disturbed; sudden changes in mood infrequent
21. (   ) Slow to adjust to a novel experience
22. (   ) Original in play
23. (   ) Is easily distracted from task at hand
24. (   ) Gives up easily; lacks persistence
25. (   ) Submits to any child who takes the initiative
26. (   ) Dominates children of his own age (either sex)
27. (   ) Will submit to a specific child only
28. (   ) Submits to a leader only after a struggle to dominate
29. (   ) Is a follower to one specific group only
30. (   ) Occasionally dominates a group
31. (   ) Usually leads a small group
32. (   ) Decides who shall participate in the group activities
33. (   ) Can organize the activities of a group to carry out a definite purpose
34. (   ) Leads or follows as the occasion demands
35. (   ) Neither leads nor follows; plays alone

Table 12-2 Inventory of Motor and Self-Help Skills of Head Start Children

Child's Name _____ Date of Birth _____

Date of Test _____ Teacher's Name _____

1.	Puts together 3-piece puzzle	____Yes ____No
2.	Snips with scissors	____Yes ____No
3.	Picks up pins or buttons with each eye separately covered	____Yes ____No
4.	Paints strokes, dots or circular shapes on easel	____Yes ____No
5.	Can roll, pound, squeeze, and pull clay	____Yes ____No
6.	Holds crayons with fingers, not with fist	____Yes ____No

7.	Puts together 8-piece (or more) puzzle	____Yes ____No
8.	Makes clay shapes with 2 or 3 parts	____Yes ____No
9.	Using scissors, cuts on curve	____Yes ____No
10.	Screws together a threaded object	____Yes ____No
11.	Cuts out and pastes simple shapes	____Yes ____No
12.	Draws a simple house	____Yes ____No
13.	Imitates folding and creasing paper 3 times	____Yes ____No
14.	Prints a few capital letters	____Yes ____No
15.	Copies a square	____Yes ____No
16.	Draws a simple recognizable picture (e.g., house, dog, tree)	____Yes ____No
17.	Can lace shoes	____Yes ____No
18.	Prints capital letters (large, single, anywhere on paper)	____Yes ____No
19.	Can copy small letters	____Yes ____No
20.	Cuts pictures from magazines without being more than ¼ inch from edge of pictures	____Yes ____No
21.	Uses a pencil sharpener	____Yes ____No
22.	Folds paper square two times on diagonal, in imitation	____Yes ____No
23.	Prints name on paper	____Yes ____No
24.	Kicks large ball when rolled to him	____Yes ____No
25.	Runs 10 steps with coordinated, alternating arm movement	____Yes ____No
26.	Pedals tricycle five feet	____Yes ____No
27.	Swings on swing when set in motion	____Yes ____No
28.	Climbs up and slides down 4-6 foot slide	____Yes ____No
29.	Somersaults forward	____Yes ____No
30.	Walks upstairs, alternating feet	____Yes ____No
31.	Catches ball with 2 hands when thrown from 5 feet	____Yes ____No
32.	Jumps from bottom step	____Yes ____No
33.	Climbs ladder	____Yes ____No
34.	Skips on alternate feet	____Yes ____No
35.	Walks balance beam forward without falling	____Yes ____No
36.	Runs, changing direction	____Yes ____No
37.	Jumps forward 10 times without falling	____Yes ____No
38.	Jumps backward 6 times without falling	____Yes ____No
39.	Bounces and catches large ball	____Yes ____No

Blueprint for Motor and Self-Help Skill Inventory

Developmental Levels	Large Motor			Fine Motor			Self-Help
3-4 Years	24	25	26	1	2	3	
	27	28	29	4	5	6	
	30	31	32				
4-5 Years	33	34	35	7	8	9	
	36	37	38	10	11	12	
	39			13	14	15	
5-6 Years							

Checklists require a great deal of structuring; the items to be noticed in a behavioral situation are clearly established beforehand (Brandt 1972). This criterion should be familiar to you, because the idea of structuring and defining "items to be noticed" applies to many of the methods already discussed. Structuring and defining are also part of the characteristics of openness/closedness and degree of selectivity. It is important to recognize that any recording scheme that marks a category, item, or answer on an observation sheet, is a form of checklist; therefore, its categories must be carefully defined.

Open vs. Closed

Checklists are closed, because they reduce raw data to a tally that indicates the presence or absence of a specified behavior.

Degree of Selectivity

The degree of selectivity is high, because the behavioral items to be recorded are identified and defined before beginning the observation.

Degree of Inference Required

The inferences required in using checklists by themselves are similar to those required when checklists are incorporated into other methods (for example, time sampling, event sampling, and frequency counts). You must define in advance the behaviors or events that properly belong in your observational categories. However, there will be times when you will see a behavior that is ambiguous and does not clearly fit the categories. In that case, you will have to decide then and there whether the behavior fits your definition.

Table 12-3   Motor Skills Checklist

Child Observed _____

Child's Age _____

Observation Setting _____

Date _____

Time _____

1.	Imitates a 3-cube bridge	___Yes ___No
2.	Uses both hands to steady a cube tower	___Yes ___No
3.	Uses scissors to snip inaccurately	___Yes ___No
4.	Copies a circle	___Yes ___No
5.	Imitates a horizontal line and a cross	___Yes ___No
6.	Feeds self independently with a spoon	___Yes ___No
7.	Dresses/undresses with assistance for front, back, snaps, laces	___Yes ___No
8.	Jumps in place	___Yes ___No
9.	Pedals tricycle	___Yes ___No
10.	Washes/dries hands	___Yes ___No
11.	Bounces ball at least three times	___Yes ___No
12.	Holds crayon between thumb and first two to three fingers	___Yes ___No

---

Advantages

Checklists have the advantage of being usable in many different situations and methods. They are efficient and easy to use. The checklist is efficient, because it reduces complex descriptive information to a single tally or notation, thus providing easily quantifiable data. The notation often signifies a category such as social exchanges, quarrels, or task-oriented activity. These categories are defined by a group of behaviors that share certain characteristics. The checklist eliminates the need to record all the details of behavior. It can also be an advantage that a checklist used in any format or method requires careful prior preparation.

Disadvantages

As with any method that does not preserve raw data, the checklist loses the details of the observed behavior and its context. This means that the observation record will consist mainly of action fragments or isolated impressions of the children observed. This makes it important to match carefully any recording method with your observation objectives.

Summary

The checklist is a method with many uses and is very simple to use. A checklist is any record that denotes the presence or absence of something. Two types of this method were discussed. One type of checklist records static descriptors, which were defined as "a set of descriptive items" that pertain to "highly stable characteristics of research subjects or settings." Age, sex, race, and socioeconomic status are examples of static descriptors. The second type of checklist records actions, which are simply behaviors. An action checklist records the occurrence of a behavior during the period of observation. Several examples of checklists were discussed.

The number of checklists is so great that it might be difficult to recognize some of them as checklists. The *Denver Developmental Screening Test* was offered as an example of a test that is also a form of checklist but may not be easily recognized as such.

Checklists are closed and highly selective: they do not preserve raw data, and behaviors to be recorded are identified and defined before the observation begins. Inferences are required with this method, because prior decisions must be made concerning what behaviors or events fit the categories chosen for observation and recording. Further, as with other methods that involve inferences, behaviors will at times be ambiguous and not clearly fit the predetermined categories. An interpretation will therefore be necessary before recording or not recording the behavior.

Checklists have the advantage of being usable in many different situations and methods. They are efficient and require little effort. A chief disadvantage is their closedness; the checklist will provide a record that will be composed of action fragments and isolated impressions of behavior and context.

Study Questions

1. What characteristics do checklists share with frequency counts and time sampling? How are they different?
2. Describe or list five examples of checklists (different from any discussed in this manual). What does your list suggest about the possible uses and kinds of checklists?
3. Construct a brief checklist and then describe how you went about making it up, what use you had in mind, what factors you had to consider, and so on.
4. How might a multiple choice examination be considered a form of checklist? Could an essay examination also have any features of a checklist?

chapter thirteen
Application: Recording Methods in Action

This chapter applies several recording methods to an imaginary child, Melissa. The intent is to illustrate how observational data might look in each method, and how the appearance of these data might change from one method to another. A specimen record will begin this illustration. Imagine that in each example, the observer sees the behavior and context described in the sample specimen record.

Bear in mind that this is one example chosen from among many possibilities. Depending on your objectives, these recording methods could follow different formats, and the final product could look quite different from what follows.

Table 13-1 Specimen Record

Child Observed   *Melissa*
Child's Age   *4 years*
Setting   *Preschool classroom*
Time   *9:20 to 9:30*
Activity   *Free play*

Objective Behavioral Description	**Interpretations**
9:20-9:22 Melissa arrives about 35 minutes late; puts her coat in her cubby. She stands in the doorway of main classroom and looks around; remains motionless for ½ minute, moving only her eyes as she glances briefly at other children and their activities.	Melissa seems shy, almost withdrawn. From moment of arrival, she seemed reluctant to enter into things. May be because she didn't want to come in first place.

9:22-9:24   M. finally walks toward reading area on far side of room from cubbies. Moves slowly at first, scraping the toe of her right foot at each step, for about 5 feet. She passes by the puzzle table where 2 children are seated; no communication exchanged. She now walks more briskly to a table with some books lying on it. Tina, Ralph, and Morton are seated at the table; Ralph and Morton are sharing a book, Tina is watching them "read." Melissa says nothing to the three children as she sits down.

Melissa still seems uncertain; even her motor behaviors seem restricted; she walks slowly, shuffling, as though unsure of herself and of her relationship with the other children or her environment. Seems to have trouble deciding what to do. Not at all communicative; makes no overtures to any of the children who were "available" for such.

9:24-9:29   Ralph and Morton don't look up or acknowledge Melissa in any way. Tina says, "Hi, Melissa, wanna read a book with me?" M. cocks her head to one side and says softly, "I don't know how to read." T. replies "We can look at the pictures." M. looks over toward the big block area and without looking at T., says "OK." Tina smiles broadly and goes to a shelf containing a number of books. M. picks up one of the books and flips slowly through the pages.

Tina is outgoing and friendly as Melissa approaches; M. is still uncommunicative; still seems shy and uncertain; speaks softly as though afraid of being heard. Tina persists in spite of M's lack of enthusiasm. M. also seems distractable or inattentive. She shies away from T's efforts to get close physically. Tina moves at a quick pace—much more energetic than M.

T. returns with a book and says "I like this one, let's look at this one." M. merely nods; T. sits down close to M, but M. moves slightly, keeping a distance of about 6-8 inches between her and T.

9:29-9:30   Ralph looks up and says "Hey, you two, wha'cha doin'?" T. tilts her head upward, thrusts out her chin slightly and says "Never mind, we're busy." M. says nothing, but gets up from the table and walks slowly toward big block area. Morton still reads.

Tina is much more outgoing and sure of herself than M. T. didn't interact too much w/Ralph and Morton; may have felt left out of their activity. T. definitely seemed pleased to see M.; displayed no unfavorable response to M's "unsocial" behavior. T's response to Ralph quite assertive, but in a friendly way; almost like she claimed Melissa as *her* playmate, maybe in retaliation for the two boys ignoring her earlier. M. still seems uninterested, even uncertain of what to do.

Using the same specimen record data, let us see what a time sample might look like. This format uses a sign system, and the data are restricted just to Melissa, Tina, Ralph, and Morton. Because this time sampling data is obtained from the previous specimen record description (focusing primarily on Melissa), there will be no information recorded for Tina, Ralph, and Morton until the recording interval matches the time in the specimen record when their behaviors would actually have been observed. In a real time sampling session, of course, the observer would have recorded Melissa's behavior (if appropriate), then he would have observed Tina, then Ralph, then Morton, and so on, for the entire class. The present illustration merely simplifies the description.

The numbers in the cells (boxes) refer to the behaviors that define the major categories. The procedure for this example would have been the following: Procedure—Observe a child for 5 seconds, record for 5 seconds; wait 50 seconds, then repeat the process with the next child until all children have been observed.

Table 13-2   Time Sampling—Interactions with Others and with Environment

Children Involved   *Melissa, Tina, Ralph, Morton*
Children's Age   *Four Years*
Observation Setting   *Preschool Classroom*
Time Began   *9:20 to 9:30*
Activity   *Free Play*

Behavior Category

General Response to Setting

1. Enters setting willingly (specify which area involved—big block area (BBA), reading area (RA), etc.)
2. Enters setting reluctantly
3. Refuses to enter setting

General Response to Equipment/Materials

4. Uses equipment/materials freely
5. Limited or sporadic use of equipment/materials
6. No use of equipment/materials

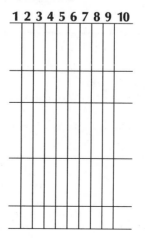

Recording Intervals   Child

1 2 3 4 5 6 7 8 9 10

General Response to Others

Recording Intervals   Child

1 2 3 4 5 6 7 8 9 10

7. Seeks or is in contact with peer
8. Seeks or is in contact with adult
9. Avoids or breaks contact with peer
10. Avoids or breaks contact with adult
11. Reluctant contact with peer; contact lacks motivation or concentration on part of child
12. Reluctant contact with adult; contact lacks motivation or concentration on part of child

The example of time sampling just given does not specify details; it merely provides the basis for determining rather broad categories of behaviors— for example, "avoids contact with adults." In practice, all of these behaviors would be *operationally defined*. For example, you could operationally define "avoids contact with adults" as "maintains a physical distance between herself and any adult; initiates no speech with an adult; does not ask for assistance or directions; does not immediately obey an adult's commands or requests." Operational definitions frequently are tested in the field; if there is ambiguity or vagueness, or if there are disagreements between observers as to how to classify given behaviors, the definitions are reworked and refined until they permit accurate decisions by the observer.

Now let us look at Melissa's social behavior within the event sampling format. Recall that the event sampling is selective and does not record all behaviors. In this example, only Melissa's social contacts or interactions are events of interest. The event sample is presented by itself through narrative description and not in combination with any other technique. Remember, though, that checklists and time sampling could be used in combination with event sampling.

Table 13-3   Event Sampling—Social Behavior

Child Observed   *Melissa*
Child's Age   *Four Years*
Observation Setting   *Preschool Classroom*
Activity   *Free Play*
Behavioral Event   *Social Interactions*
Time   *9:20 to 9:35*

Event Description	**Interpretations**
9:24-9:29 Melissa slowly approaches the reading table where Tina, Ralph and Morton are seated. M. sits down, but says nothing to the others. Tina responds immediately to M's presence; greets her with "Hi, wanna read a book with me?" M. replies that she (M.) can't read. T. replies that they can look at the pictures. M. agrees with a softly spoken "ok." Tina smiles and goes for a book. M. does not look at or speak to Ralph and Morton, nor they to her. T. comes back and tries to sit close to M., who resists by moving away slightly keeping about 6-8 inches between them. Ralph speaks to the two girls, asking them what they're doing. T. responds, "Never mind, we're busy." M. says nothing but gets up from the table and moves slowly toward the cubby area.	Melissa seems shy, withdrawn, apathetic. She doesn't respond to Tina's greeting, barely even looks at her; seems not even to notice Ralph and Morton, who also ignore her. M. avoids close contact with Tina; seems to reject physical or psychological proximity. M. is easily distracted, does not focus well socially, as evidenced by her lack of eye contact with Tina and by her looking around the room as T. tries to engage her in a social exchange. M's actions don't appear to stem from any dislike of Tina; no evidence of hostility—indeed, M. is emotionally bland. Appears to have no interest in the company of others.
9:29-9:30 M. breaks contact with Tina and Ralph and walks toward big block area.	Melissa still seems withdrawn and uninterested; she makes no response to Ralph's friendly overture.

The anecdotal record is one more method that could be used to observe and record the behavior of Melissa. The anecdotal record might be appropriate if a teacher noticed Melissa's seeming lack of social responsiveness and decided to follow up with some additional observations. This would be a topical use of the record (Irwin and Bushnell 1980) if the teacher wanted to focus just on social behavior. The teacher could also decide to accumulate a series of behavioral incidents with the intention of learning about Melissa from a broader perspective. Our hypothetical teacher might also decide to use a frequency checklist to determine whether Melissa's "nonsocial" behavior occurred very often or whether she was simply having a "bad day."

Table 13-4 Anecdotal Record

Child Observed   *Melissa*
Observation Setting   *Preschool classroom, during free play*
Observer   *Mrs. Thompson*
Date   *9/23/92*

Melissa came to school late today. She stood in the doorway to the main classroom and just looked around for about half a minute at the other children involved in various activities. She finally walked across the room toward the reading table, scraping the toe of her right foot for about 6 steps or so. She then picked up her pace a bit and, on reaching the table, sat down. Tina, Ralph, and Morton were already seated at the table. Tina had been watching the two boys "read" a book together; she greeted Melissa with a bright "Hi, Melissa, wanna read a book with me?" The boys neither looked up nor said anything. Melissa told Tina that she (Melissa) couldn't read, but Tina replied that they could look at the pictures. Melissa agreed with a softly spoken "ok;" she made no eye contact with Tina—in fact, she looked over toward the block area as she spoke her consent. As Tina went to get a book from the shelf, Melissa began idly flipping through some pages of a book that was lying on the table. Tina returned with a book, saying "I like this one; let's look at this one." She tries to sit close to Melissa, but she moves away slightly, putting 6-8 inches distance between them. Ralph asks, "Hey, you two, wha'cha doin'?" Tina responds with "never mind, we're busy." As she says this, she tilts her head upward and sticks out her chin slightly. Melissa makes no response; she gets up from the table and walks slowly toward the big block area. Mrs. Johnson announces clean-up time, but Melissa again does not make any relevant response; she doesn't participate in clean-up.

Comments

This is the second time in three days Melissa has been late for school. As I recall, on the other occasion, she also seemed different from her "usual self."

Melissa stood in the doorway as though reluctant to leave her position there. I sensed that, momentarily at least, she would have rather been somewhere else.

M's response to Tina's suggestion to look at pictures uncharacteristically lacked enthusiasm. She usually likes to look at books.

I can't understand M's reaction to Tina's trying to sit close to her. It's almost as though M. is rejecting Tina. The contrast between Melissa's and Tina's behavior seems especially marked.

Note: I'll have to do some follow-up observations of Melissa. Her seemingly apathetic, unsocial behavior needs to be checked—it may just be a bad day for her. Must check with some of my staff; they may have noticed she's become somewhat withdrawn over the past several days. Bring this up at next staff meeting.

chapter fourteen

Interpretation of Observations, Implementation of Findings, and Ongoing Evaluation

Objectives

After studying this chapter, you will be able to

- discuss the relationship among the activities of observation, interpretation, implementation of findings, and ongoing evaluation
- discuss the two roles or types of interpretation
- analyze the concept of bias in interpretation
- discuss the several meanings of implementation of findings
- analyze the components of implementation
- describe the process of ongoing evaluation

This chapter will address the topics of interpretation, implementation, and evaluation. These topics will be discussed to point out the importance of each one in its own right, as well as their relationship to one another.

Interpretation of Observations

Considerable space has already been given to the subject of interpretation, and yet, part of another chapter is devoted to this topic. This is done for two important reasons.

The more fundamental reason is to reemphasize the broad, inevitable role interpretation plays in our lives. Our entire beings are involved in our views of the world, in the way we "see" people, objects, and events. There are no self-evident facts. But, we do become so accustomed to certain "facts" in our world, that they seem self-evident and require no further interpretation or processing. Once we understand what a dog is, we do not attach an interpretation to our every observation of a dog. We simply see a dog.

In this broad sense of interpretation, our knowledge, values, attitudes, and experiences act as "filters" through which what we observe must pass. Naturally, not everything that exists "out there" in the real world gets through our filters. Some things do not even get noticed; we sometimes fail to get a conscious sense impression of an object, person, or event. The incompleteness of our observations is partly the result of our interest at the time, level of concentration, bodily states such as fatigue or illness, what aspects of the situation we think are important, and the amount of time we have to observe. So, we may not see Jerry sharing a toy with Jacob, or Tanya tripping over the corner of the rug, although we may be looking directly at the situation. We are not cameras and cannot merely point our eyes in some direction and register everything that occurs. This is a liberal use of interpretation, and the term personality can summarize the influence of who we are on what we see and on the meaning we derive from what we see.

A stricter use of interpretation involves an additional step. In this use, we interpret something when we consciously try to make it clear and give it a meaning that goes beyond our empirical data. If you can recall, explanation was defined earlier as "making clear or understandable . . . to give or show the meaning or reason for" (see page 16 ff.). A major point here is that to explain, to make clear or understandable, often involves moving from something that is directly observable to something that is not directly observable or observed. For example, you repeatedly hear four-year-old Margo asking Mrs. Bergman for approval—something observable—and you conclude that Margo is an emotionally dependent child whose parents probably reinforce that kind of behavior at home—something not observed.

When one interprets, one is really imposing a bias on some fact. The word "bias" is not meant in a negative sense. It refers to the inevitable absence of *total* objectivity and the inevitable presence of the observer's own unique filters. Since no two individuals are exactly alike, no two individuals will see the same phenomenon in entirely the same way or to the exact same extent. We have referred to "personal biases and perspectives," which again, are made up of our experiences, abilities, attitudes, and knowledge. There is another kind of bias that is more the product of formal learning and purposeful adoption than of forces and influences over which we often have no control. This is the bias (filter) provided and shaped by a theory, hypothesis, conceptual framework, or philosophy.

Theoretical biases may seem more important than personal ones. They are merely different, however, though related and interdependent. Learning a theory and using it to interpret behavior are most assuredly dependent on some of your personal characteristics—intelligence, aptitude, and potential to become a competent observer. Moreover, your values and general views about children can affect which theoretical position you feel most comfortable with emotionally and intellectually. If you believe that children learn on their own if opportunities are provided them, you are not likely to enjoy an educational approach that rigidly structures the classroom and its activities.

Biases formed from theories also have another effect on what you see. They direct your attention only to certain parts of a situation, event, or behavior. Mussen, Conger, Kagan, and Huston (1984) describe this state of affairs: "Each scholar comes to the infant armed with a set of biases about what qualities are important, puts his or her observation 'lens' closest to those phenomena, and chooses words to describe them." It is not only theoretical biases that create this limited attention; our everyday biases do it, too. Can you imagine a father watching his four-year-old son Billy playing with some children in a schoolyard? Suddenly, while the father is looking right at them, Billy pushes a playmate; a fight breaks out between them and the other child hits Billy on the arm. It is not inconceivable that the father might blame the other child, that he might not "see" Billy as the instigator of the conflict. Indeed, all the father might see is the other boy hitting his son. This is called "selective perception," meaning that people often see only what they want to see, or place importance only on what they think is important, ignoring everything else. The result of this is that just as we assign different degrees of importance to different events in our daily affairs, different theories assign different degrees of importance to various phenomena. Piaget, for example, focused his attention on cognitive or intellectual development, but Freud was interested in personality development. It follows, therefore, that if Piaget and Freud were able to observe a child together, each would concentrate on different facets of the child's behavior, and each would make different interpretations.

In summary, then, even the most simple, straightforward, and informal observations and encounters with the environment involve some form of interpretation. We must put what we see and experience into a relationship with what we already know. We often can do this without much conscious deliberation. More formal interpretations, on the other hand, require us to look at a phenomenon and make sense of it within a particular perspective or conceptual framework—a theory, for example. And this might require conscious thought.

The second reason for discussing interpretation again is that it is the foundation of implementation of findings and ongoing evaluation. Your interpretations will determine the nature of your findings, what you think is significant, or even whether you find anything at all. This is also the case with ongoing evaluation. Evaluation involves making judgments about the value, effectiveness, or appropriateness of something. It stands to reason that such judgments involve some interpretations, and quite possibly both formal and informal interpretations, as previously discussed. In short, implementation and evaluation require you to make sense out of your observations before you can put them to some relevant use. Uses and purposes vary, of course, and can range from merely wanting to understand some facet of a child's development and behavior, to wanting to assess whether an existing program is doing what it claims to be doing, to wanting to initiate a new program.

Implementation of Findings

Implementation is a broad topic. It is probably as broad as the number of reasons for observing and the number of observation methods you can use. This statement is based on the assumption that your reasons for observing should be determined before entering the child's "behavior stream." The phrase "implementation of findings" implies a predesignated purpose and method. In this respect, observation, whether formal or informal, is not very different from a research study or experiment.

An experimental psychologist, for example, has to know certain things before she even enters her laboratory. She must first identify and define a research question or problem. Why does she want to do the experiment? What knowledge does she hope to gain? She must then try to predict under what circumstances or conditions she is likely to find the answers to her question. *Conditions* refer to many factors: the physical and psychological characteristics of the experimental setting (crowded space, stress-provoking experimental tasks); the age, sex, and other characteristics of the subjects participating in the study (IQ, socioeconomic level, level of education, personality traits); how long the experiment will take—simple frequency counts of the occurrences of some response, or perhaps open-ended expressions of personal opinion. She must also decide beforehand how the data will be analyzed; what kinds of statistical tests will be used to determine the reliability and accuracy of the answers to her research problem.

Observation need not be as complicated as all this, of course, but the same fundamental principle applies to observation as to formal research; you have to know why you are observing before you "throw your net into the child's behavior stream." This principle was expressed in an earlier chapter by the statement that observation is not just casually looking *at* something; rather, it is looking *for* something.

Implementation or *to implement* means to "fulfill or satisfy the conditions of; to perform; to put into effect" (Webster 1981). This is a very inclusive definition, because there are broad limits to what one can perform, put into effect, or satisfy the conditions of. For that reason, implementation of findings at some point has to be considered in the specific context of your own observation purposes. For instance, you could "satisfy the conditions of" an observation exercise by obtaining a specimen record of a child's behavior during school recess. You might do nothing further with the record, but still have accomplished the goal of gaining experience in describing behavior in a detailed, narrative form. A teacher, however, might use the record to monitor a child's progress in various developmental areas or to establish the basis for modifying the child's behavior.

The word *findings* must be carefully considered. If findings are given too limited a meaning, observation will predominantly serve to support research. This would rule out observing children simply to learn about them, to see if they behave as psychologists describe. In this sense, findings take on a much broader meaning and perhaps can even be defined as objectives or purposes. Implementation of a purpose can be accomplished when you satisfy the condition of learning how Adam responds to the social behaviors of his peers, or when you learn the characteristics of Margaret's speech.

Ongoing Evaluation

Making judgments is an unavoidable activity we all do for various reasons. To evaluate is to make a judgment, and to make a judgment is to make a *comparison* between some event, object, or behavior, and a *standard* or *criterion*. The notion of comparison seems obvious even in the simplest of circumstances. For example, you try a different route to class or work, but you decide that your old route is better than the new one. It is quicker, more scenic, and it passes by a store where you sometimes shop. Your standards here, among possible others, are time, aesthetic pleasure, and the convenience of not having to go out of your way to shop.

Comparisons are essential, for without them, we could not perceive or know anything; we could not even distinguish the familiar from the unfamiliar. We must make comparisons with what we already know to recognize what we do not know. The critical factor in all of this is the *selection* of the standard. Selection is the basis of observation itself, of any implementation of findings, as well as of ongoing evaluation. All three of these activities require comparison with a standard. In this general sense, therefore, a standard is any framework or context within which one can make a judgment, decision, or comparison.

Let us return to some familiar territory. Some of our standards are determined by our personalities. A theory is also a standard by which comparisons, judgments, and decisions are made. A theory is a formal standard, whereas our personalities might be called informal standards.

If evaluation involves comparison with a standard, then *ongoing* evaluation is a continuous comparison, with the implication that whatever is being evaluated can or will change. It is also possible for the standard to change. Indeed, when evaluating children, the standard has to change. Parents' expectations and demands regarding their child's behavior change as the child's abilities change with maturation and experience. Demands and expectations are therefore standards that are modified to keep step with the child's ability to meet them.

Selection of the standard, as mentioned above, is critical in many cases, because the standard will determine whether the child's performance satisfies the adult's conception of what she can and should be able to do. For example, standards governing toilet training are applied by parents in relation to the child's bowel and bladder control. If the parents are realistic in their assessment of the child's physiological maturity, there may be no problem. The parents will adjust their standard to fit the child. In contrast, the parents could have unrealistic expectations (standards) for their child's toileting behavior, and they could misapply the standard—or apply the wrong standard. They could demand that she sit on the potty, not wet or soil her pants, and tell them when she has to go to the toilet, when the child simply is not capable of such behavior.

Matching the standard to the child's capabilities involves several factors. First, the parents have to know the approximate age a child can be successfully toilet trained. This could be thought to involve an explanation or interpretation, in the sense that success is explained by the concept of *maturational readiness*. Second, implementation of findings is the result of learning about this maturational readiness, evaluating the child's present level of readiness, and then either applying or not applying the standard, depending on the outcome of the evaluation. If the child is not deemed ready for serious toilet training, further evaluation is necessary. The parents might reevaluate her a month or so later, updating their information and making another comparison between the child's apparent readiness and their standards for toileting behavior.

The above example is a simple one. Ongoing evaluation occurs in much more complex ways; but regardless of the level of complexity, the same process occurs as in the toilet training illustration.

Some Practical Examples of Implementation   Although implementation of findings is a broad topic, it does have very specific and very practical effects. Let us look at some hypothetical examples of how observational findings could be used in various contexts.

Illustration # 1

Mrs. Parrish wants to encourage independent behavior among the children in her preschool classroom. She is new to this particular setting, however, and she does not yet know the children and how they play or use the equipment and materials. She believes that independent behavior can be encouraged and fostered by the type and arrangement of the physical objects in the environment. Mrs. Parrish therefore decides to observe the children's play activities and, using an event sampling technique, record instances of dependent behavior displayed by the children. She chooses to first observe *dependent* behavior so as to identify the conditions under which such behavior occurs. She then hopes to modify those conditions in a way that will foster independent behavior.

Mrs. Parrish notices very quickly that every time any child wants to play with a puzzle, the alphabet game, record player, or paints, she has to ask an adult for help. When these materials are involved, the children almost invariably exhibit dependent behavior, simply because the shelves are too high for them to reach. If an adult must hand the materials to the children, Mrs. Parrish concludes, that hardly fosters independence and self-sufficiency.

As a result of this extremely simple observation and interpretation, Mrs. Parrish has the storage shelves lowered to a height accessible to the children. Ongoing evaluation finds that the incidents of children asking for help getting equipment is reduced almost to zero.

Illustration # 2

Most preschools want to encourage cooperation and sharing among the children in their programs. Cooperation and sharing are learned behaviors, however, and one cannot count on them to occur simply as a matter of course. Ms. Crenshaw, the teacher of a class of four-year-olds knew this, but she had to plan ways to allow the children to learn to cooperate. She had to determine how to arrange various classroom situations to bring about cooperative rather than competitive interactions among the children. She decided to observe the children and her staff to see what kinds of situations led to cooperation or competition.

The following scene was observed by Ms. Crenshaw on the morning following her decision to look for instances of cooperative and competitive behavior.

9:30 A.M. It was time for rhythm band activity, and Mrs. Wilson was in charge. She placed the box containing the rhythm instruments on the floor and told the children to get the instruments they wanted to play. (The box contained six triangles, one tambourine, one block and drum stick, and two rattles.) Immediately, there was a scramble toward the box. Martin got there first and grabbed a tambourine. Sally was right behind him and she got her hand on the same tambourine. Martin tugged against Sally's grasp, saying "It's mine; I got it first." "But I want to play it today," Sally responded. While this battle was going on between Sally and Martin, eight other children were milling around the box trying to get an instrument. Juan picked out the only wooden block and drum stick and ran over to the corner of the room. Carlisle had picked out one of the triangles. Willard also grabbed a triangle, but there were six of those, and so no arguments broke out over that particular instrument. Mrs. Wilson finally had to break up the fight between Sally and Martin. She asked Sally to let Martin play the tambourine today and she could play it tomorrow. Sally reluctantly agreed. Martin walked off, a big smile on his face. Sally picked out the last remaining triangle and walked over and stood beside the children who had got their instruments. After nearly two minutes of rather frantic activity, each child got an instrument, although not without some continued grumbling from the two or three children who did not get the one they desired.

From this observation, Ms. Crenshaw decided there must be a better way to start the rhythm band activity than by putting the box of instruments in the middle of the floor. She came to the conclusion that rather than fostering cooperation and sharing, this approach really created competition. After all, thought Ms. Crenshaw, what other message could the children get when, in effect, they were told "Ok, kids, it's first come, first served, and the fastest and strongest among you will get the instruments you want." She instructed Mrs. Wilson that, in the future, the box was to be passed among the children, permitting each child to choose the instrument he or she wanted that day. The teacher was also to explain that the next time, another child could pick an instrument that he or she was unable to choose the time before. In this way, every child would eventually get to play the instrument he or she desired.

Subsequent observation of this activity confirmed Ms. Crenshaw's interpretation. Except for an occasional complaint from a child who did not want to wait until the next day to play his favorite instrument, the children accepted the new routine. There were even instances when a child would relinquish her turn with an instrument and give it to a friend.

Illustration #3

Mrs. Gonzales believes that children are active participants in their own development, and therefore should be allowed to direct many of their own activities. Her preschool classroom has a wide variety of equipment and materials selected purposely to accommodate children who vary widely in interests and skills. Mrs. Gonzales also believes that children should be encouraged to "stretch" beyond their present level of ability to promote the development of new skills and interests. Consequently, she uses her observation skills to document each child's behavior and activities in various parts of the classroom. She observes and records data about the equipment and materials the child uses and the skills and knowledge they require of the child. She also observes how long and how often the child plays in any given area. Mrs. Gonzales would like the children to strike a reasonable balance in their use of materials and activities, believing that such a balance will further their overall development.

In the course of her observations, Mrs. Gonzales notices that Victor, a new boy in her class of five-year-olds, plays with the other children using equipment and materials that demand gross motor skills, but he avoids fine motor activities unless he is by himself. From time to time, Victor will watch some of the children as they play with small puzzles, cut out pictures with scissors, or string beads, but he never joins them. If, when he is by himself and in the middle of a fine motor activity, another child approaches, he immediately stops what he is doing and walks away. Mrs. Gonzales notices, however, that Victor's fine motor skills are quite good, and so she tentatively rules out poor coordination as a cause of Victor's behavior. Because she cannot identify anything in the classroom that might contribute to his avoidance of these activities with other children, she decides to consult with Victor's mother or father. She recognizes that a child's experiences at home can affect his behavior at school.

From a conference with Victor's mother, Mrs. Gonzales learns that Victor's older brother (seven years old) is an exceptionally well-coordinated youngster, with motor abilities that are ahead of what one would predict for his age. Unfortunately, however, the brother ridicules Victor's less well-developed fine motor skills, even though Victor holds his own when it comes to running, jumping, climbing, and wrestling. Mrs. Gonzales tentatively concludes (infers) that Victor's self-image is poor in this area because of his brother's frequent disparaging remarks. Apparently, Victor refuses to play with the other children in these activities for fear they will also ridicule him.

Mrs. Gonzales decides to test her interpretation, to implement her findings regarding Victor's home situation. Over the course of several weeks, she manages to draw Victor into a series of activities that increasingly involve fine motor abilities. She always makes it a point to comment favorably on Victor's performance, as well as on the performances of the other children. She has no real concern that anyone will make fun of Victor's fine motor abilities, because she knows that his are as good as most of the other children's in the class. Ongoing observation and evaluation confirm Mrs. Gonzales's interpretation. Within a month, Victor plays with other children in both large and small muscle activities. Now, Mrs. Gonzales notes, Victor is striking more of that balance she thinks is so important.

The first illustration might seem the simplest scenario one could paint. Mrs. Parrish notices that the children cannot reach some of the toys because the shelves are too high. She defines their asking for adults' help in getting the toys as dependency behavior. She then reasons that changing the conditions under which toys can be got will change the children's behavior. The shelves are lowered, and the children act independently.

The finding in this first illustration was the relationship Mrs. Parrish saw between shelf height and dependent behavior. She implemented her finding by changing the nature of the relationship from high shelves and high dependency, to lower shelves and independence. What is important to note here, however, is that the "finding" was given a particular meaning; children asking an adult for help in getting toys was interpreted as dependency behavior and evaluated as undesirable. Another teacher might have thought differently, possibly believing that the interests and goals of the preschool are better served by the staff maintaining control over equipment and materials. This second teacher would have looked for dependency in other kinds of behaviors.

The second illustration is only a little more complicated than the first. Much depended on the meaning Ms. Crenshaw put on the children's scrambling for the band instruments. The connection between placing the box on the floor and the children's behavior is not difficult to see. Two key elements, however, are the meaning of the children's responses, and how they should be handled. Ms. Crenshaw saw the milling, shoving, and arguing as unacceptable behaviors that contradicted her goal of fostering cooperaion and sharing. She implemented her finding (the connection just mentioned) by structuring the distribution of instruments so that the children had to take turns.

Another teacher might have seen the children's scrambling for the instruments as a natural part of growing up and of learning not only to share, but also to assert themselves. He may have allowed some competition because he believes competition is an inevitable part of life. A second possibility is that the other teacher agrees with Ms. Crenshaw's objective of promoting sharing and cooperation among the children, but disagrees with her method. He might implement his finding by trying to teach the children *general rules* of conduct. Instead of making it impossible to compete by giving each child an instrument, the second teacher might use suggestions or reminders of the rules. As Sally and Martin fought over the tambourine, he might have said something like, "Now Sally, Martin got the tambourine first. What did I tell you children about sharing toys. If someone gets a toy before you do, you have to wait until he is done playing with it, and then it is your turn." The second teacher would be counting on the children to *internalize* the rules and eventually behave cooperatively because it is the appropriate thing to do. In either case, ongoing observation and evaluation would determine the effectiveness of the two teachers' ways of interpreting and implementing their findings.

The final illustration involves more observational data and inferences than the other two illustrations. Mrs. Gonzales sees the children's behavior through her philosophy (and "filter") of balanced activities and providing experiences that help the child progress beyond her current level of ability and development. Within that philosophy, Victor's failure to participate in fine motor activities with the other children violated the balance she thought so important. She progressively, though tentatively, ruled out various possible explanations for Victor's behavior. She finally made the inference that some situation at home might be the cause. When she learned about Victor's brother, she interpreted Victor's behavior as being a result of a poor self-image and fear of being ridiculed by his peers in school. She acted on that interpretation (implemented her finding) by gradually involving Victor in activities that increasingly required small muscle skills. When he learned that the other children did not make fun of him as his brother did, Victor became a regular participant in fine motor activities.

Summary

Interpretation can be thought of in terms of personality and formal theory. In either case, interpretation is the foundation of implementation of findings and ongoing evaluation. A finding is a finding only if it has some meaning, which can then be applied to a specific situation or problem. Ongoing evaluation depends on interpretation, because evaluation involves making a comparison between something observed and a standard. This, in turn, requires making sense out of your observational data and seeing the relationship between the data and the standard you have selected.

Implementation involves a performance, satisfying the conditions of something, or putting something into effect. If you find that Fred fights with Elizabeth whenever they are together in the big block area, you might implement that finding by directing one of them into a different activity. Your response implies that you have certain objectives for the children's behavior, and you interpret or see their behavior in terms of those objectives. Implementation, therefore, is based on a predetermined purpose.

Ongoing evaluation requires comparisons. Comparisons are essential, because without them we could not perceive or know anything. Selection of the standard is critical to observation, implementation, and evaluation; all these activities require some sort of standard. In this broad sense, therefore, a standard is any framework within which one can make a judgment, decision, or comparison. Our personalities are informal standards, and theories are formal ones. Ongoing evaluation often necessitates modifying the standard one applies to a situation. This is especially true when evaluating children's behavior, which naturally changes as they grow and develop.

Study Questions

1. How do observation, interpretation, implementation of findings, and ongoing evaluation depend on one another? Describe their interrelationship.
2. What is meant by the term "bias" as it is used in this chapter? List some of your biases, and describe how they might affect what you see when you observe children, and your interpretations of your observations.
3. What happens when an observational finding is implemented? Describe the steps involved, the roles of observation, and interpretation.

Part 3

Observation Exercises

Introduction and Preparation

Introduction and Preparation

Your observation exercises emphasize behavior and development. The major goal of the exercises will always be for you to learn about the child, whether from a broad developmental viewpoint or the immediate and more narrow viewpoint of the child's situation and setting. A related goal will be to enable you to do something with the information you gain from the observations. What you do with that information depends on your reasons for observing and the meaning the information has for you.

Many textbooks on children divide the life span into developmental or functional areas such as physical, motor, social, emotional, and language. This way of studying the child might give the impression that these areas are independent of one another. This is not the case. It is for the convenience of the psychologist, teacher, and others who are involved with children, that the child's development is segmented in this way. This procedure is useful and perhaps even necessary, because it brings the study of the child down to a manageable size. No one can examine simultaneously every facet of development and behavior. Nonetheless, a child is a unified, integrated whole, and his physical self is part of his intellectual self, which are parts of his social self, and so on.

As you observe children of different ages, you will be conducting something similar to a *cross-sectional* study. You will be gathering data that could be used to compare, for example, children's language development from infancy to about six years of age. You could also use this data to determine how closely a particular child's behavior matches the norms for that behavior. For example, does eighteen-month-old Jamie walk by himself, as norms predict he probably will? Or, do the social behaviors of four-year-old Christine agree with normative descriptions of four-year-olds?

There is one other important feature of your exercises. Extensive use is made of questions, which serve at least two purposes. First, they give you information about some of the specific *content* of the developmental areas. They help you focus on specific behaviors as targets of observation and recording. Remember, however, that such a focus may not always be necessary, depending on the methods you use. Consider the specimen description, where any behaviors the child exhibits while you are in her "stream" are suitable for recording.

A second reason is that the questions can be useful aids in interpreting or classifying recorded behaviors. For example, the question "How capable is the child of balancing?" not only gives you information about an observable feature of motor behavior; it also suggests that if you observe a child walk across a balance beam, you could make some interpretive comments about his coordination and control in that activity. Asking questions is an important part of the observation process.

The observation exercises begin with the period of infancy. You will be asked to observe a newborn (birth to one month of age) and a fifteen-to eighteen-month-old infant. There are several observation exercises dealing with certain aspects of development and behavior for each age period.

The second set of observation exercises covers early childhood, or what is often called the preschool years. This portion of the lifespan begins at age two and goes up through age five. The changes that occur after infancy in areas such as physical growth are relatively slower and steadier than during infancy. Generally speaking, you will see greater differences between a six-month-old and an 18-month-old than you will between a two-year-old and a three-year-old. Therefore, in Chapter 17, you will observe children at intervals of years.

Each observation exercise also provides some brief background information concerning the specific developmental or behavioral area covered.

chapter fifteen
Observing the Newborn: Birth to One Month

Exercise 15-1: Physical Characteristics of the Newborn

Background Information

A newborn's physical appearance is easily recognized and typical of most newborns. The birthweight of the average full-term baby ranges between 5½ and 9½ pounds, the average length between 19 and 22 inches. Characteristically, the skin is wrinkled, blotchy, and covered with fine hairs *(lanugo)* that fall off during the first month. At birth, the skin may be pale to pink in color, or it may have a yellowish appearance due to what is called *normal physiological jaundice.* The eyes of Caucasian babies are generally blue and do not take on their true color until sometime during the first year.

The head may have a misshapen appearance created by passage through the narrow birth canal, but this disappears by the end of the second week. The head comprises about one-quarter of the newborn's total length, which creates a disproportional appearance. The neonate has a very short neck, no chin, and a flattened nose—what some refer to as a "baby face." There are six soft spots or *fontanels* on top of the newborn's head. These allow the head to change its shape during the birth process, and they allow for brain growth during the first years of life. They close by around 18 months of age.

The external genitalia of both sexes may look enlarged, a temporary condition caused by the mother's female hormones passing to the baby during pregnancy. The newborn's legs are bowed slightly, and the feet turn inward at the ankles until the soles are almost parallel.

Observation Objectives

To observe and describe the physical characteristics of a newborn infant, with the eventual objective of comparing them with an older infant.

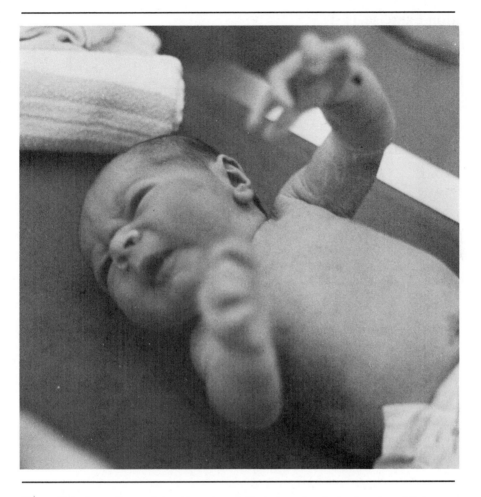

Figure 15-1 Face of a newborn. Note the relatively large head, short neck and flat nose. (Photo by Warren R. Bentzen)

Procedure

Describe in as much detail as you can the physical characteristics of a newborn (one month old or less). You will need a measuring tape to measure certain physical features. It is suggested that you write your original notes on ordinary paper, then transfer them to a more formal observation sheet that follows the format provided below.

Observation Exercise 15-1

The Physical Characteristics of the Newborn

Observer's Name _____

Child Observed (code name or number) _____

Child's Age _____ Child's Sex _____

Observation Context (Home, day-care center) _____

Date of Observation _____ Time Begun _____ Time Ended _____

Brief Description of Setting/Situation

Objective Description:

Total Length of Newborn _____ Weight of Newborn _____

Length of Head _____ Ratio of head to total body length _____

Length of Trunk _____ Ratio of Head to Trunk _____

Describe the characteristics of the following:
HEAD AND FACE (shape, eyes, ears, mouth, nose):

TRUNK (e.g., size in relation to head, overall appearance):

ARMS AND LEGS (positioning, shape):

HANDS AND FINGERS (positioning, shape):

SKIN (color, texture, general appearance):

Question Guides:

1. What are the newborn's most noticeable physical characteristics? How would you describe her body proportions? facial features? the shape of her legs and their typical positioning?
2. Is there anything about the newborn's physical features that a parent or caregiver might find attractive, or that might motivate a parent or caregiver to feel protective of the newborn?
3. Is there anything about the newborn's appearance that strikes you as unusual? If so, explain.

Exercise 15-2: Infant States and Responsiveness to Stimulation

Background Information

The newborn is frequently described in terms of *states,* which are levels of arousal such as asleep, drowsy, alert, and crying (see Table 15-1). Papalia and Olds (1993) define state as "a periodic variation in an infant's cycle of wakefulness, sleep, and activity" (p. 136). A state has three important characteristics: it is "a behavioral condition that (1) is stable over a period of time, (2) occurs repeatedly in an individual infant, and (3) is encountered in very similar forms in other individuals" (Hutt, Lenard, and Prechtl, 1969, cited in Papalia and Olds, 1979). States are important to the study of the neonate and young infant for several reasons: (1) States describe all infants, which makes them consistent patterns of behaviors; and (2) the infant's state affects the abilities she exhibits and the responses she makes to stimulation at any given time. Besides the characteristics of these states, one can also consider such factors as (1) how frequently a newborn is in a particular state, (2) for how long, (3) what kinds of stimulation put her there, and (4) what amount of stimulation is necessary to arouse her.

There are several forms of stimulation or interaction that are known to quiet a crying baby. Papalia and Olds (1992) note that "the age-old way to soothe crying babies involves steady stimulation—rocking or walking them, wrapping them snugly, or letting them hear rhythmic sounds or such of pacifiers" (p. 96). In their earlier edition, Papalia and Olds (1979) also cited feeding as a soothing stimulus to a restless infant, as well as "immersing a foot in warm water" and putting the infant "in a warmer place" (Papalia and Olds, 1979, p. 112-113).

Observation Objectives

To observe states of arousal of the newborn, to describe some of their defining characteristics, and to observe and record how a newborn's state affects his responses to the environment.

Table 15-1 Infant States

Regular Sleep This state is characterized by closed eyes, regular breathing, and a lack of muscle or eye movements, except for sudden generalized startle responses. Mild stimuli will not arouse the infant who is in this state, which makes regular sleep the low point on the overall arousal continuum.

Irregular Sleep The infant's eyes are still closed, but breathing is irregular and more rapid than during regular sleep. There are slight muscle movements or stirrings from time to time, but no generalized movements. The infant may exhibit facial grimaces, smiles, mouthing movements, and puckering of the lips. There may also be eye movements, which can be discerned through the closed lids.

Periodic Sleep　This state falls between regular and irregular sleep. The infant displays sudden bursts of facial and body movements; there are also changes in the rate of breathing.

Drowsiness　This condition typically occurs when the infant is waking up or falling asleep—what is sometimes called the "twilight zone." The eyelids open and close. If the lids are open, the eyes are unfocused and appear dull or glazed. An infant in the drowsy state will exhibit more activity than when in regular sleep, but less activity than when in irregular or periodic sleep.

Alert Inactivity　Here the infant is awake but not very active. The eyes have a bright and shiny appearance. A state of *alert activity* can usually be seen after three or four weeks of age. This state is similar to alert inactivity except the infant displays considerably more motor behavior.

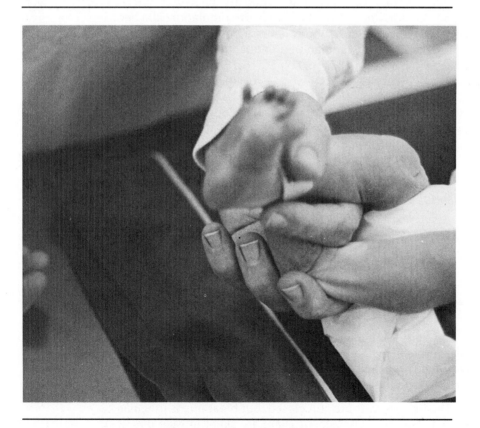

Figure 15-2　The Babinski reflex. Note the spread toes. (Photo by Warren R. Bentzen)

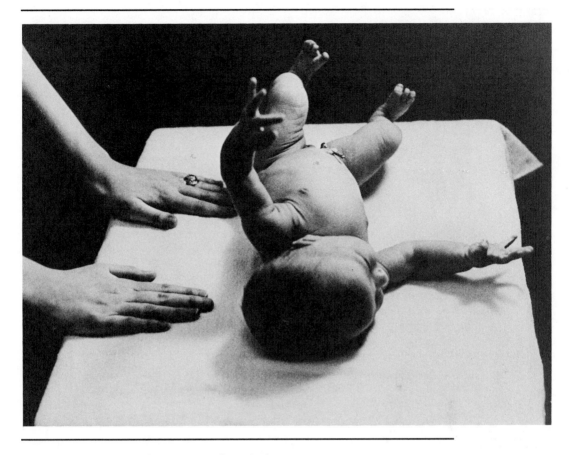

Figure 15-3 The Moro Reflex (Courtesy of Mead Johnson)

Waking Activity In this state one sees frequent bursts of generalized motor activity; the eyes are open; the infant does not cry but may utter other vocalizations such as moans, grunts, or whimpers. Breathing is quite irregular.

Crying Crying here refers to a sustained or prolonged cry. Facial grimaces, flushing of the face, and closed eyes may accompany the crying. There is frequently generalized motor activity.

Based on the work of Wolff (1973). This table adapted from Gander and Gardiner (1981, 109-110)

Procedure

As a first step, carefully describe characteristics of the physical and social environment that could be sources of stimulation for the newborn

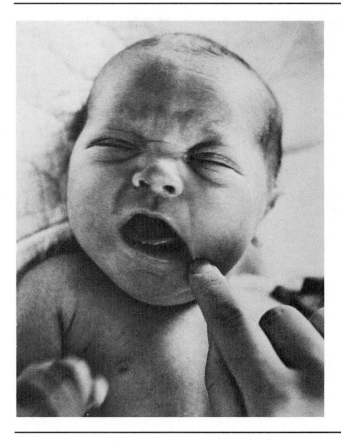

Figure 15-4   Rooting (Courtesy of Mead Johnson)

—e.g., background noises, talking, objects within sight or reach of the baby, direct stimulation provided by the caretaker (talking to him, caressing him), and so on. This description of the environment is the background against which you will assess the newborn's responsiveness when in various states. As a second step, describe in detail the newborn's behaviors using the specimen record technique. Make note of the small components of responses, such as respiration rate and rhythm, muscle movements, facial expressions, and eye movements (as seen through closed lids if asleep). Classify the behaviors according to the categories defined in Table 15-1.

It is suggested that you observe for about five minutes at a time, striving for at least three five-minute sessions over a total period of an hour to an hour-and-a-half. Since newborns tend to sleep a good part of the day, spacing out your recording sessions will help reduce fatigue and increase your chances of seeing the child in more than one state.

Observation Exercise 15-2

Infant States and Responsiveness to Stimulation

Observer's Name _____

Child Observed (code name or number) _____

Child's Age _____ Child's Sex _____

Observation Context (Home, day-care center) _____

Date of Observation _____ Time Begun _____ Time Ended _____

Brief Description of Setting/Situation

Objective Behavioral Description: **Response to Stimulation**

Session 1:

Session 2:

Session 3:

Parent's/Caregiver's Responses
to Newborn's State Behaviors:

Question Guides:

1. How many different states of arousal does the newborn exhibit during your observation of him?
2. How long does he remain in each state?
3. Is he in one state more than any other? Which one?
4. Is there any one feature of each state observed that best distinguishes it from other states?
5. What, if any, stimulation changes the newborn's state? How does his state affect his response to stimulation—is there an apparent general relationship between state and responsiveness to stimulation? What is it?
6. How does the parent or caregiver respond to the newborn while he is in various states? Is the parent or caregiver aware of the newborn's differing sensitivity to stimulation when in various states?

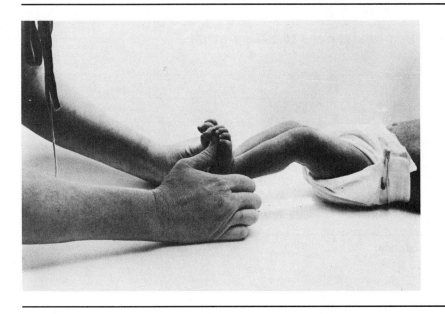

Figure 15-5   The Plantar Reflex (Courtesy of Mead Johnson)

Exercise 15-3: Individual Differences and the Newborn

Background Information

Psychologists speak of individual differences even among newborns. Individual differences exist in such areas as spontaneous behaviors, soothability, states, physical characteristics, and temperament.

Spontaneous behaviors are internally generated rather than responses to outside stimuli. They include such observable behaviors as "random startles, fleeting smiles, kicking, erections, and random mouthing and sucking movements" (Gander and Gardiner 1981). As Gander and Gardiner note, infants differ markedly in how often these behaviors occur, their type, and the sequences in which they occur. *Soothability* refer to how easily a crying or upset infant is comforted by such adult responses as holding, rocking, swaddling, warming, or giving a pacifier.

Perhaps the most interesting assessment of individual differences was made by the research team of Thomas, Chess, and Birch (1968, 1970). They describe infants by the terms "easy," "slow-to-warm-up," and "difficult." These descriptions are the result of infants' and children's responses on six personality dimensions: activity level, rhythmicity, approach/withdrawal, adaptability, intensity of reaction, and quality of mood. The infant or child is rated as either high or low on each dimension, depending on the characteristic ways she responds to various situations. These characteristic responses identify the child's *temperament*. Temperament is an important concept, because the infant's response tendencies can interact with the personalities of her parents and with the environment. This interaction can result in either a compatible or an incompatible relationship between the infant and her physical and social environment. For example, imagine a child with a vigorous, physically active temperament born to parents who are inactive physically. Of course, the relationship would not be determined solely by the temperaments of the parents and child. Nonetheless, temperament can have an effect on the child's development and behavior; and since qualities of temperament seem to be stable over the first ten years of life, they deserve attention. Table 15-3 presents the responses of a two-month-old who would be rated high and low on each of the six personality dimensions identified by Thomas, *et al.*

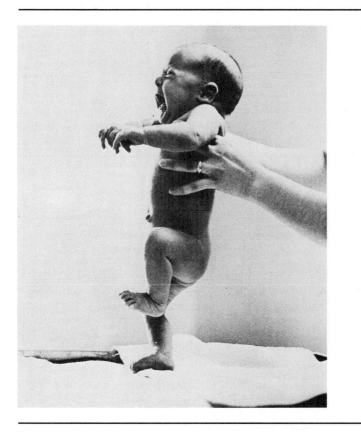

Figure 15-6 The Stepping Reflex (Courtesy of Mead Johnson)

Observation Objectives

To observe the differences in the soothability, spontaneous behaviors, and the temperaments of two newborns.

Procedure

This exercise ideally requires you to observe two newborns; however, if that is not possible, you can complete the exercise with just one newborn. Although the behaviors you will be observing are useful for studying individual differences, they will also give you information about a single child. It is suggested that you use the specimen record format for observing and recording. Observe each of the two newborns for at least three five- to ten-minute sessions within a total period of 60 to 90 minutes in each case. If you find it difficult to obtain much information on the newborns' temperamental qualities just by observing, you may ask the parent or caregiver about the child's typical responses in various situations. For this, refer to Table 15-2, which provides a general description of behaviors related to the Thomas *et al* nine personality dimensions (also refer to Table 15-3).

Table 15-2   Temperamental Qualities

Activity Level   Activity can begin in the uterus, where an active fetus can kick frequently. Active babies move around in their cribs or basinettes; they prefer to climb or run rather than engage in more placid activities. Other babies show much less vigorous activity levels.

Rhythmicity   Rhythmicity is characterized by regular cycles of activity—eating, sleeping, and bowel movements that occur pretty much on schedule. Other infants are not as predictable.

Approach/Withdrawal   Approach is an attitude of delight or acceptance when confronted with something new—laughter at first bath, readily eating new food. Withdrawal is a refusal to accept new situations.

Adaptability   Characterized by rapid adjustment to change; no severe negative reactions to disruption of normal routines. Some babies do not easily tolerate change or deviations from the familiar.

Intensity of Reaction   Some children laugh loudly, scream when they cry. Others merely smile, whimper or cry softly.

Quality of Mood   Some children are generally bright and cheerful; they smile easily. Other children seem generally unhappy and discontent; seem constantly to complain.

Adapted from Berger, 1991, pp. 216-217

Table 15-3   Infant Temperaments (at Two Months)

Temperament	Rating	Behavioral Characteristics
Activity level	Low	Motionless when being dressed or during sleep.
	High	Frequent movement in sleep. Squirms when diaper is changed.
Rhythmicity	Regular	On 4-hour feeding schedule since birth. Regular bowel movement.
	Irregular	Different waking time each morning. Feedings vary in size.
Approach/ Withdrawal	Positive	Smiles, licks washcloth. Liked bottle since birth.
	Negative	Rejects cereal the first time. Cries with strangers.
Adaptability	Adaptive	Passive during first bath, then enjoys bathing. Smiles at nurse.
	Not adaptive	Startles at sharp, sudden noises. Resists diapering.
Intensity of Reaction	Mild	No crying when diapers are wet. When hungry, whimpers rather than cries.
	Intense	Cries when diapers are wet. When not hungry, rejects food vigorously.
Quality of Mood	Positive	Smiles at parents. Smacks lips with first taste of new food.
	Negative	Fussy after nursing. Rocking carriage causes crying.

Adapted from Dworetzky (1987, 110)

Observation Exercise 15-3

Individual Differences in Newborns (Part I)

Observer's Name _____

Child Observed (Newborn #1 code name or number) _____

Child's Age _____ Child's Sex _____

Observation Context (Home, day-care center) _____

Date of Observation _____ Time Begun _____ Time Ended _____

Brief Description of Setting/Situation

Objective Behavioral Description:

Session 1:

Session 2:

Session 3:

PARENT'S REPORT (If needed. Identify each area reported on):

Observation Exercise 15-3

Individual Differences in Newborns (Part II)

Observer's Name _____

Child Observed (Newborn #2 code name or number) _____

Child's Age _____ Child's Sex _____

Observation Context (Home, day-care center) _____

Date of Observation _____ Time Begun _____ Time Ended _____

Brief Description of Setting/Situation

Objective Behavioral Description:

Session 1:

Session 2:

Session 3:

PARENT'S REPORT (If needed. Identify each area reported on):

COMPARISON

Newborn #1: Summary Description   Newborn #2: Summary Description

Summary Description of Differences

Soothability:

Spontaneous Behaviors:

Temperaments:

Question Guides:

1. What spontaneous behaviors does the newborn exhibit? How frequently do these occur? About how long do they last? Do they seem to follow a recurring sequence or pattern?
2. Does the parent or caregiver respond to any of the spontaneous behaviors exhibited? If so, describe.
3. Is the newborn easily soothed or comforted? What seems to soothe her the most? What different tactics does the parent or caregiver use to comfort the baby?
4. What temperamental qualities characterize the baby? Under what circumstances do you observe indications of the newborn's temperament?
5. Does the parent or caregiver seem aware of the baby's unique responses to situations? If so, how? Do the parents or caregivers of the two newborns observed differ in their responses to the babies' temperaments? How?

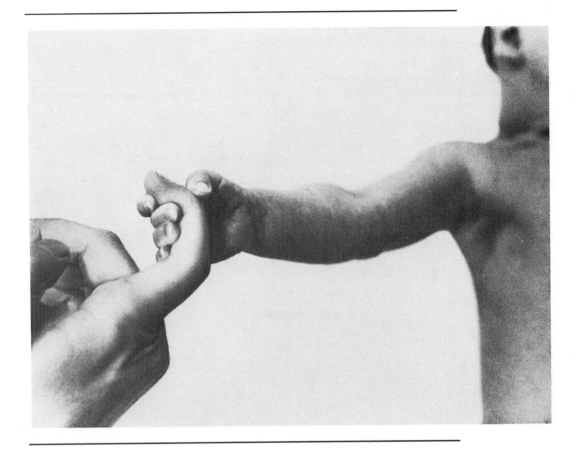

Figure 15-7   Grasping (Courtesy of Mead Johnson)

Exercise 15-4: Motor Responses of the Newborn

Background Information

The newborn's motor abilities are best characterized as reflexive. Discussion of the newborn or infant would be incomplete without mentioning these built-in motor patterns. You may see several of these reflexes during your observations, especially the more common ones such as the startle, orienting, rooting, sucking, swallowing, eye blink, and grasp reflexes (see Table 15-4). Some of these reflexes have survival value; they protect the newborn and young infant from potential harm and enable her to take advantage of the caregiver's efforts to keep her alive. The rooting, sucking, and swallowing reflexes, for example, permit the newborn to eat; the vomiting and eye blink reflexes are protective in nature. Other reflexes appear to serve no special purpose, although pediatricians use them as indications of the child's neurological development. For example, if the Babinski reflex (in which the toes curl upward and fan out when the sole of the foot is stroked) persists beyond six months or so of age, it could indicate damage of the central nervous system.

The newborn's voluntary gross (large) motor activities are limited to lifting up his head while lying on his stomach. Some newborns can lift the head to about a 45 degree angle (*Denver Developmental Screening Test* 1969). Hand functions are limited mainly to the grasp reflex. General, *undifferentiated* body movements are prominent in the newborn. Even his reactions to focused stimulation, such as a pinprick to the foot, typically involve overall movements of the arms, legs, and torso, rather than withdrawal of just the stimulated foot and leg.

Table 15-4   Infant Reflexes

Reflex	Eliciting Stimulus	Response	Age Ceases
Rooting	Stroke cheek with finger or nipple	Turns head, opens mouth begins sucking	9 mos.
Moro	Sudden stimulus—loud noise, being dropped	Extends legs, arms fingers; arches back and pulls head back	3 mos.
Grasping	Stroke palm of hand	Makes a strong fist; can be picked up	2-3 mos.
Tonic neck	Place on back	"Fencer" position with head to one side, extension of limbs on prefered side, other side flexed	2-3 mos.
Babinski	Stroke side of foot	Fans toes out and turns big toe upward	6-9 mos.
Walking	Hold under arms, bare feet touching flat surface	Makes walking motions	4-8 wks.
Eye Blink	Puff of air in face, loud noise, strong odor, bright light	Blinks eyes	

Adapted from Papalia and Olds (1979, 127; 1993, 153)

Keep in mind the general principles that govern motor development. Muscle control proceeds from the head to the feet *(cephalocaudal principle)*, and from the midline of the body to the outer extremities *(proximodistal principle)*. Thus, control of the head and neck (which includes the eyes, mouth, lips, tongue), comes before control of the trunk, legs, and feet. The infant gains control over the larger arm and shoulder (midline) movements before he can grasp small objects between thumb and forefinger (extremities).

Observation Objectives

To observe and record a newborn's reflexive and voluntary motor responses.

Procedure

In this exercise, you will be asked to deviate from a totally naturalistic approach and try to elicit some common reflexes. It is recommended that the parent or caregiver stimulate the reflexes so that you will be free to carefully observe and record the responses while they are occurring. Do not overstimulate the baby, especially when eliciting reflexes that require loud noises or sudden withdrawal of physical support. You will also observe and record the newborn's voluntary movements and motor patterns. For this, you will use a narrative descriptive format (specimen record), since movements of some kind are likely to occur for much of the time. Observe for five-minutes at at time, and try for at least three five-minute sessions over a total period of an hour to an hour and a half.

Observation Exercise 15-4

Motor Responses of the Newborn

Observer's Name _____

Child Observed (code name or number) _____

Child's Age _____ Child's Sex _____

Observation Context (Home, day-care center) _____

Date of Observation _____ Time Begun _____ Time Ended _____

Brief Description of Setting/Situation

Objective Behavioral Description:

Reflex Elicited	Stimulation Used	Response
1.		
2.		
3.		
4.		
5.		
6.		

Voluntary Responses (Describe):

Head:

Arms:

Legs:

Trunk:

Overall Description:

Question Guides:

1. What reflexes does the newborn exhibit? What specific stimuli elicit the responses? Does he get used to *(habituate)* and stop responding to any stimuli that initially cause reflex responses?
2. What non-reflexive movements does the newborn display? What are the characteristics of these movements? smooth? jerky or thrashing about? coordinated? Are movements related to one another or are they seemingly independent? Do his movements bring him into any contact with the physical environment? If so, does such contact seem to affect or influence further movements?
3. Does the newborn have control over his general movements? over individual parts of his body? Does he have more control over some body parts than others? If so, how might this difference in control be explained?
4. Does the parent or caregiver respond to his movements? Does he try to encourage them?

Exercise 15-5: Perceptual Responses of the Newborn

Background Information

Vision   Vision is the sense on which we depend the most, and even newborns' visual abilities are fairly well developed. They can "make small movements of their heads and eyes in response to visual stimulation" (Fogel 1984), although only slowly and inaccurately. Newborns may also have preferences for certain visual objects; they show this by looking longer at preferred than nonpreferred objects *(visual fixation)*. The majority of newborns can visually follow a stimulus to the midline of the body (about 80% can do this by one month of age, according to the *Denver Developmental Screening Test* 1969). The newborn's optimal range of vision is about 6 to 8 inches. Despite their limited visual acuity, newborns can distinguish some details of their environment; for example, they can "discriminate between solid gray patterns and those composed of five gray stripes" (Willemsen 1979).

Newborns are sensitive to changes in the brightness of the surrounding lighting (Willemsen 1979). Not all psychologists agree on the newborn's visual preferences. Writers such as Craig (1989), report that "infants are selective about what they look at from the beginning. They look at novel and moderately complex patterns and at human faces" (p. 156). Craig (1989) notes that the newborn's preference for the edges of a face changes, with development, to an interest in "the eyes, and even later, at the mouth of a person talking" (p. 156). There does seem to be agreement that newborns prefer to scan the edges and outlines of objects, especially curved outlines. Interestingly, there is evidence that newborns as young as two weeks of age can show a preference for their mothers' faces, even when presented as pictures rather than live (Carpenter 1974, cited in Craig 1983).

Hearing   It was once believed that newborns were deaf, but it is now known that they are sensitive to some aspects of sound. Indeed, Willemsen (1979) notes that they "react to all the major aspects of auditory stimulation— that is, pitch, loudness, timbre, and pattern (rhythm)." Papalia and Olds (1979) report that "the greater the sound intensity, the greater the babies' increase in heart rate and movement," where such increases indicate awareness of the stimulation. Their responses to intense sound helps explain why newborns and babies in general pay attention to high-pitched voices and why adults speak to them in that way. There is also evidence to suggest that newborns can distinguish their mother's voice from that of another female (Fogel 1984). Papalia and Olds (1987) suggest that the infant's "early preference for the mother's voice may be an important mechanism for initiating bonding between a mother and a baby . . ." (p. 161).

Habituation   is another important component of a newborn's response capability. Habituation occurs when, after exposure to a physical stimulus that originally evokes response, the newborn ceases to respond. She gets used to it and it no longer interests her. There are two basic reactions to novel sounds (Papalia and Olds 1979). First, the newborn will exhibit an *orienting response* by turning her head toward the source of the sound. Second, if she is doing anything else at the time, she will stop or *inhibit* that activity. It is as though she can do only one thing at a time, and the novel sound is more important than something that may already be familiar to her. But as Papalia and Olds (1979) point out, it might be difficult to observe an orienting response, because the newborn does not have good control of her eye and muscle movements. Therefore, inhibition of an activity (such as sucking) following a sound, indicates that the newborn is orienting. The inhibitory response reliably accompanies the orienting reflex (Papalia and Olds 1979).

Observation Objectives

To observe and record some of the newborn's behaviors that reflect her perceptual response capabilities.

Procedure

This exercise has two parts. In Part I, you will be eliciting some responses from the newborn. Perform the simple stimulation tasks outlined below, and record on the checklist provided whether or not the baby responded. Immediately follow with a detailed but concise description of the response. You will need a small flashlight (a penlight is preferable) to test several of the newborn's visual responses.

In Part II, using a form of event sampling, observe the newborn for any of the perceptual responses discussed in the section on Background Information. Especially look for behaviors such as the orienting and habituation responses. Notice how the parent or caregiver responds to and stimulates the baby. You may want to perform some casual testing by speaking to the newborn and comparing her reactions to your voice with her reactions to the voice of a familiar person. If there are objects hanging above the crib, observe whether she makes any visual responses to them.

Observation Exercise 15-5

Perceptual Responses of the Newborn

Observer's Name _____

Child Observed (code name or number) _____

Child's Age _____ Child's Sex _____

Observation Context (Home, day-care center) _____

Date of Observation _____ Time Begun _____ Time Ended _____

Brief Description of Setting/Situation

Part I

Stimulation	Response			Description
	Yes	**No**	**Uncertain**	
Loud Hand Clap	____	____	____	
Soft Hand Clap	____	____	____	
Loud Voice	____	____	____	

	Yes	No	Uncertain
Soft Voice	___	___	___
Object 6" from eyes	___	___	___
Object 15" from eyes	___	___	___
Tracks moving light	___	___	___

Part II

Event Sampling

Event Observed   **Description**

Question Guides:

1. Are there any objects within the newborn's line and range of vision? Does he visually respond to these objects. Does he gaze at it or follow it with his eyes if it is moved slowly in front of his face?
2. Does the newborn respond visually to the general environment? Does the newborn appear to scan the area immediately above him (assuming there are no objects suspended above his crib or bassinet) or to either side of him? If he is held, does he look around the room, as though trying to visually take in his surroundings? What leads you to believe that the newborn has made responses to particular stimuli?
3. Do some body positions seem to evoke more responses to the environment than other positions (e.g., lying on his back, held over an adult's shoulder or on an adult's lap)?
4. Is there any apparent "mismatch" between the newborn's visual competence and the visual stimuli provided for her? For instance, is there a complicated mobile hanging above her crib, when a simple square, circle, or diamond shape might be more appropriate to her ability to process visual information?
5. Does the newborn respond to background sounds? Are there any orienting responses? Has she habituated to these general noises? Why do you think she has made a recognizable response to this aspect of her physical environment?
6. Does the newborn respond to sounds that are not always present in the background? Does she orient? Does she eventually habituate? What leads you to conclude she oriented or habituated to any sounds? To what sounds are these responses made?
7. Does the newborn respond differently to continuous as opposed to intermittent sounds? If so, what are the differences, and what are the specific sounds he responds to.
8. Does the newborn respond to voices? Does she give any indication that she prefers her mother's voice to someone else's voice. If you think so, how does she demonstrate her preference?

Exercise 15-6: Emotional Functioning of the Newborn

Background Information

This last exercise is intended only as a very brief introduction to the area of emotional behavior and functioning, a topic that is continued in Chapters 16 and 17. We draw here on the work of Stanley and Nancy Greenspan (1985), who identified six "emotional milestones." We are primarily concerned in this chapter with the first of these six milestones or stages, but for the sake of providing you with a feeling of continuity and with a larger context, we include the second stage as well.

The first two of these stages or milestones concern the capacities of *self-regulation* and the *use of the senses* to take an interest in the world. The Greenspans refer to these milestones as "two simultaneous challenges" (p. 4). They are challenges because the newborn, after nine months in the darkness and relative quiet of the womb," is suddenly catapulted, as it were, into a world filled with a variety of sensations that are completely new to her. In the first milestone, which takes place between birth and three months of age, the newborn must organize these sensations and at the same time feel comfortable in their presence and actively engage them in ways that are appropriate to her level of developmental maturity—e.g., show interest in the sights and sounds around her and not find them painful (Greenspan and Greenspan, 1985).

This then permits achievement of the second milestone (two to seven months), which is that of "taking a highly specialized interest in the *human world*" (p. 5, italics original). An assumption here is that if the baby does not find these environmental stimuli pleasurable, he may be unlikely to progress to the stage where the world of human beings "is seen as the most enticing, pleasurable, and exciting of all experiences" (p. 4). The pleasure that one wants the baby to feel, say the Greenspans, can be seen in her "enraptured smiles and eager joyfulness" as she "gazes excitedly at your face" while she feels the movements of your body and hears your voice.

Observation Objectives

Your objectives here are quite abbreviated relative to the preceding exercises. We simply want you to attempt to assess how well a newborn is achieving the Greenspans' first emotional milestone. Your objective is to observe and record the newborn's interest in and responsiveness to the sounds, sights, and things that are in his environment. We are aware that responsiveness is already heavily involved in the other exercises in this chapter. Nonetheless, we want to place emphasis on emotions and, in the case of the newborn, on the foundation or precursors of his subsequent emotional growth, development, and behavior.

Procedure

In this exercise, use the event sampling technique. Watch a newborn (a child between birth and one month of age and no older) for any behavioral evidence that she is *spontaneously* interested in the sights and sounds around her and that she does not "find them painful" (i.e., she does not appear disturbed or distressed by them). "Spontaneously" means that the newborn is not reacting to *your* efforts to evoke some kind of response from her; she is responding on her own.

Observe for about five minutes at a time over three separate sessions. Pool or combine the information from the three sessions to draw your conclusions or inferences.

Observation Exercise 15-6

Emotional Functioning of the Newborn

Observer's Name _____

Child Observed (code name or number) _____

Child's Age _____ Child's Sex _____

Observation Context (Home, day-care center) _____

Date of Observation _____ Time Begun _____ Time Ended _____

Brief Description of Setting/Situation

Objective Behavioral Description   **Interpretations**

Summary Comments on Newborn's Emotional Functioning
(Greenspans' First Emotional Milestone)

past and present on the stage of active memory" (p. 40). Let's look briefly at these with respect to some normative ages of particular accomplishments.

Kagan says that the three-month-old infant "can recognize a familiar event in her perceptual field because it shares properties with her schemata" (p. 40). Sharing properties with her schemata means that the familiar event previously encountered by the infant is perceived as being similar in some respects to her memory of that event. During the first six months, however, this recognition will disappear if too much time passes between successive experiences of the event.

The second element of memory development, the ability "to retrieve a schema when there are minimal clues . . . in the immediate field" (p. 40), becomes functional, Kagan says, after the first six months. This ability to retrieve a schema can be measured by hiding an attractive toy and making the infant wait before he is allowed to reach for it. Kagan cites research that found that in a group of infants studied from the ages of eight to twelve months, "no eight-month-old was able to remember the toy's location with a one-second delay . . ." (p. 41). By twelve months of age, all the infants could find the toy when their search for it was delayed for three seconds, and a majority could perform this task even with a seven-second delay.

The third memory achievement involves the ability to retrieve the past over longer and longer lapses of time. Kagan notes that "When older children and adults read a sentence or listen to a conversation, they are able to integrate the incoming information with their knowledge over a period of time that can last as long as thirty seconds" (p. 42). Kagan calls this process of integration *active memory*, which, he says, becomes stronger and more functional around eight months of age (p. 42). Thus it is that "The infant now automatically relates the present to the immediate past, which means she is comparing information from two sources" (p. 42).

V. *Representational/Symbolic*

Representation, which is having one thing "stand for" another, possibly quite different, is, says Fogel, the "crowning achievement of cognitive development in the first three years of life" (p. 6). He also includes symbolic thinking, the most significant of which is the use of language. (For a detailed discussion of representational ability, see Chapter 17, Exercise 3.) Of course, one major function of *linguistic symbols* is precisely to represent something else: the word 'chair' stands for the actual object we sit in, or 'dog' can stand for a particular furry, four-legged animal we pass everyday on our way to work (or perhaps "Rover" stands for *our* dog). Fogel indicates that it is late into the second year of life before children can grasp "the relation between the symbol and the actual object . . ." (p. 6). This simply means that symbol use is essentially "unthinking" or "uncritical," and it serves predominantly practical purposes, such as in the practical connection between, say, the word 'milk' and the actual glass of white liquid that the parent gives the child following his utterance of the word.

VI. *Communicative/Linguistic*

This competency area is close to the representational/symbolic competency just discussed. One important difference is emphasis on the use of language *to communicate*. There is, of course, the complicated business of learning the meaning of words, proper grammar, and so on, but the ultimate use of language is to convey one's ideas, thoughts, and feelings to other people. Communication also involves knowing when to speak and when to listen (the reciprocal character of communication), learning about the environment, understanding what others are trying to make known, and making known one's own messages in socially appropriate ways. In short, language is a social skill as well as an intellectual skill.

VII. *Social/Interactive*

Fogel initially emphasizes social/interactive competence in the context of language usage, especially the skill of taking turns in conversation. He mentions the naturally occurring "bursts and pauses in their behavior" as potential forerunners of such conversational skills, but he quickly points out that "any semblance of taking turns seems to be created by the adult partner who learns to skillfully insert her smiles, coos, and words into the natural silences left by the infant" (p. 7). Fogel indicates that the infant's awareness of his or her role as a *partner* in an interaction with an adult does not come about before the age of five or six months. Although there are other facets of social competence, of course (the next basic competency area is one of these other facets), it is important to recognize that infants start to learn social skills far ahead of any learning of words.

VIII. *Expressive/Emotive*

Feeling and expressing certain kinds of emotional states is an important element of the infant's social skills (Fogel, p. 7). What emotions an infant can experience apparently depends upon age or developmental level. Fogel says there is general agreement that "infants do not know the feeling of fear before about eight months, and they cannot experience complex feelings like guilt, pride, or shame until they are almost three years old" (p. 7). Control of the kinds of emotions they want to express is not achieved before two or three years of age (Fogel, p. 7). Kagan (1984) offers some informative comments on the relationship between emotional states and age, as well as on the general development of emotion.

> The popular belief that a child's emotions do not change with growth requires the improbable assumption that maturational changes in the brain that produce new cognitive evaluations and special feeling tones have no influence on the older person's emotional experiences. However, because one often uses the same language to name emotions in two- and twenty-two-year-olds, it is easy to believe that the emotional

experiences are the same. American mothers also assume, incorrectly I believe, that three-month-olds can experience the emotions of interest, anger, joy, or fear that are attributed to adults. (Kagan, 1984, p. 172)

IX. *Self-Regulatory/Coping*

Whether consciously aware of it or not, parents, teachers, and other adults who work with children, are concerned over the practical issues of a child's self-control and her ability to deal constructively with various aspects of the environment; they are also pleased (if not downright relieved) when a child in fact achieves these abilities. As Fogel puts it, "The development of self-regulatory skills is greeted by parents with a sense of relief that goes beyond delight. The ability of an infant to cope with the stresses of everyday life takes from the parent's shoulders a considerable burden" (p. 7). Among the indicators of "successful self-regulation," Fogel lists "sleeping through the night, waiting patiently while a meal is being prepared, handling the fear and distress of separation from the parents, fighting assertively to retrieve a toy from a meddling older sibling" (p. 7).

These skills can be put into the general category of autonomy, which, of course, tends to free adults from some of the tasks associated with being a child's parent or caregiver (see Fogel, p. 8). This freedom gives credence to the relief and delight that adults feel upon the child's achievement of self-regulatory and coping skills.

Why is Infancy Important?

Let us get back briefly to the reasons why infancy is such an important topic of study. Here we shall follow Bower's lead, because he also asks the same question. "Why," he asks, "should 2 percent of a lifespan merit such attention?" (p. 1; "such attention" refers, among other things, to his own book on infancy). We like his answers, because they are ones over which probably few would quibble. We offer you an extensive quote from his *Primer*.

Probably more of the skills that separate human beings from other animals are acquired in infancy than in all the rest of childhood together. By the end of infancy the baby is sociable and cooperative. He has learned what is necessary for language, possibly the most important of all human skills. He can walk on his own two feet. He has refined the manual skills that man shares with no other animal. He can use tools to a limited extent, but an extent greater than any nonhuman. He has acquired some very basic and important concepts of space, causality, number. All this happened in eighteen months, grown from what look like most unpromising beginnings. (pp. 1-2)

David Elkind, a well-known author and Professor of Child Study at Tufts University, also specifies the particular concerns, and therefore the potential accomplishments, of the infancy period. He writes as follows:

From birth until about two years of age infants are concerned with constructing a world of permanent objects, attaching themselves to significant others, and establishing what now retired Harvard professor Erik Erikson called a sense of "trust." These three attainments constitute the major intellectual, social, and emotional developments of the infancy period. (Elkind, 1981; p. 98)

Have you any doubt that all of these cited accomplishments are indeed important and that they form the very foundation for everything that is to come in subsequent developmental periods?

Of course, the nine competency areas just discussed are, in and of themselves, the occasions for celebrating this first portion of the life span. Although one could argue that the adult also functions within, as well as adds to, these skill areas, he or she does not do so for the first time as an adult (or older child). Let's turn now to a practical application of the ideas presented above.

Exercise 16-1: Physical Characteristics and Motor Abilities of the Infant/Toddler (One to Twenty-Four Months)

Background Information

Physical Characteristics: You will find some striking differences in physical appearance between the newborn and the 15- to 24-month-old infant or toddler. Indeed, you need not wait very long before seeing some dramatic changes. Let's first look briefly at the changes that take place in the child's weight and height. Faw and Belkin (1989), in their excellent college review book on child psychology, report that the first four months of life result in a doubling of birth weight, which brings the infant up to a bodyweight of 14 or 15 pounds. (Craig, 1989, indicates a range from 12 to 15 pounds. We mention this only to point out that such norms will vary at least slightly from source to source; any specific norm probably should not be considered a precise figure.) Weight triples to an average of 20 pounds (Papalia and Olds report 22 pounds) by the end of the first year. Interestingly enough, subsequent weight gain during the whole second year, according to Faw and Belkin, amounts to only about five pounds. This sharp decrease in gain is attributed to the child's increased physical activity and resulting increased consumption of calories.

Height gains during the first four months come to about 3 to 4 inches (Faw and Belkin, p. 130). By the end of the first year, the child grows yet another 6 inches, achieving a length (on average) of 29 to 31 inches. As with weight increases, growth in height slows down during the second year to a "mere" 4 (to 5) inches. The height of the average two-year-old is 33 to 35 inches (Faw and Belkin, p. 130). Height of the two-year-old, by the way, is approximately one-half of what it will be when he or she is an adult.

As you can recall from Chapter 15, the newborn's head is misshapen and disproportionately large relative to her body, which gives the child an appearance that is peculiar if not outright distorted. The growth following this first month or two of life is, say Faw and Belkin, an attempt of the body to " 'catch up with' the head" (p. 131). The trunk gains some 50 percent in length during the first two years, while the arms increase their length by 60 to 75 percent (Faw and Belkin, p. 131).

Motor Characteristics and Abilities: At one month, the newborn exhibits a number of involuntary reflex responses, and his voluntary movements are random and poorly controlled. This random aspect of early muscle movement is referred to as mass action and is the opposite of the specific action that refers to the older child's more coordinated muscle movements. Use of the hands is limited to a grasp reflex, and he seems totally unaware that he even has hands. By 18 months, the infant has accumulated the achievements of head control, sitting, rolling over, crawling, creeping, standing, walking, and running. His ability to reach for, grasp, and manipulate objects has also undergone dramatic change. By about three months of age, he begins swiping at objects and becomes aware of his hands; by 18 months, he can turn pages of a book one at a time. At one month, his only way to communicate is to cry; by 18 months, he uses words and exhibits other true social behaviors. (See Tables 16-1 and 16-2). Of course, all of these accomplishments have depended on the development and maturation of the nervous system, which in turn have depended on many other factors, not the least of which was a supporting and nurturant physical and social environment.

Craig (1989) offers a useful "overview" of an infant's competencies at the ages of four, eight, twelve, eighteen, and twenty-four months. For the area of motor competencies, we shall take advantage of Craig's format and briefly present some of the developmental milestones that are typical at the ages indicated above.

Four Months: The infant can usually hold up his chest when in the prone (on the stomach) position. The four-month-old can also hold his head steady while sitting up supported by an adult. He can roll over from front to back and vice versa. Craig notes that "most four-month-olds can reach and grasp for an object, although they frequently do not make contact" (p. 145). Faw and Belkin (1989) say that the infant of two and one-half months of age is in what they call the "early reaching period," in which she reaches for objects she sees but does so with very poor coordination and control, and frequently her efforts fail. (The development of reaching and grasping behavior will be discussed in greater detail in a separate section below.) These authors report that by the age of four months, "visual reaching and hand reaching become coordinated" (p. 145). This skill is evidenced by infants "visually following their hand and arm as they reach for an object, and their attention alternates between the object to be grasped and the grasping hand itself" (Faw and Belkin, p. 145). Incidentally, Faw and Belkin view *visual tracking* as a form of visual reaching, even though it is not coordinated with hand and arm movements. Visual tracking is following an object with the eyes, and it appears at about three and one-half months of age.

Eight Months: Craig reports that most eight-month-olds can get into a sitting position on their own, and almost all infants of this age can maintain a sitting posture once they are put into it by another person. Faw and Belkin (1989) note that most six- to seven-month-olds can sit in a high chair, but that accomplishment comes slightly before the ability to sit without external support. Craig indicates that more than half of all eight-month-olds can stand while holding on to a support, and about half can bring themselves to a standing position (p. 147). Some smaller proportion can move about in a sidewise stepping motion while holding on to the sides of a crib or playpen; some even have the early ability to walk while holding on to a piece of furniture for support, an ability sometimes referred to as "cruising."

The typical eight-month-old can move from place to place by crawling (with the body on the ground) or by creeping on the hands and knees (Craig, p. 147). Faw and Belkin note that at about seven months, infants might thrust "one knee forward as they lie on their stomach." This, say Faw and Belkin, "is the initial stop in learning to crawl" (p. 140). These authors claim that by eight months ("34 weeks"), the average child has the capacity to crawl, but they point out that because there is not sufficient arm and leg strength, he cannot yet keep the stomach off the ground by creeping on the hands and knees.

With regard to hand and arm control, Craig indicates that most eight-month-olds can "pass objects from hand to hand, and some are able to use the thumb and finger to grasp" (p. 149). She also reports that infants of this age can usually "bang two objects together . . ." (p. 149). Craig also notes that most eight-month-olds can hand an object back and forth to an adult, an activity they very much enjoy doing.

Twelve Months: Faw and Belkin (1989), distinguishing between "supported walking" and "independent walking," (p. 141) report that children typically take their first unsupported (independent), albeit unsteady, steps a short time after their first birthday. Subsequent development of the ability to locomote progresses quickly from that milestone accomplishment, say Faw and Belkin. Craig writes that twelve-month-olds "actively manipulate the environment. They are able to undo latches, open cabinets, pull toys, and twist lamp cords" (p. 149). She also mentions the acquisition of a *pincer grasp*, which should be distinguished from the *ulnar grasp*, which Berk (1989) describes as "a clumsy motion in which the fingers close against the palm" (p. 147). The pincer grasp enables the infant to oppose the thumb and forefinger. This *cortical opposition* ability, in turn, enables the child to pick up quite small objects such as hairs, pins, coins, and so on. With this and other new abilities, however, the child can also get into many more things (and much more trouble) than she could heretofore: she can "turn on the television set and the stove, . . . explore kitchen cupboards, open windows, and poke things into electrical outlets" (Craig, 1989; p. 149).

Eighteen Months: Children eighteen months of age are almost without exception walking alone. They often like to carry things in their hands or push or pull some kind of object as they walk. (Craig, 1989, p. 150) They have a very hard time as yet doing such things as kicking a ball, jumping, or pedaling a tricycle. (Craig, p. 150).

Eighteen-month-olds, according to Craig, are generally capable of "stacking from two to four blocks to build a tower, and often they can manage to scribble with crayon or pencil" (p. 150). At this age, children frequently show increased ability to feed themselves and can even partly undress themselves. (Craig, p. 150) Dressing oneself, however, is apparently an appreciably more difficult task than taking clothes off, and for that reason, dressing comes later in development.

Twenty-Four Months: The gains in abilities between 18 and 24 months of age seem quite astonishing. As Craig (1989) puts it,

> Two-year-olds can not only walk and run, but they can usually pedal a tricycle, jump in place on both feet, balance briefly on one foot, and accomplish a fairly good overhand throw. They climb up steps and, sometimes, come down again with assistance. They crawl into, under, around, and over objects and furniture; they manipulate, carry, handle, push, or pull anything they see. They put things into and take things out of large containers. They pour water, mold clay, stretch the stretchable, and bend the bendable. They transport items in carts, wagons, carriages, or trucks. They explore, test, and probe. (Craig, (1989) p. 151)

Perhaps her concluding statement is of the greatest importance, to wit: "All this exploration provides a vital learning experience about the nature and possibilities of their physical world" (p. 151). This, of course, is what development is all about.

To bring this section of this first exercise or unit to a close, we would like to present in summary form Faw and Belkin's discussion of the "phases of object manipulation." We do this because the ability to reach for, grasp, and manipulate objects is such a critical ability. Indeed, it could be argued that our hand or manual dexterity is among *the* central attributes that set us apart from the rest of the animal kingdom, with language or symbol use certainly being another key distinguishing characteristic of human behavior and ability.

The authors identify a "prereaching period" and an "early reaching period" (p. 144). The first period comprises about the first two or two and one-half months, during which time the newborn or infant does not reach for objects but merely stares at them if they come into view. (See also Laura Berk, 1989, for reference to, and a discussion of, prereaching.) The second, early reaching period, begins at about two and one-half months of age, when "children begin to reach for objects that they see" (p. 144). Again, however, such behavior is poorly controlled and usually fails to hit the intended target. Let's look now at the two phases discussed by Faw and Belkin.

Phase I, say Faw and Belkin, evidences "various stages of object manipulation," but they write in terms of the characteristics of the skills that represent those stages. We present those characteristics immediately below.

PHASE I

1. Reaching and grasping are not engaged in as separate acts. That is to say, they lack *differentiation* and demonstrate instead the characteristics of *mass action*. Faw and Belkin also point out that this aspect of hand use demonstrates the principle of *proximo-distal development*. This is simply development that proceeds from the midline (proximo) of the body outwards to the extremities (distal).
2. The infant in Phase I cannot yet use two arms at the same time.
3. Control of hand and arm movements is relatively absent. Once initiated, the infant in Phase I cannot stop a reaching movement, nor can she adjust a reaching movement if it is inaccurate and off target.
4. Grasping in this Phase is not performed in conjunction with how the object feels to the infant. Instead, reaching and grasping are directed by the visual presence of the object as well as by the object's visual relationship to the hand.

Adapted from Faw and Belkin (1989; p. 144).

Faw and Belkin indicate that the "obvious switching of attention back and forth between the grasping hand and the object to be grasped" ends by five months of age, and the infant now "moves his or her hand directly to the object" (p. 145). The authors note that although the movements are well coordinated, they nonetheless still belong in Phase I, because "the reach and grasp are controlled by the visual presence of the object sought and are a unitary action rather than two separate actions" (p. 145). They also note, importantly, that a grasping response will still be made once the reaching is initiated, even if the hand does not actually touch the object. This phenomenon occurs because the infant cannot yet completely control bodily actions. It's as though once begun, a movement or gesture simply must be finished, despite the fact that nothing will be accomplished by it.

Five months of age, say Faw and Belkin, denotes the division or transition between Phase I and Phase II. Phase II has the following characteristics.

PHASE II

1. In this phase, infants reach and grasp with two hands, not just one.
2. Infants are able to correct errors in reaching once they are detected.
3. Reaching and grasping now become separable activities and each can be engaged in independently of the other.

4. Visual presence of the object is no longer the primary impetus for grasping; now contact with the object is the controlling factor.

Adapted from Faw and Belkin (1989; p. 146).

Some of the objectives found in this chapter will provide you with a number of options that are absent in the other exercise chapters. The age span from one to twenty-four months comprises a large number of devel-

Figure 16-1   Face of a toddler. See the difference in proportion as compared to the newborn. (Courtesy of Mead Johnson)

opmental changes that cannot be observed and recorded by any single individual. Moreover, it's also likely that you will have less opportunity to observe infants and toddlers than you will children of preschool age. This fact almost necessitates that we give you enough alternatives so that you can observe the behavior of at least one child in this important first stage of life.

Observation Objectives

(1) To observe and describe the physical characteristics of a child anywhere between one month and twenty-four months of age and compare them with the physical characteristics of the newborn observed in Exercise 15-1; and/or (2) to observe and record the motor behavior of an infant between one and twenty-four months of age. This objective should be done in conjunction with objective (1) above, which means that you can observe the same infant for both parts of the assignment; and/or (3) to compare and contrast the motor skills of at least two infants who are of appreciably different ages (say, for example, 10 months and 18 months)— the goal here is to chart, in a cross sectional way, the developmental progress an infant makes over the space of several months.

Procedure

For objective (1) of this exercise, measure the child's weight, total height, and the length of the head, trunk, and legs. Compare these measurements with those you obtained on a newborn and summarize the differences. Also compare the toddler's height and weight with the figures given above for the fiftieth percentile. If a comparison with a newborn is not possible, simply determine whether the infant's physical characteristics correspond to what you would normatively expect for his or her age.

For objective (2) of this exercise, use the event sampling format and observe and record all of the infant's motor behaviors for two or three five-minute periods. Distribute your observations so as to get a varied sample of the infant's abilities rather than an extended display of pretty much the same behaviors. In other words, try to get examples of reaching and grasping, crawling or creeping, walking, cruising, and so on, depending on the infant's age or developmental level. Compare the infant's abilities with norms for his or her age.

For objective (3), you will observe and record in event sampling format two infants' large and fine motor skills as specified in the observation exercise sheet. You may have to encourage the infants to exhibit some of the skills listed if they do not display them spontaneously. Encourage here means demonstrating what you want them to do. We shall permit such encouragement in this instance because we want you to compare and contrast the two infants' abilities on the same tasks.

You should have on hand such items as a few raisins, 4-6 small blocks, a small container with lid (large enough to hold several of the blocks), beads and a piece of string, a book or magazine, playdough, and a crayon. Some of these items may already be part of the infants' or toddlers' toy collection. Observe and record the following fine motor tasks: (1) stacking several blocks (determine how many they can stack); (2) picking up a raisin (what grasping technique do they use?); (3) placing some of the blocks in the container and removing them again; (4) pulling, squeezing, or pounding playdough; (5) turning the pages of a book; and (6) scribbling with a crayon. The large motor skills you are to observe are self-explanatory. Ideally, pick subjects who are old enough to display at least some of the behaviors described above, but who are sufficiently different in age to show developmental differences in performance or competence.

This exercise falls under Fogel's sensorimotor/tool-using competency area. Can you observe the infants using an object in any way that qualifies as tool use? Naturally, the probability of tool-using behavior increases as the infant's age increases. Therefore, don't look for such behavior in a very young infant.

There is no set amount of time you are to observe, but complete the exercise.

Observation Exercise 16-1

Physical/Motor Characteristics and Skills of the Infant or Toddler (One to Twenty-Four Months)

Observer's Name _____

Child Observed (code name or number) _____

Child's Age _____ Child's Sex _____

Observation Context (Home, day-care center) _____

Date of Observation _____ Time Begun _____ Time Ended _____

Brief Description of Setting/Situation

Objective (1): Physical Characteristics

Total Length of Child _____ Weight of Child _____

Length of Head _____ Ratio of head to total body length _____

Length of Trunk _____ Ratio of Head to Trunk _____

Describe the characteristics of the following:

HEAD AND FACE (shape, eyes, ears, mouth, nose, etc):

TRUNK (e.g., size in relation to head, overall appearance, etc.):

ARMS AND LEGS (positioning, shape):

HANDS AND FINGERS:

Comparisons with Newborn (These may be made using published norms if actual observations of a newborn are not possible or wanted):

Length:

Weight:

Ratio head to total body length:

Ratio head to trunk:

Child's height and weight relative to norms cited:

Objective (2): Motor Skills of the Infant (1-24 Months)

Observer's Name _____

Child Observed (code name or number) _____

Child's Age _____ Child's Sex _____

Observation Context (Home, day-care center) _____

Date of Observation _____ Time Begun _____ Time Ended _____

Brief Description of Setting/Situation

Event Sampling

Objective Behavioral Description   **Interpretation**
(Note specific behaviors observed)

**Comparison of Infant's Functioning
With Age Norms:**

Objective (3): Fine Motor Abilities
(If children were tested by observer, describe how they were persuaded to perform)

Fine Motor Task   **Description of Response**

Child 1: (Age

Stacking Blocks

Picking Up Raisin

Putting Blocks in Container; Removing Them

Stringing Beads:

Response to Playdough:

Scribbling with Crayon:

Turning Pages:

Hand and Leg Preference:

Indications of Tool Use:

Child 2: (Age   )

Stacking Blocks

Picking Up Raisin

Putting Blocks in Container; Removing Them

Stringing Beads:

Response to Playdough:

Scribbling with Crayon:

Turning Pages:

Hand and Leg Preference:

Indications of Tool Use:

Comparison (Similarities) of Child 1 and Child 2:

Contrast (Differences) Between Child 1 and Child 2:

Gross Motor Abilities

Child 1: (Age   )

Event   **Description**

Walking

Running

Climbing Stairs

Walking Sideways, Backwards

Jumping From Low Height (one step)

Other (crawling, creeping, scooting, etc.)

Child 2: (Age   )

Event   **Description**

Walking

Running

Climbing Stairs

Walking Sideways, Backwards

Jumping From Low Height (one step)

Other (crawling, creeping, scooting, etc.)

Comparison of Child 1 and Child 2:

Contrast Between Child 1 and Child 2:

Question Guides:

The following questions use language that seemingly emphasizes the observation of two infants. If you cannot perform that objective, simply refer to the questions in terms of one infant; none of the meaning will be lost.

1. If you observe a toddler, does he or she possess any physical-motor characteristics that might explain the term "toddler"?
2. What is the *overall* character or quality of the two infants' large muscle actions? generally smooth and accurate, or rough and imprecise? How do they differ? What differences would you predict based on their respective ages or developmental levels?
3. Are there large muscle actions that the infants perform easily and others they have difficulty with? Is there any apparent relationship between their abilities and the kinds of activities they choose? That is, do they try things that they do not do very well, or do they seem to stay with those activities they do best?
4. Do the infants show any signs of preferring one foot over the other? one hand over the other? If so, how do they demonstrate their preference (e.g., kicking a ball, the foot they lead with when stepping up a stair, the hand they use to pick up objects)?
5. How many blocks can the infants stack? What best characterizes their efforts to stack blocks? quick and sure? slow and uncertain?
6. When picking up a small object such as a raisin, which fingers do the infants use? What part do their thumbs play? Are they at first unsuccessful in their efforts and then succeed by changing their approach or grasping style?
7. Are there any differences between the way the infants grasp a large object such as a block and a small object such as a raisin?
8. How do their large and fine motor skills compare with the norms for children their age? What skills or responses would you predict they could do fairly well, and which would you predict they could not do at all? Can you rank them in order of increasing difficulty, based on the norms provided, and then rank order them based on how well they actually performed? How do the two rankings compare with each other?
9. What locomotor skills do the infants exhibit? If an infant is just beginning to walk, what proportion of time does she spend walking as opposed to crawling or creeping?
10. Which of Faw and Belkin's phases of reaching and grasping development describe the two infants? On what specific behaviors do you base your conclusion?

Exercise 16-2: Social Behavior of the Infant (One to Twenty-Four Months)

Background Information

When two or more persons take each other into account and influence each other in some way, their behavior is social behavior. The infant most assuredly influences others, and, in an elementary way, he also takes others into account. The infant exerts influence every time an adult responds to his crying, smiling, and vocalizing. When the child changes his behavior to adjust to someone else's characteristics and responses, he is taking that person into account.

There are a few infant behaviors that adults consider especially significant socially. Crying is an important response from the moment of birth; it signals that something is wrong and requires attention. Throughout childhood, crying continues to be a form of communication; it is often disturbing to adults, who take quick action to stop it. Smiling, along with specific eye contact, is particularly gratifying to adults, and the first true social smile—which appears by around six weeks—often makes parents ecstatic. Bower (1977) offers several reasons why infants smile: "(1) . . . human beings around them. (2) . . . any high contrast stimuli, which elicits attention from those around them and causes the infant to link the human face with pleasure. (3) . . . at discovering a relationship between their behavior and events in the external world" (from Travers, 1982, p. 56).

Discussions of the infant's social behavior and competence often include the subject of *attachment*. Attachment is considered present when one person is dependent on another person for emotional satisfaction. One psychologist defines attachment as ". . . an affectional tie that one person forms to another specific person, binding them together in space and enduring over time . . ." (Ainsworth, 1973 p. 1, cited in Travers, 1982, p. 329). Seifert and Hoffnung (1987), also citing Ainsworth, emphasize an additional aspect of attachment by indicating that attachment is "a relationship that is characterized by reciprocal affection and a *shared desire to maintain physical closeness*" (p. 271; italics added).

Attachment develops in stages that have been described by a number of researchers. It is thought to be essential to healthy development, and some psychologists believe that attachment forms the basic foundation for much of the child's future social development and relationships. Table 16-3 depicts some typical characteristics and behaviors associated with attachment, and Table 16-4 presents Mary Ainsworth's (1967, 1973) three stages in the development of attachment (adapted from Travers, 1982, p. 331).

The concept of basic trust versus mistrust is another aspect of social behavior. *Trust versus mistrust* is the first of eight *psychosocial* stages in Erik Erikson's theory of personality development. Psychosocial stages, according to Craig (1989), are "periods in life during which the individual's capacities for experience dictate that he or she must make major adjustments to the social environment and the self" (p. 41). The adjustment to be made, however, is determined by the individual's developmental level and receptiveness to experience. Basic trust versus mistrust should be resolved during the first 18 months to two years. If things go well, the infant will resolve this first conflict by establishing a stronger sense of trust in his physical-social environment than of mistrust. Whether trust or mistrust becomes the stronger feeling depends on how the infant is treated and on whether or not he sees the world as a predominantly safe, nurturing, and reliable place. Achieving feelings of trust requires interactions between the adult and child that are consistent and effectively match the psychological characteristics of both of them. As Gander and Gardiner (1981) put it, "Trust results when mother and infants coordinate their behaviors to one another's temperaments and needs and are consistent and reasonable" (p. 201). The physical environment must also be perceived as reasonably safe and predictable. This perception is affected by the infant's learning that his behaviors have predictable consequences. For example, he shakes his crib and a mobile above him moves. Or, as he learns to control his body, he increases his sense of security and confidence as he functions in a world of space, objects, and natural laws.

Observation Objectives

To observe and record: (1) the infant's general social behaviors and interaction patterns with others; (2) behaviors that indicate attachment; and (3) the effect of observed and reported qualities of the infant's temperament on the interactions between her and others in her familiar surroundings. Also, to use data from different recording methods to draw conclusions about the child's social behavior and temperament, and about the usefulness of different methods in a particular situation.

Procedures

This is a three-part exercise. Each part, however, can stand as an independent exercise. In Part I, you will use the specimen record method of recording. You should observe for about three ten-minute sessions within a 60- to 90-minute period, depending on your circumstances. Refer to the guide questions that are provided. You will be asked to record your interpretive comments. Make certain your inferences are related to your observed data: Do not make an interpretation that is not supported by your objective behavioral description. The information from Part I will also be used in Parts II and III.

In Part II, you will use a time sampling and frequency count format. You will also be using the observation data obtained in Part I. You will note on the checklist whether the infant displays attachment behaviors during the specified time intervals. In this part of the exercise, *you* are asked to determine the observing and recording intervals to be used. As a general procedure, you may want to divide your recording time into a series of equal intervals, such as ten ten-second periods. Choose another short period of time (ten seconds, for example) between each recording interval during which you will only observe. Wait for a time (perhaps five minutes) and repeat the process at least twice more. For this part of the exercise, the parent or another familiar caregiver must be with the child or he is not likely to show attachment behaviors. After you have collected your data, answer the questions that follow Part II.

Part III requires you to integrate information on the infant's general social responses and interaction patterns, which you will have obtained in Part I, and information on the child's temperament. Data on temperament will be acquired from your observations and the parent's report. Table 16-5 describes the characteristics of various temperaments. First observe and record the infant's behavior over two or three ten-minute sessions using the specimen record format. When the data are collected, analyze the record for examples of behaviors and descriptions of characteristics that fit any of the information on temperament in Table 16-6. In the second phase of this exercise, ask the parent specific questions about the child's temperament. The information given in Tables 16-5 and 16-6 can help you formulate these questions.

Finally, answer the questions that follow Part III. It is in answering these questions that you will integrate the two sets of information referred to above.

Observation Exercise 16-2

PART I: Social Behavior of the Infant (1-24 Months)

Observer's Name _____

Child Observed (code name or number) _____

Child's Age _____ Child's Sex _____

Observation Context (Home, day-care center) _____

Date of Observation _____ Time Begun _____ Time Ended _____

Brief Description of Setting/Situation

Social Behaviors and Interaction Patterns

Objective Behavioral Description   **Interpretation**

Question Guides, Part I:

1. Does the infant initiate social contacts with others in the environment? How does he go about it? by verbalizing? by establishing physical contact? by crying? by sharing a toy?
2. How does the other person react to the infant's social behaviors? Does the adult *focus* her attention on the infant and try to sustain the interaction, or does she cut short her response to him as though his overtures were an inconvenience?
3. Does the infant smile? How frequently, and at what? How do others react to his smiling? Does their reaction have any observable effect on the child's subsequent behaviors?
4. How does the infant respond to you, the observer? Does he show fear and uncertainty? withdrawal? Does he approach and try to engage you in play or other interaction? If he approaches you, how long does it take him to do so? Is there a period of "adjustment" on his part? How long is that period?
5. What physical features of the infant or toddler do you think *might* be attractive to the adult in his setting or to adults in general? Does the adult present during your observations make any comments about baby features she finds appealing? If so, does she respond in any way to those features?
6. What is the adult's response to the child's crying? How tolerant does the adult seem to be of the baby's crying? Is the adult's response immediate, delayed slightly, delayed for a long time? How does the infant respond to the adult's efforts to stop his crying? If the adult is successful, does she stop her interactions with the child, or does she take the opportunity to engage in further social contacts? Does the child seem to cry excessively?
7. Is there specific eye-to-eye contact between the adult and the infant? How does each respond to such contact? How long does the baby maintain this contact? How and for how long does the adult try to establish contact if he is not immediately successful?
8. Where does the child fit in terms of Fogel's social/interactive area of competence? Does the infant have any concept of sharing or taking turns? Is the infant old enough to be aware of his role as "a partner in an interaction with an adult" (p. 236 of this manuscript)?

Observation Exercise 16-2

PART II: Social Behavior of the Infant (1-24 Months)

Observer's Name _____

Child Observed (code name or number) _____

Child's Age _____ Child's Sex _____

Observation Context (Home, day-care center) _____

Date of Observation _____ Time Begun _____ Time Ended _____

Brief Description of Setting/Situation

Time Sampling of Attachment Behaviors

Recording Intervals	1	2	3	4	5	6	7	8	9	10
Behavior Categories										
Looks at Mother										
Makes Physical Contact with Mother										
Smiles at Mother										
Shows Object to Mother										
Moves Closer to Mother										
Establishes Visual Contact with Mother										
Cries When Mother Leaves Room										
Negative Reaction to Stranger's Approach										

INTERPRETIVE COMMENTS:

Partly adapted from Willemsen (1979, 250)

Questions, Part II: *(These are not guide questions. They are questions you are to answer in writing.)*

1. What percentage of the total time observed did the infant exhibit each of the attachment behaviors sampled? What percentage of the total time observed did the child exhibit non-attachment behaviors? How do these frequencies compare with each other and what is the ratio between them?
2. Analyze your specimen record data (from Part I) for attachment behaviors. If there are any, count how often they occurred. How does this frequency count compare with the count obtained from your time sample? Do you feel more comfortable with one set of figures than with the other? If so, why? Was time sampling an appropriate method to use under the circumstances? Why or why not?
3. On the basis of Ainsworth's three stages of attachment (Table 16-4) and the information given in Table 16-4, can you tell from your time-sampled data which stage of attachment the infant is in? Can you tell from your specimen description? Is one a better basis for judgment than the other? If so, which one, and why?

Observation Exercise 16-2

PART III: Social Behavior of the Infant (1-24 Months)

Observer's Name _____

Child Observed (code name or number) _____

Child's Age _____ Child's Sex _____

Observation Context (Home, day-care center) _____

Date of Observation _____ Time Begun _____ Time Ended _____

Brief Description of Setting/Situation

OBJECTIVE BEHAVIORAL DESCRIPTION   **Qualities of Temperament Noted**
(Specimen Record)

Session 1:

Session 2:

Session 3:

PARENT INTERVIEW

Questions Asked Parent   **Parent's Response**

Questions, Part III: *(These questions are to be answered in writing.)*

1. How do your decisions or judgments regarding the child's temperament compare with the parent's reported descriptions of her temperament? Going back to your specimen record data, whose conclusions about the child's temperament seem more accurate?
2. Does the child's behavior as you observed it correspond with the parent's report? That is, could you have used the parent's perceptions of the child to predict the infant's behaviors with reasonable accuracy?
3. What general conclusions do you reach about the usefulness of the concept of temperament? Why do you draw the conclusions you do?

Exercise 16-3: Cognitive and Language Behavior of the Infant (One to Twenty-Four Months)

Background Information

Many of the behaviors you have observed to this point are related to the infant's cognitive and language development. From Piaget's theoretical perspective, motor and perceptual functions (the essential components of the *sensorimotor period*) are the foundation of cognitive development. Early motor responses first allow the infant to handle objects, to bang, pull, push, drop, and roll them. These are necessary activities, says Piaget, because the child learns about objects by doing something with them. He cannot yet learn about the world by thinking and reasoning. Eventually, the infant becomes mobile, which puts him into more direct contact with the environment. Progressing from having objects brought to him, to going to objects on his own, changes both the quantity and the quality of his experiences.

The infant, like everyone else, gets information about his world through seeing, hearing, touching, tasting, and smelling. But merely receiving information is not enough; he must do something with it. Language and cognition, which includes thinking, knowledge, memory, problem solving, reasoning, concepts, provide the means of processing and using information.

There are several aspects of cognitive behavior that are relevant to the infant. One aspect is *concept*. Gander and Gardiner (1981) write that "A *concept* may be thought of as a mental representation or memory of something" (p. 143, emphasis original). Ault (1977) notes that concepts "represent the attributes common to several different events" (p. 89). Piaget's *schema* is a mental representation of events in the world. Concepts, however defined, provide ways of classifying and organizing our sensory information; they bring together features and qualities that are shared by concrete things or abstract ideas. For example, dog is a concept. When someone says "dog," we might think of such things as many different species (collie, German shepherd, terrier), four-legged animal, fur bearing, carnivorous, domesticated house pet, and "Rover."

Habituation is used by some psychologists (see Willemsen 1979, or Sroufe and Cooper 1988, for example) to infer the presence of concepts or memory even in the newborn. "When something new is perceived in the environment," write Sroufe and Cooper (1988), "attention tends to be focused on it. If it is repeated over and over, it loses its ability to draw attention" (p. 149). This is the phenomenon of habituation. If the infant (or anyone else) *reorients* to a *new* stimulus, it is logical to believe that he must have a concept of the first stimulus in order to know that the second one is different in some way. Sroufe and Cooper (1988) note that habituation "has provided the basis for a very powerful research technique used to study infants" (p. 150). Stranger anxiety also requires the possession of concepts. The child has to recognize that what he perceives about a stranger is somehow different from his concept of a familiar person.

For Piaget, *object permanence* is the crowning achievement of the sensorimotor period and provides the basis for all further cognitive development. When a child has the concept of object permanence, he understands that objects continue to exist even when out of sight or hearing. "Out of sight, out of mind" characterizes the infant who has not yet achieved object permanence. Object permanence develops through a series of stages (see Table 16-7) and is complete by the end of the sensorimotor period at about two years of age.

The sensorimotor period is divided into the six subperiods depicted in Table 16-8. Piaget used the idea of *sensorimotor schemes*, which are organized actions or sequences of actions that permit the individual to interact with the environment. Schemes become modified through learning and provide the foundation for more complex schemes and learning.

There are two other Piagetian concepts that help explain cognitive development and behavior throughout the lifespan: *assimilation* and *accommodation*. Assimilation occurs when the person attempts to make a stimulus or event fit what she already knows or knows how to do. The infant deals with reality by using existing sensorimotor schemes. For

Figure 16-2 Sensorimotor behavior is displayed by the child using this stacking toy. (Reprinted from Lesner, Pediatric Nursing, figure 9-9)

example, if she can pick up large objects with a palmar grasp, she may try to pick up small, flat ones in the same way. But, if efforts to assimilate do not succeed, then progress depends on the infant's making changes in her sensorimotor scheme. She has to *accommodate* to the novel features of the situation. The infant in the above example will have accommodated if she changes her grasping scheme from a palmar grasp to a thumb and forefinger (pincer) grasp to pick up the small, flat object. Accommodation does not occur automatically; the child must be developmentally ready for it.

The reinforcement theory of learning has also had a significant impact on developmental psychology. This view holds that individuals behave as they do because their behavior has led to consequences they found rewarding: the response is *reinforced*. This form of learning is known as *operant conditioning*. A key point about operant conditioning is that an individual is more likely to repeat a behavior if its consequences are satisfying than if they are unpleasant and punishing.

A second major type of learning is *classical conditioning*. An important aspect of classical conditioning is that it involves involuntary behavior, which is behavior over which we have little to no control. What is especially significant about classical conditioning is that emotional responses can be learned in this way. Classical conditioning begins with an event that naturally causes a response (as when hunger causes a dog to salivate in the presence of food). This event can become associated with a second event that does not cause the response (the *sound of a bell*, for example, does not cause salivation). Through a pairing of these two events, the second event (the bell) can acquire the ability to produce the response (the salivation) originally produced only by the first event (hunger). Imagine a child who is constantly punished by her uncle. Punishment causes anxiety and fear. Those emotions become associated with the uncle, and, eventually, his mere presence makes the child anxious and fearful.

Language   Language could be the single most significant accomplishment of the human species. Language is a complex set of written or spoken symbols that are combined according to special rules of grammar or syntax in order to communicate various kinds of information.

Language is acquired in a predictable series of stages that can be distinguished according to whether or not the child speaks intelligible words. Vocalizations that occur prior to speech are called *prelinguistic*, and those that include true words are called *linguistic*. Thus, we have two distinct periods of language development that are further subdivided into stages. These periods and stages are depicted in Table 16-1.

Observation Objectives

To observe and record various behaviors that indicate the level and characteristics of the infant's cognitive and language functioning, including such abilities as memory and conceptual thinking. To identify situations in which operant and classical conditioning might be occurring.

Procedure

This exercise has three parts. In Part I, you will test the infant's concept of object permanence. You will need an attractive toy and two pieces of cloth large enough to completely cover the toy. Your test consists of the following steps: Step (1) Seat the child in a chair and, after holding a toy in front of her so she can see it, drop the toy on the floor. Observe and record her response (refer to the Guide Questions). Step (2) Seat the child at a flat surface. Show the child the toy, making certain she sees it; then place the toy under the cloth while the child watches you do it. Observe and record her response. Step (3) As the child watches, move the toy from under the first cloth and hide it under the second cloth (*visible displacement*).

Observe and record her response. Step (4) Hide the toy under the cloth as the child watches. Then, while she cannot see what you are doing, hide the toy under the second cloth, but leave the first cloth in its original position (*invisible displacement*). Observe and record her response. (In all of these steps, refer to the Guide Questions.)

In Part II, observe the child for two to three ten-minute sessions and record in specimen record form the child's behaviors and relevant characteristics of the context. When you have completed your observations, analyze the specimen record for behaviors that indicate anything about what she has learned and her level of cognitive functioning. Look for behaviors that indicate whether the child is in Piaget's sensorimotor period; look for behaviors that identify which *substage* of the sensorimotor period the child is in. Also look for occasions when operant or classical conditioning might be occurring, such as when the parent responds with "Good boy, Billy!" when the child brings her a favorite toy, or when the parent punishes the child.

In Part III you will be using an event sampling procedure to observe and record the infant's language behavior. Spend about 20 or 30 minutes in the child's context, but remain as inconspicuous as possible. Record verbatim the child's speech, to whom he speaks and under what circumstances, and the reactions of others to his communications. Also note behaviors that reflect the child's *speech reception* abilities—how much speech he *understands*. Also take note of the physical gestures the child might use in his efforts to communicate.

Observation Exercise 16-3

PART I: Cognitive and Language Behavior of the Infant (1-24 Months)

Observer's Name _____

Child Observed (code name or number) _____

Child's Age _____ Child's Sex _____

Observation Context (Home, day-care center) _____

Date of Observation _____ Time Begun _____ Time Ended _____

Brief Description of Setting/Situation

PART I—Object Permanence:

Behavior Observed   **Description of Response**

Step (1) Dropping the Toy

Step (2) Hiding Toy While Child Watches

Step (3) Visible Displacement of Toy

Step (4) Invisible Displacement of Toy

Comments:

Question Guides, Part I:

1. How does the child respond visually when the toy is dropped? Does she look for it? Does she look in the right place; that is, does she seem to know the path the toy will take as it falls?
2. How does the child respond when you hide the toy under the cloth in Step (2)? Does she look for the toy under the cloth or somewhere else? Does she make any emotional or motor responses, for example, facial expressions that indicate delight or amusement, or gross muscle movements that indicate excitement?
3. How does the child respond to Step (3)? Does she continue to look under the first cloth where she first saw you hide the toy, or does she look under the second cloth? Again, what emotional or motor responses does she make as she participates in this game?
4. How does the child respond to the invisible displacement of the toy? Does she persist in looking under the first cloth, or does she go immediately to the second cloth?
5. Given the child's age, what responses would you predict from her in the area of object permanence (what do the norms indicate about her probable level of response)? What stage is the child in with respect to the development of object permanence?

Observation Exercise 16-3

PART II: Cognitive and Language Development of the Infant (1-24 Months)

Observer's Name _____

Child Observed (code name or number) _____

Child's Age _____ Child's Sex _____

Observation Context (Home, day-care center) _____

Date of Observation _____ Time Begun _____ Time Ended _____

Brief Description of Setting/Situation

PART II—Objective Description: **Interpretive Comments**

Session 1:

Session 2:

Session 3:

Question Guides, Part II:

1. What evidence is there that the infant is in Piaget's sensorimotor stage of cognitive development? That is, what responses seem typical of the infant, and how do these responses fit into Piaget's theory?
2. What responses does the infant make that are classifiable as sensorimotor schemes? Why do they fit that category rather than the category of random or unpatterned activity?
3. Are there any indications that the infant possesses concepts? What behaviors can be interpreted as showing possession of concepts?
4. What evidence does the infant show that he or she remembers?
5. Are the infant's behaviors being reinforced in any way? What responses are reinforced, and how does the reinforcement occur—by a smile from the adult, by picking the child up and making a fuss over her? What behavior changes result from the reinforcement (changes in the basic nature of the behavior)? in its frequency?
6. Are there any indications that classical conditioning could be taking place? What are the circumstances of the conditioning process? What is the originally neutral stimulus, and what stimulus is substituted for it? What is the resulting change in behavior? emotional changes? changes in motor activity? avoidance of an object or person?
7. Does the infant give evidence of accommodation; for example, does he change his approach to a problem when the initial approach does not succeed? If the child accommodates, how does her behavior change as a result? What behaviors indicate that assimilation is occurring? Does the infant show signs of Fogel's "internalized selection of courses of action"? (see page 6 above).
8. Are there any occasions for learning created just by the adult's normal caregiving activities; for example, verbalizing about an event or object while she changes the infant's diapers? What kind of learning might be taking place? What specific adult activities contribute to the infant's learning opportunities?

Observation Exercise 16-3

PART III: Cognitive and Language Development of the Infant (1-24 Months)

Observer's Name _____

Child Observed (code name or number) _____

Child's Age _____ Child's Sex _____

Observation Context (Home, day-care center) _____

Date of Observation _____ Time Begun _____ Time Ended _____

Brief Description of Setting/Situation

PART III—Event Sampling Language:

Objective Behavioral Description   **Interpretations**

Question Guides, Part III:

1. What in the physical or social environment stimulates vocalizations? inhibits them? What are some possible explanations for either of these effects?
2. What are the main characteristics of the infant's vocalizations? Are they babbling sounds? one-word phrases? telegraphic speech? What effect do these vocalizations have on others? How do they respond? Do their responses affect the infant's subsequent vocalizations?
3. When does the infant cry? What happens when he cries? Do the effects of his crying on adults change the crying pattern? Does he use crying often as a means of communication, or does he more often use language to communicate?
4. What physical gestures does the infant use to try to get his meaning across to others? Does he point? take the person by the hand and lead her to the "situation"? Do his gestures seem to match or fit his verbalizations; that is, does he seem to coordinate the timing of his gestures with his speech?
5. What responses give evidence of the infant's ability to understand language; that is, what are his receptive skills? What commands and directions is he able to understand and obey? Are his reception and production abilities different from each other? Does the infant understand more than he can speak, or the opposite?

Exercise 16-4: Emotional Development and Behavior in the Infant (Two to Eighteen Months)

Background Information

Emotions are an extremely important part of human behavior, and as Greenspan and Greenspan (1985) make clear, emotional development begins almost from the moment of birth. You can recall from Chapter 15 that the *first milestone* of emotional development (which occurs between birth and three months of age) involves the newborn's capacity of self-regulation. This first milestone also involves the infant's taking an interest in the world. The Greenspans put it this way:

> Your newborn is faced with two fundamental and simultaneous challenges during the first weeks of life. The first is self-regulation—the ability to feel calm and relaxed, not overwhelmed by his new environment. The second is to become interested in the world through his senses—what he hears, sees, smells, tastes, and touches, and what he experiences through his sense of movement. (p. 14)

These tasks are challenges because the newborn, after nine months in the "darkness and relative quiet of the womb," is suddenly catapulted, as it were, into a world filled with a variety of sensations that are completely new to her. The newborn must organize these sensations and at the same time feel comfortable in their presence and actively engage them in ways that are appropriate to her level of developmental maturity—e.g. show interest in the sights and sounds around her and not find them painful (Greenspan and Greenspan, 1985). This then permits achievement of the second milestone, which is that of "taking a highly specialized interest in the *human* world" (p. 5, italics original).

The *second milestone* (from about two to seven months) is described by the Greenspans as "falling in love." They write that

> As your newborn moves along into the second, third, and fourth months of life, she will begin to show selective interest in the most special part of her world, namely, you.

It's assumed that if the baby does not find environmental stimuli pleasurable, he may be unlikely to progress to the stage where the world of human beings "is seen as the most enticing, pleasurable, and exciting of all experiences" (p. 4). The pleasure that one wants the baby to feel, say the Greenspans, can be seen in her "enraptured smiles and eager joyfulness" as she "gazes excitedly at your face" while she feels the movements of your body and hears your voice. They indicate further that the "baby is now becoming more responsive to external social interactions, whereas earlier she was more influenced by her inner physical sensations (e.g., hunger, gas bubbles)" (p. 41).

The *third milestone*, which occurs between three and ten months of age, is founded on this special interest in the human world, but now the baby in effect says "love alone is not enough—I now want a dialogue" (p. 4). Dialogue here does not mean sitting down and talking with the adult. It refers instead to the such things as the baby smiling in *response* to the parent's smile, or reaching for an object that is held out to him, or making sounds in response to the parent talking to him. The baby is communicating in his own way, and the communication is *intentional*. Indeed, the authors call this milestone "developing intentional communication." The Greenspans also note that the baby is learning that the world is "a cause-and-effect world" (also a cognitive achievement on the baby's part), which means he learns that his behaviors lead to behaviors from others. when he smiles, for example, so does his mother or father. He is also learning some negative emotions, such as anger when you try to take away a toy.

The *fourth milestone*, which occurs between nine and eighteen months of age, is characterized as the "emergence of an organized sense of self." In this stage the child extends her "emotional dialogue" another step and "learns to connect small units of feeling and social behavior into large, complicated, orchestrated patterns" (p. 5). The increased skill becomes especially evident near the middle of the fourth stage, which is at fourteen or fifteen months of age, when the child can integrate or combine newer and more complex behaviors with behaviors accomplished earlier. If Susan wants to play, for instance, she is no longer confined to pointing to a toy and making sounds that her mother may or may not understand. Instead, Susan can pick up the toy and carry it to her mother, thereby making her intentions rather clear.

The ability to combine relatively complex social and emotional patterns also indicates increasing cognitive abilities. As the Greenspans write, "The emerging ability to piece together many small activities and emotions into a pattern, known as the ability to organize, is crucial to the development of higher-level thinking and planning" (pp. 83-84). In the example of Susan just above, she demonstrated that she knew the "meaning" of objects, the toy, in this case, and of the action of taking the toy to her mother to play. Again, as the Greenspans put it, "This is the beginning of a 'conceptual' attitude toward the world. Objects now have functions" (p. 5). Equally important, however, people, especially parents, also come to have functions for the child; they serve special purposes. Furthermore, they "take on attributes" (p. 5). Parents show feelings and display actions whose functions or meanings the child eventually recognizes.

Observation Objectives

To observe and record behaviors that indicate an infant's level of emotional development according to Greenspan and Greenspan's (1985) second, third, and fourth "emotional milestones."

Procedure

We suggest you observe an infant between the ages of 2 and 18 months in order to maximize the possibility of getting data that are relevant to the stages of emotional development specified in the objectives above.

We shall suggest that you use the event sampling technique. Specifically look for those behaviors or capacities that define the emotional milestone (stage) that corresponds to the age of the infant you have chosen. We suggest that you observe for at least three or four ten-minute periods; this should give you ample opportunity to see the behaviors that are of interest to you. Try to get a varied sampling of emotional behaviors, behaviors that demonstrate more than just one aspect of your particular infant's stage of emotional development.

Observation Exercise 16-4

Emotional Development of the Infant (2-18 Months)

Observer's Name _____

Child Observed (code name or number) _____

Child's Age _____ Child's Sex _____

Observation Context (Home, day-care center) _____

Date of Observation _____ Time Begun _____ Time Ended _____

Brief Description of Setting/Situation

Objective Behavioral Description   **General Interpretations**

Behavioral Summary:

Infant's Probable Emotional Stage:

Supporting Evidence:

Question Guides:

1. What specific behaviors did the infant exhibit that led you to classify his or her level of emotional development as you did?
2. Did the infant exhibit any behaviors that are found in the next higher stage? If so, were they too infrequent to allow you to put him or her into that next stage? Or, did you classify the infant in the lower stage because of his or her age?
3. Was the infant ahead of his or her age with respect to emotional development? Was he or she behind?

chapter seventeen
The Young Child: Ages Two Through Six

Introduction

This chapter focuses your observations and recordings on the period referred to as the preschool years. Although many significant things occur during this span of four years, the rate of growth and developmental change seen during the 18 to 24 months of infancy probably will never again be equaled in any comparable period of time.

The observation exercises in this chapter are approached differently from those in the previous chapters. Unlike the period of infancy, the preschool period will not be divided up into smaller units such as four one-year periods, with separate exercises for each year. The entire preschool period is covered as a single entity, even though it comprises a greater amount of chronological time than infancy.

A second difference in approach concerns the organization of the material. The Question Guides are presented before the Exercise Sheets, and some of the background information is included among the questions, rather than in a separate section. The background information is a starting point for your observations. There are other sources of information you can consult about child development and various theories as additional points of view from which to "see," understand, and interpret children's behavior.

The numbered questions (Question Guides) from Exercises 17-2 on are based in part on the works of Lay and Dopyera (1977) and Lay-Dopyera and Dopyera (1982).

Exercise 17-1: The Preschool Child in the Physical Environment

Background Information

Our physical surroundings exert a powerful influence on all of us. How much space we have, the objects and their arrangement in that space, and the social-psychological "meaning" of the space, combine to determine and direct our behavior. A preschool classroom, a playground, or the child's home are particular spaces with equipment, materials, people, and arrangements that are used even if they are not designed for special purposes. As the child's cognitive and language abilities become more sophisticated, she also comes to understand that spaces have definitions. These definitions dictate what she may do in that space, that is, what others will allow her to do. Also important, however, is the child's learning what she can do in the space because of the physical properties of the objects and materials it contains.

Observation Objectives

To familiarize you with the physical environment in which you are observing and to learn how children respond to and are influenced by their physical surroundings.

Procedure

Your first task is to draw a diagram of the indoor and outdoor environments. On each diagram, name the equipment and materials and show their locations. With your diagram in hand, anyone should be able to walk into the observation setting and find anything that is there (bookshelves, toilets, art area). Similarly, the diagram of the outside environment should locate swings, slides, boxes, jungle gyms, and other equipment. It is advisable to describe equipment and materials if their names alone do not supply information about their important characteristics.

The second part of your assignment concerns how children use the areas available to them, and how different areas have different effects on behavior. Begin by selecting two areas of the classroom or other setting that differ significantly in the activities and behaviors allowed there. For example, one would expect behavior in the big block area to be quite different from that in the dramatic play or story-telling area. The differences can be partly the result of the teacher's enforcement of rules governing behavior. But, spaces themselves also affect behavior. What can be done in a given space is determined by what is there to do something with. If there are no blocks on hand, there obviously will be no playing with blocks. If puzzles are stored on shelves out of the children's reach, playing with puzzles will have to depend on an adult's help.

Observe and record the behavior of two children in the two areas; follow them as they move around the room. Then compare and contrast their behavior in one area with their behavior in the other. Note whether their actions are in keeping with the requirements and expectations of the location. Summarize the specific ways their behavior changes (if in fact it does) from one location to another. For this exercise, use the specimen record method, since you are not looking for any particular event or behavior; you are interested in everything that occurs related to the child in the physical environment.

Observation Exercise 17-1

PART I: The Preschool Child in the Physical Environment

Observer's Name _____

Observation Context (Home, day-care center) _____

DIAGRAM OF PHYSICAL ENVIRONMENT

Inside

Outside

Observation Exercise 17-1
_____

PART II: The Preschool Child in the Physical Environment

Observer's Name _____

Child Observed (code name or number) _____

Child's Age _____ Child's Sex _____

Observation Context (Home, preschool) _____

Date of Observation _____ Time Begun _____ Time Ended _____

Brief Description of Setting/Situation

_____

OBJECTIVE BEHAVIORAL DESCRIPTION   **INTERPRETATIONS**

Location 1:

Location 2:

Summary of Behavior Differences:

Question Guides:
1. Do the children's behaviors change from one location to another? If so, how?
2. What behaviors would you expect in each of the two locations you observe the children? Do their behaviors conform to your expectations (or the space's definition)? If so, how? If not, why not? Does the teacher have to remind the children of the proper way to behave in any area?
3. What in the environment holds the children's interest? How do they express that interest?
4. Do the children use the equipment and materials in an appropriate manner?
5. How would you assess the overall arrangement of the classroom or playground? Is there enough space for the children to move around freely? to engage in the activities for which the space is intended?

Exercise 17-2: Physical Growth and Motor Functioning

Background Information

Physical characterisitics and motor abilities are probably the most noticeable and easily measureable aspects of human growth and development. These characteristics and abilities are often of major importance to parents, who point with pride to the gains their child makes in height, weight, and ability to walk, run, and manipulate objects. Since everything we do in some way involves a physical body, it makes sense to say that our physical and motor development and abilities form the foundation for our behavior.

In certain respects, this exercise will be easy to accomplish. Young children are usually active physically, and many of their motor behaviors are obvious. On the other hand, there are some subtle aspects to motor behavior that can be overlooked. For example, all "normal" children walk and run, but each does so in her own unique style. For some, walking is smooth and well-coordinated, with no significant peculiarities; for others, toes might point noticeably outward, feet may be somewhat widely spaced, or balance while running might be poor. Moreover, there are behaviors that do not have obvious physical-motor components. Sitting at the snack table eating is not a vigorous activity like free play in the big block areas. And yet, there are things to be considered; for example, the child's posture (does he slouch, sit on one leg, cock his head to one side?), the child's skill in handling eating utensils, pouring juice, or wiping crumbs from the table.

The behaviors of interest in this exercise fall into three general categories: (a) physical characteristics, (b) gross (large) motor movements or abilities, and (c) fine (small) motor movements or abilities. All of the child's physical-motor functioning will fall into one of these three categories. Recall that developmentally, the child first becomes adept at gross muscle activities, at movements and skills that involve large muscles. Later, she acquires fine motor skills. Therefore, a child who seems to perform mostly large muscle activities, might be lacking fine motor skills; however, do not make such a judgment based on just a few observations. It could be that the child does not like the fine motor activities available in the classroom, and so she plays mostly in the large motor areas.

Observation Objectives

To learn about preschool children's physical characteristics and motor abilities and how they are alike and how they are different from one another in these areas.

Procedure

If possible, select two children of differing ages (a two- or three-year-old and a five-year-old would be good choices). If that is not possible, simply select any two children who are reasonably active physically. Using an event sampling format, describe in detail (1) the children's physical appearances and (2) their motor activities as they play during the observation session. Observe each of the two children for about 10 to 15 minutes. Then examine your data and compare and contrast (that is, describe the similarities and differences between) the two children; draw some general conclusions as to their motor skills, degrees of coordination, and preferred activities.

The Question Guide provided will be give you information about the components of motor development and behavior and will direct your observations and interpretations.

Question Guides (Partly adapted from Lay and Dopyera 1977)

1. Is there anything about the child's body build that sets her apart from the rest of the group?
2. What can you say about how the child holds his body? For example, how does the child stand, sit, walk, and run? Is the child stoop-shouldered? Is the head carried high or does the child look down?

Gross Movements and Abilities Gross movements and abilities involve the large muscles of the body. Movements controlled by these muscles are large, sweeping movements such as climbing, swinging, walking, running, throwing, and jumping. There is an important consideration for this exercise. When a child is just learning a skill, she tends to practice only that skill, isolating it from others already mastered. This process of learning and practicing a behavior is called *differentiation*. This is the process in which a new skill differentiates or separates out of old, existing skills. During differentiation, the child must devote his entire attention to the unfamiliar task. Once the task is perfected, however, the child can combine the new skill with his existing skills to form an integrated whole. These existing skills are not necessarily physical-motor skills, but may be verbal or cognitive skills. For instance, a child might climb up and down the jungle gym using the hands and feet in a number of different ways, while at the same

Figure 17-1 Gross motor skills, or use of large muscles is demonstrated by these preschoolers on riding toys. (Reprinted from Lesner, *Pediatric Nursing*, figure 19-7)

time shouting to a friend, "Look at what I'm doing." This is an example of *integration*.

When you observe a motor behavior, note if it is combined with other behaviors to form a more complex pattern (integration), or whether the behavior is exhibited by itself and in a repetitive manner (differentiation) (Lay and Dopyera 1977).

Children are capable of a wide variety of motor actions, although individual differences exist. Some children will be able to run, jump, climb, intentionally fall down (with control), and do somersaults and cartwheels. Certain of the child's motor behaviors are basic skills (e.g., walking and running), and some children will be able to perform variations of these basic skills. For example, a child may be able to walk and run backwards or sideways. Be alert to the range or variety of motor actions the child can perform. Remember, developmental level, which is to some degree indicated by age, is a strong determinant of what a child can do.

3. How many different motor behaviors can the child perform?

Children demonstrate their ability to balance in many ways. They walk across balance beams elevated off the floor, they walk on cracks or lines on the ground; they walk stepping from one rock to another. When recording instances of these behaviors, try to indicate how much balancing ability is required. For example, how wide is the beam the child walks across? How quickly does she move on these balancing tasks? Can the child do these things without help, or must her hand be held? How does she compare with the other children? Can the child perform other actions while balancing (integration)?

4. How well does the child perform balancing activities?

You may be able to gauge the child's strength only by seeing how much he can lift, pull, or push compared with his peers. You may not be able to determine his strength in terms of the *most* he can lift, pull, or push. Children demonstrate their strength in a number of ways: they lift and stack blocks, pull each other in wagons, hang from ladders or jungle gyms, and wrestle with each other. What behaviors show the child's strength? How much strength is needed for a particular behavior? For example, how many blocks did the child lift at one time; how many children did she pull in the wagon at the same time, and so on.

5. How strong is the child?

Some children seem to do everything at their top rate of speed, whereas others have a more leisurely pace. How quickly does the child do various things such as walk, run, and climb? Does his rate of movement vary depending on the particular activity or piece of equipment used (keeping in mind that such things as rate of movement also depend upon the child's level of skill)? Are the child's movements coordinated and well timed, or does he do things faster than his coordination will allow?

6. How quickly can the child move or perform various activities?

How long can the child perform a given activity without resting? Can the child go from one activity to another without seeming to get tired? How many times can the child perform a given movement without stopping to rest? Endurance may be partly determined by comparison with the child's peers.

7. How much endurance or stamina does the child have?

Many activities require a sense of rhythm, an ability to move one's body in a properly timed sequence (e.g., in dancing). What evidence is there that the child has this rhythmic capacity? Can she keep time with music and bounce a ball? Can she hop or skip half way across the room without losing the correct pattern of motion? Can the child perform one non-rhythmic activity while simultaneously performing a rhythmic one; for example, can she talk with someone while at the same time make dance movements to music?

8. What are the child's abilities to perform rhythmic movements?

Fine Motor Movements and Activities   This category involves movements of the small muscles of the body; for example, those used in picking up small objects, zipping a jacket, writing with crayon or pencil, and buttoning a shirt. Fine motor behavior evolves or differentiates out of gross motor movements; it therefore occurs later in the motor development sequence.

Activities such as eating, dressing, and general grooming typically require small muscle skills. To what extent can the child dress himself? This includes buttoning and zipping shirts and jackets, putting on one's socks and shoes, tying laces, and putting on shirts. Eating requires many small muscle actions: holding a fork or spoon and bringing it to the mouth in a controlled manner; pouring liquid; cutting meat with a knife; and serving food from a larger dish onto a plate. General grooming involves combing one's hair, washing one's face and hands, drying oneself with a towel, and brushing one's teeth.

9. What is the range and variety of the child's fine motor skills involved in self-help behaviors?

_____

_____

Figure 17-2   Fine motor skills, the use of small muscles, are demonstrated by this child.

The preschool environment is full of materials that provide opportunities for small muscle activities. There might be tools such as screwdrivers, hammers, and pliers; jugsaw puzzles with small parts to be fitted together; small blocks to build. Simply turning the pages of a book requires fine muscle skills. Be alert to the child's functioning in these areas. Try to draw some conclusions regarding his skill in various activities, as well as the extensiveness of his small muscle abilities.

10. What is the child's ability to handle and use various kinds of toys, objects, and tools? How extensive are his abilities in this area?

Observation Exercise 17-2

Physical Growth and Motor Functioning

Observer's Name _____

Child Observed (code name or number) _____

Child's Age _____ Child's Sex _____

Observation Context (Home, preschool) _____

Date of Observation _____ Time Begun _____ Time Ended _____

Brief Description of Setting/Situation

OBJECTIVE BEHAVIORAL DESCRIPTION   **INTERPRETATIONS**

(Event Sampling)

Child 1 (age   ):

Child 2 (age   ):

Comparisons:

Exercise 17-3: Cognitive and Intellectual Development and Behavior

Background Information

This exercise is concerned with the child's mental functioning: how he perceives and thinks about the world, and the factual knowledge the child has and how he uses it. Jean Piaget distinguishes between two kinds of knowledge: (1) knowledge of specific facts and information, which he called knowledge in the "narrow sense;" and (2) knowledge that involves the child's thinking processes and how she reasons about reality, which he called knowledge in the "broad sense." Knowledge in the broad sense also concerns the relationships that the child forms among the various facts he has learned in the narrow sense (see Kamii and DeVries 1977).

One of the characteristics of children's thinking has to do with what Piaget called egocentrism. *Egocentrism*, which is perhaps the best known of the cognitive contents, is concerned with the extent to which children view themselves as the center of reality. Charles Brainerd (1978) offers an interpretive rule of thumb when he writes that "Any behavior that suggests children are preoccupied with themselves and/or unconcerned with things going on around them may be termed egocentric" (p. 103). It's important to recognize that egocentrism results from the young child's *cognitive inability* to take someone else's point of view or to separate himself from various aspects of his environment. Don't confuse this with *egotism*, a label we usually reserve for older children or adults who are intellectually capable of seeing the world from another's perspective, but for whatever reason choose not to do so.

Egocentrism can be expressed by the child who makes a remark about another child, not realizing that the remark could hurt that child's feelings. Or, a child might tell you a story and mention names or describe events only she knows about; yet, she assumes you are as aware of these persons and events as she is.

1. Look for examples of egocentric behavior.

    There are many cognitive abilities that adults take for granted. For the young child, however, these abilities must develop over a long period of time. Piaget argued that some abilities cannot be taught directly; rather, they are the result of maturation, a lot of general experience, learning from others (social transmission), and the processes of assimilation and accommodation.

    One of these cognitive abilities is known as *classification*. This is the process of sorting objects into groups according to perceived similarities. Classification requires that the child notices similarities and differences in the properties of objects. Then he must group those objects on the basis of their similarity on a particular property—for example, color, size, shape, or function. Properties of objects are also called *stimulus dimensions*. There are many dimensions that can form the basis of classification.

For example, does the child put all the toy sheep in one group in the "barnyard" and all toy cows in another group? Does the child put square things and round things into two different, mutually exclusive groups? Can the child sort objects on the basis of more than one attribute at a time—according to *both* size and shape, for example?

2. Observe how the child sorts objects. How does she perceive things to be alike or different? On what basis does she note similarities and differences?

Another important cognitive ability concerns the concept of *number*. Number includes the ability to count, but it also involves such things as one-to-one correspondence and conservation of number. *One-to-one correspondence* is the process of matching two groups of objects, lining up one object of one group with one and only one object of the other group. A child who has this ability can, for example, give each child at the snack table one glass of juice, or place a chair at the table for each child there. Note that this ability does not require counting, but only the ability to see that each child is to get one glass, one chair, or what have you.

Conservation of number is the understanding that the way objects are arranged in space has no effect on their quantity—if no objects are added to or subtracted from the group, their total number remains unchanged. For example, you show a child two equal rows of pennies (say, five in each row). She agrees that the rows are "the same." Then, while she watches, you spread out the pennies in one row so they take up more space than the other row. If the child cannot conserve number, she will tell you the altered ("spread out") row has more pennies than the unaltered row. If she can conserve number, she will not be fooled by the altered row's appearing to have more pennies, and she will tell you the two rows are still the same.

3. Can the child put objects into one-to-one correspondence? Can you give an example? Does he have the concept of number? How does he show that understanding? If he does not understand the number concept, what does he do that indicates the absence of the number concept?

Another cognitive ability that interested Piaget is called seriation. *Seriation* involves the sequential arrangement of objects or ideas according to a particular attribute. Specifically, seriation requires the child to compare and coordinate differences among objects. Thus, arranging sticks of different lengths from shortest to longest is an example of object seriation. Knowing that if Billy is older than Tommy, and Tommy is older than Mary, then Billy is older than Mary, is an example of an abstract seriation.

4. Can the child seriate? According to what criteria does the child arrange objects or events? How many objects can the child arrange in some kind of order?

A child may be able to arrange three sticks according to length, but has difficulty with more than three sticks. He may simply put a larger group of sticks into several groups of three each, although each set of three may be seriated correctly. For example, given nine sticks of different lengths, the child may sort the sticks into three groups of three sticks each, but each smaller group may be seriated correctly.

The concept of conservation applies not only to number but to anything that can be measured; for example, amount of liquid and amount of substance. In these cases, does the child understand that putting equal amounts of liquid into two differently shaped containers does not change their quantities. Or, given two balls made of equal amounts of clay, does the child understand that flattening one of them into a pancake does not change its quantity?

5. Does the child have any understanding of conservation of liquid and substance? How does she show this understanding?

The concepts of causality, space, and time are also important aspects of cognitive functioning. *Causality* is the child's comprehension of cause and effect relationships and how he attempts to explain various phenomena. For example, does the child see the relation between the weather and how one should dress? Or, how does the child try to explain why one object floats and another one sinks?

According to Charles Brainerd (1978), there are three "general features of preoperational children's causality concepts: *finalism, artificialism,* and *animism*" (italics original; p. 106). We would like to deal with these in some detail so that you will be able to recognize their presence in children's thinking.

Brainerd (1979) discusses Piaget's definition of *Animism* as follows:

> By 'animism,' Piaget means more or less the same thing that the dictionary means—i.e., preoperational children attribute life to things that are not actually alive. Or, more precisely, they attribute life to things that adults do not believe are alive (p. 108).

Animism can, we believe, be a bit difficult to discern in children. This is because it's tempting to confuse or equate animism with symbolic play. In the latter, the child simply *pretends* a doll is alive, for example, but does not *literally* believe it is alive. Furthermore, as Brainerd points out, Piaget's definition poses some problems, because adults don't always agree among themselves about what is alive and what is not.

It might be worthwhile to give you a brief description of the four substages through wich Piaget believed the development of animism must pass. The first two substages occur during the preoperational stage of cognitive development, whereas the last two occur during the period or stage of concrete operations. We'll give you these as well in case you observe a precocious child who might be exhibiting an advanced development of animism relative to his preoperational peers. For this discussion, we draw on Brainerd's descriptions (pp. 108-109).

Substage I: In substage I, the essential criterion for life is "the effect that an object has on people." If an object can do anything at all that has some consequences for humans, it's said to be alive and to have a will of its own. Lamps, bicycles, cars, and stoves (Brainerd, p. 108) would qualify as having life under this criterion.

Substage II: Here, life has the necessary attribute of mobility: "To be viewed as living, an object must be capable of moving" (p. 109). But as Brainerd points out, movement must be "one of its [the object's] normal functions" (p. 109), even though it need not move spontaneously or by itself. Thus, tables and lamps would not qualify as living things because they do not (ordinarily) move. Interestingly enough, a stone would be considered alive because it can move "by rolling" (p. 109).

Substage III: In this substage movement plays a continuing role, but now it must be spontaneous movement, movement that does not require the intervention of human beings. Stones and bicycles no longer qualify, as they did in substage II, but the sun does since it moves (albeit only apparently) on its own around the earth.

Substage IV: Life in this substage is attributed only to plants and animals, which are the categories of objects that adults normally think of as alive.

The second causality concept is *finalism*, which, says Brainerd, is "the manner in which preoperational children answer the interrogatives 'why,' 'what,' 'where,' and 'how'—but especially the interrogative 'why'" (p. 106). According to Brainerd, Piaget believed that most adults attribute two basic meanings to "why." One of these refers to the goals or purposes of one's behavior. This meaning is captured in the question "Why did you do that?" (p. 106). The second meaning relates to the causes of events. This meaning is captured in the question "Why does the sun shine?" (p. 106). In sum, the first meaning of "why" has to do with effects, or as Brainerd puts it, with "where things are going" (p. 106). The second meaning concerns causes, or as Brainerd again puts it, with "where things come from" (p. 106).

Piaget apparently argued that preoperational children are not able to distinguish between the cause and effect meanings of "why," which can explain the difficulty adults have answering questions to children's satisfaction. Children deal simultaneously with causes and effects, and they talk about these two variables as though they were interchangeable.

Finalism also involves the preoperational child's belief that everything has an identifiable cause. As Brainerd writes, "When Piaget says that preoperational thinking is 'finalistic,' he means that it searches for a simple and direct cause for even the most trivial and accidental occurrences" (p. 107). Simply put, finalism does not account for the basic principle that *"some events happen entirely by chance"* (p. 107).

The third causality concept is *artificialism*. This is the belief that everything that exists has been created by human beings or by a god who builds the way people do, which is according to some blueprint or plan. Natural phenomena such as lakes and mountains are seen as having been purposely constructed by humans for human uses. Brainerd notes that artificialism, like finalism, "implies that no event can occur spontaneously" (p. 107). Everything has a place in some overall plan or design. From this belief, says Brainerd, comes a concept of causality that "fails to differentiate physical causes from psychological ones" (p. 107).

6. Does the child show animism, finalism, or artificialism in his thinking? What behaviors give evidence for this kind of thinking? What evidence is there for the child's general understanding of causality, of cause and effect relationships?

The *space* concept involves awareness of how objects are located in space, of objects' relative positions, and of the amount of space needed to accommodate or contain an object. Some concept of space is needed just to move from place to place without bumping into things, or to find one's way without getting lost.

The concept of *time* involves an understanding of past, present, and future, and of duration, which is how long something lasts. Does the child refer to something he did yesterday or is going to do tomorrow? Does he have a grasp of relational terms such as *before, during* and *after*? Does he say such things as, "I have to wash my hands before I eat" or "Daddy always drinks coffee after he eats"?

7. Does the child demonstrate an understanding of space and time? How does he show this understanding? How complete does it seem to be?

You should also be alert to the child's factual knowledge. What general kinds of information does she have? Can the child name many objects, persons, or animals? Does she know where she lives (address, city); does she have knowledge of some events that are current in the news? This factual information is knowledge in the "narrow sense" and can be thought of as part of the child's intellectual development and behavior.

8. What factual information does the child have, and how does he use those facts in his dealings with others?

There are other cognitive "contents" that are relevant to the "preschool period" of the lifespan, but we obviously cannot cover all of these. There is one other kind of ability, however, that we feel is especially appropriate to your understanding of preschool children's intelligence, namely the ability to represent mentally the world and its various aspects. Ruth Saunders and Ann Bingham-Newman (1984) offer an excellent account of six characteristics of representation ability. These characteristics can be said to identify the types or levels of representation that are possible for the preoperational child (and for older children and adults, as well). Let's look at these briefly (please see Saunders and Bingham-Newman, pp. 137-138).

(1) The ability to have three-dimensional objects represent or stand for other objects. This ability can be expressed under at least three conditions or circumstances: (a) when both objects are very much alike (p. 137); (b) when both objects are not much alike; and (c) when the child constructs a model of some real object by using a variety of other objects.

(2) The ability to recognize and use two-dimensional objects such as pictures or drawings to represent another real object or setting. The authors cite an example of "using a picture of a doctor's office to create the atmosphere for a dramatic play episode" (p. 137).

(3) The ability to denote objects by exhibiting actions that are usually performed on or with those objects, such as "making a pounding motion to stand for a hammer or a dribbling motion to stand for a basketball" (p. 137).

(4) The ability to represent beings that are alive by mimicking actions or behaviors that are associated with them—for example, moving one's arms to imitate an elephant's trunk (p. 137).

(5) The ability to represent a real event through the use of an abbreviated action or series of actions. This can involve making just a few movements to stand for a lot of movements that, in an actual situation, take a considerably longer period of time. Saunders and Bingham-Newman give the example of a child bringing "a spoon to the mouth three times to stand for eating breakfast" (p. 137).

(6) The ability to express an idea in a number of different ways.

Observation Objectives

To sensitize you to the way children think and to the kinds of information they might know and are capable of learning. To observe how children differ in their cognitive abilities and styles. To become aware of how preschool, preoperational children mentally represent their world.

Procedure

If you can, select two children of different ages as the subjects of your observations. A five-year-old and a two- or three-year-old would be best. If this is not possible, randomly select two children who are in the observation setting. Using the specimen record method, record in as much detail as you can the children's behaviors and the context of those behaviors. Devote about 10 or 15 minutes to each child. Then examine the specimen record and describe each child's cognitive characteristics. Write a summary cognitive profile of the two children. How well do the children fit Piaget's sensorimotor stage of development? What representational abilities do the children demonstrate? Describe specifically the behaviors or characteristics that, to you, indicate functioning within a particular category of representational ability. As a final step, compare the two children's level of mental functioning. What can the older child do that the younger one cannot? Which child demonstrates more egocentric behavior? How do they differ in the way they mentally represent the world and its objects or events? As well, how are they alike in all of these areas of cognitive functioning?

Observation Exercise 17-3

Cognitive and Intellectual Behavior

Observer's Name _____

Child Observed (code name or number) _____

Children's Ages _____ Children's Sex _____

Observation Context (Home, day-care center) _____

Date of Observation _____ Time Begun _____ Time Ended _____

Brief Description of Setting/Situation

OBJECTIVE BEHAVIORAL DESCRIPTION   **INTERPRETATIONS**

Child 1 (Age):

Child 2 (Age):

Summary Child 1:

Summary Child 2:

Comparison of Child 1 with Child 2:

Contrast Between Child 1 and Child 2:

Exercise 17-4: Language Development

Background Information

Language is one of the more prominent behaviors in the preschool child. The preschooler is rapidly acquiring speech vocabulary and is refining his grammar and syntax to conform more closely to adult speech patterns. For many people, language is an indication of intellectual and social progress. In this exercise, you will be concerned with describing and analyzing the child's speech, determining such things as the depth and variety of her vocabulary, characteristic sentence structure, and the syntactical forms the child is capable of using. In later exercises, you will be asked to observe and record children's social uses of language beyond the present unit's emphasis on egocentric and sociocentric speech.

Let us look at the child's speech in terms of Piaget's concepts of egocentrism and sociocentrism. *Egocentric speech* is speech that does not take the other person into account; it is speech that, for all practical purposes, is private. There is no real effort to communicate with the other person; therefore, whatever is said is meaningful only to the speaker. Piaget identified three types of egocentric speech: (a) *monologue*, in which the indival talks only to himself and with no other persons present; (b) *repetition*, in which the individual repeats words and phrases over and over again as if to practice them or as if he simply enjoyed making the sounds; and (c) *collective monologue*, in which two or more persons are talking together but none of them is paying attention to what the others are saying. Each "conversation" is independent of the other conversation.

Socialized Speech, on the other hand, is public speech. It is intended to communicate with someone and each person takes into account what the others are saying and responds accordingly.

1. Does the child engage in egocentric or socialized speech? What are the circumstances under which these types of speech are used?

Vocabulary is the foundation of speech. We communicate by putting individual words together into properly constructed sentences and paragraphs. Presumably, the greater the number of words in our vocabularies, the greater the number and variety of sentences and ideas we can utter and transmit to others. Words have different meanings and serve different purposes. Moreover, words must be placed in the correct position within a sentence; thus, there are rules of grammar and syntax.

2. What do you observe about the child's vocabulary?

In particular, examine the child's speech for words that express relations and oppositions, for example, words such as *and, or, not, same, different, more, less, instead, if, then,* and *because.* Also, how varied or rich is the child's vocabulary when she talks about the world and the people and things in it? Think in terms of general classes or categories of objects, persons, and events, and then assess how many different words the child uses to discuss those categories. For example, one can talk about animals, people, colors, shapes, vehicles, feelings, weather, food, and buildings, among many others. Each of these words (or concepts) represents a general class of phenomena. Therefore, how many different animals can the child specifically name or talk about: dog, cat, squirrel, tiger, fox, sheep, lamb, and so forth? The child may have only a few specific words representing members of the class, animals. Assess the child's ability in the other categories in the same way.

Sentence structure is also an important aspect of speech. Structure refers to such things as the *types* of sentences the child uses: questions, imperatives (i.e., commands or directions), sentences that contain a subject and an object. Does the child form compound sentences (two sentences separated by a conjunction); sentences containing a main clause and a subordinate clause (e.g., "I'll go with you if you play with me first."); and sentences containing *relative clauses* (e.g., "The boy who hit me is over there.").

3. Examine the child's speech for the type of sentences he uses. What is the apparent extent of such usage; that is, does the child have a wide or narrow variety of sentence types?

Finally, there is the area of *syntactical forms.* These refer to how various types of words are used within a sentence to convey meaning. Syntactical forms also refer to how various words in a sentence are positioned relative to one another to convey meaning. For example, we speak of forms of *to be,* as illustrated by sentences such as "Johnny *is* big" and "My mommy *was* here." There are also words that take the "ing" ending: "Sam is hitt<u>ing</u> Billy" and "The children were walk<u>ing</u> across the street." Then there are words that take the *infinitive form,* such as "I want <u>to</u>

watch TV" and "He wanted *to go* with his mother." There are also the various *tenses;* past, present, and future, to mention only the simple tenses. ("I <u>went</u> to the store"; "She <u>is playing</u> here with me"; "My mother <u>will go</u> to work on Monday.")

4. What kinds of syntactical forms does the child use in her speech? What can you say about how she uses the various parts of speech that include:

singular and plural forms: one bird and two birds; one man and two men.

possessive forms: my book; their house; his car.

verb forms (singular and plural): They don't eat here. He doesn't come very often. The boxers hit each other hard.

pronouns: you, me, they, us, I, him.

adverbs: She walked *slowly* across the room. He ate *quickly* and left.

adjectives: The *red* shoes; the *big* building.

prepositional forms or phrases: He went *to* the blackboard; The cat hid *under* the couch.

Observation Objectives

To learn about the language production abilities of preschool children, and how children of preschool age use language as a means of social interaction.

Procedure

In this exercise, you will most likely be performing a group observation. You are to choose <u>two to three children</u> who are playing together or are involved with each other in some way. (A legitimate exception to a group observation is any occasion when a child is talking to him- or herself, such as in the case of self-regulation of behavior, or in language play [see Exercise 17-5 for a description of this kind of play], or in other circumstances in which the child is exhibiting language skills outside of a social context.) If the group breaks up during the observation session, complete your notes and then find a similar group and repeat the process. Your purpose is to observe and record the language behaviors of children who are engaging in social exchanges. You will be using the <u>event sampling method</u> to record instances of language use. You will also record the children's specific use of language to communicate with one another. As much as possible, record their speech word for word; also be sure to include data about the social and emotional aspects of the situation.

Observation Exercise 17-4

Language Development and Behavior

Observer's Name _____

Child Observed (code name or number) _____

Children's Ages _____ Children's Sex _____

Observation Context (Home, preschool) _____

Date of Observation _____ Time Begun _____ Time Ended _____

Brief Description of Setting/Situation

OBJECTIVE EVENT DESCRIPTION   **INTERPRETATIONS**

Descriptive and Interpretive Summary of the Group's Language Behavior

Exercise 17-5: Play

Background Information

Play is considered by some psychologists to be the most important activity in which the young child engages. Indeed, play activities pervade the lives of children from infancy throughout childhood. Some play seems obviously linked to the child's observation of adults; other play seems to stem from the child's fantasies and from experiences that she finds particularly enjoyable.

There are a number of explanations of the major purpose of play. These range from play as getting rid of excess energy to play as a means of socio-emotional expression. Play can be a group or an individual activity. Play is distinguished from non-play behavior by its special characteristics, the most important of which are its voluntary nature and its complete structuring by the participants, with little regard for outside regulation. When play is governed by consistent rules, we say children are playing *games*. These rules give play a social dimension. The participants must put their own personal wishes into the background and abide by the requirements of the game and the wishes of the larger group.

Figure 17-3 Children engaged in parallel play—playing beside but not with each other.

It is important to note that not everything children do is play, although they will sometimes try to make play out of what adults intend to be serious. We say this even though in some sense, play is serious business. But, we must not confuse play as having important (and therefore serious) consequences for children's development, with the notion that play is essentially *equivalent* to work, study, exploration, and other kinds of nonplay behaviors.

Grace Craig (1989) specifies six categories or *forms* of play that depend on particular characteristics and functions. As Craig notes, these categories of play will overlap with one another; they are not mutually exclusive or exhaustive:

1. *Sensory Pleasure.* "The aim of this kind of play," says Craig, "is sensory experience in and for itself" (p. 255). This kind of play instructs children regarding their "bodies, senses, and the qualities of things in their environment" (p. 255).

2. *Play with Motion.* This is physical movement enjoyed for its own sake. As Craig points out, "play with motion is often begun by an adult and provides infants with some of their earliest social experiences" (p. 255).

3. *Rough-and-Tumble Play.* Craig notes that although this kind of play is often discouraged by teachers and parents, there is evidence that it is beneficial to children. Along with exercise and the release of energy, rough-and-tumble play teaches children how to "handle their feelings, to control their impulses, and to filter out negative behaviors that are inappropriate in a group" (p. 255).

4. *Play with Language.* This kind of play involves experimentation with language rhythms and cadences, the mixing up of words to make new meanings, the use of language to poke fun at the world and to verify their grasp of reality (Craig, p. 255). There apparently is no concern with using language to communicate; children concentrate on the language itself by manipulating its sounds, patterns, and meanings. Interestingly enough, Craig also notes that children use language play "as a buffer against expressions of anger" (p. 255).

Citing Judith Schwartz (1981), Craig describes three kinds of language play.

1. There is the regular repetition of "letters and words in a steady beat: La la la / Lol li pop / La la la / Lol li pop" (p. 257).

2. There is play consisting of patterns of words "as if they were practicing a grammatical drill or sentences using the same words: Hit it / Sit it / Slit it / Mit it. And: There is the light. / Where is the light? / Here is the light" (p. 257).

3. There is "the less frequent kind of play" in which "children play with the meaning of words or invent words to fit meanings" (p. 257). She gives the examples of "San Diego, Sandiego, Sandi Ego / San Diego, Sandi Ego / Eggs aren't sandy!" (p. 257).

Craig proposes that children engage in language play because it is funny, it gives them the opportunity "to practice and master the grammar and words they are learning," and it allows them "to control their experiences" (p. 257). She notes that older children use language to structure their play, perhaps through the use of rituals that, when followed, allow them to control the experience.

5. *Dramatic Play and Modeling.* The taking on of roles or models is considered a major type of play. This involves such activities or behaviors as playing house, imitating a parent going to work, pretending to be a policeman, nurse, or truck driver (Craig, p. 257). What's entailed here, says Craig, is not just an imitation of whole patterns of behavior, but also such elements as "fantasy and novel ways of interaction" (p. 257). She notes further that children come to understand various social relationships, rules, and other aspects of their culture by way of imitative play.

Figure 17-4   Solitary play—the child is focused exclusively on his own activity.

6. *Games, Rituals, and Competitive Play.* This last type of play is perhaps the most sophisticated. It involves rules and specific goals, decisions about taking turns, setting up guidelines about what is and is not allowed, and so on. These games and the activities they require help to develop cognitive skills—learning rules, understanding the sequence of cause and effect, realizing the results of various actions, learning about winning and losing, and learning to fit and adjust one's behavior to certain permissible patterns and rules (in Craig, p. 257; see also Herron & Sutton-Smith, 1971; Kamii & DeVries, 1980).

John Dworetsky (1987) cites what he calls "five descriptors" of play. He draws from the work of Rubin, Fein, & Vandenberg (1983) and Smith & Vollstedt (1985), who conclude that "the greater the number of descriptors that can be applied to any given situation, the more likely people are to call those circumstances play (Dworetsky, p. 368). Let's look briefly at these descriptors, which in essence simply isolate different aspects of behavior that are considered to be indicative of play.

1. *Intrinsic motivation.* This simply means that behavior is motivated or prompted from within the individual, and it's "done for its own sake and not to satisfy social demands or bodily functions" (p. 369).
2. *Positive affect.* Play is pleasurable or fun to do.
3. *Nonlaterality.* This means that the behavior "does not follow a serious pattern or sequence"; it has a pretend quality about it (p. 369).
4. *Means/end.* Here the means are emphasized rather than the ends of the activity. Primary interest is in the behavior itself and not in any goals or outcomes that may be achieved.
5. *Flexibility.* This simply means that the behavior isn't rigid but shows pliability in form and context across various situations.

Observation Objectives

To study play behavior from a group or an individual perspective. To analyze children's behavior according to specific descriptive criteria and thereby determine whether that behavior is play or non-play.

Procedure

In this exercise, you will be using a <u>specimen description format</u>. You may observe and record individuals, groups, or both. <u>Observe at least three individual children, or two groups, for 10 to 15 minutes on each occasion</u>. Then analyze your descriptive data and draw conclusions as to whether the activity you have recorded is play or non-play activity. Support your decisions by interpreting your data according to Craig's six types of play and Dworetsky's five descriptors discussed above. Indicate, where possible, the kind of play you have observed in each instance and which of the descriptors seem to apply to the behaviors you have recorded. If you believe a behavioral episode is not play, explain also why you reached that decision.

Observation Exercise 17-5

Play

Observer's Name _____

Child Observed (code name or number) _____

Children's Ages _____ Children's Sex _____

Observation Context (Home, preschool) _____

Date of Observation _____ Time Begun _____ Time Ended _____

Brief Description of Setting/Situation

PLAY DESCRIPTION AND CLASSIFICATION

Unoccupied Behavior:

Solitary Play:

Onlooker Behavior:

Parallel Play:

Associative Play:

Cooperative Play:

Summary of Interpretive Comments:

Exercise 17-6: Emotional Behavior

Background Information

Emotions are such a basic part of our psychological beings that we sometimes take them for granted. Some of our emotions are clearly identifiable by us. We know when we are angry, frightened, or joyous. At other times, however, we can have feelings that are not so clear; we may not be able to label what we feel. Whatever the case, emotions are internal experiences that are private and directly accessible only to the individual experiencing them. This being so, we cannot state with certainty what emotion another person is feeling. She must tell us, or we must *infer* the emotion on the basis of the individual's behavior, facial expressions, and the event that preceded and might have caused the feeling. A child's emotional behaviors become more refined and extensive as she matures. Therefore, a four- or five-year old will typically be more emotionally expressive than a two-year old. But, what is the role of emotions; what is their significance? Let us examine for a moment the concept of emotions from a more developmental or perhaps theoretical perspective.

Carroll Izard, in his book *Human Emotions* (1977), asks whether there is a need to study emotions. He notes that "there is a wide range of scientific opinion regarding the nature and importance of emotions" (p. 3). He goes on to give some of these scientific opinions, but very early on, he reaches his own conclusion: "My view is that the emotions constitute the primary *motivational system* for human beings" (italics added, p. 3).

Regardless of your own specific opinion on this question, it's a fact that emotions are here to stay. It's also a fact that on a personal level, emotions—our own and those of children—are extremely important. They are also important on a "professional level." Traditionally, for example, early childhood education programs emphasized children's social and emotional development, and the current stress on cognitive development is of relatively recent origin.

Stanley Greenspan, a practicing psychiatrist involved in research in infant and child development, and his wife Nancy Thorndike Greenspan, a health economist, wrote a book entitled *First Feelings* (1985), in which they deal with the emotional development of children from birth to age four years. Of interest to us are the six "milestones" that characterize or define children's emotional growth and development. In this chapter, we shall briefly discuss only the fifth and sixth emotional milestones, which begin at 18 months of age and go through 48 months of age. This span covers the preschool years, and we intend that you use them as guidelines for determining a child's approximate stage of emotional development or maturity. The earlier stages (1 through 4) are covered in Chapters 15 and 16. The Greenspans' six emotional milestones were arrived at by "closely observing babies' behavior, emotional reactions, and ways of relating to us" (pp. 3-4). You will be asked to do something similar, but in your case, the theoretical groundwork has already been laid. You will only be asked to put your observations into this theoretical framework and to draw some conclusions regarding a child's level of emotional development. This is very much like putting a child's intellectual development and behavior into Piaget's theory of cognitive development, which you may have already done in Exercise 17-3.

Let us point out again, however, that our major purpose is not to provide you with a means of *intervening* in children's lives as therapists, or even as teachers. Rather, in this exercise, we want to give you a theoretical framework within which to observe and record children's actions in the particular area of emotional development and behavior.

Emotional Milestones During the Preschool Years

The fifth stage or milestone identified by the Greenspans occurs between eighteen and thirty-six months of age. By the time children reach this stage, they have learned how objects work, and they continue to improve their ability to "organize complicated social and emotional patterns . . ." (p. 5), an ability that becomes evident in stage 4. This stage 4 competence increases to enable the child to "create . . . objects in his own mind's eye" (Greenspan and Greenspan, p. 5). Mental images of his mother, for example, allow him to deal with her—and with objects—even in her absence. As the Greenspans also point out, this ability to form mental images and impressions (to "create [one's own] experiences" or "construct her own ideas," say the Greenspans) also gives the child the ability to dream "in an adult way" (p. 6). This occurs later than fifteen months of age—perhaps by about two or two and one-half years of age. A child in this stage can also engage in pretend play.

The sixth and final milestone, which occurs between thirty and forty-eight months, takes children into what the Greenspans describe as "the emotional realms of pleasure and dependency, curiosity, anger, self-discipline or setting their own limits, even empathy and love" (p. 6). Additionally, children learn "to separate make-believe from reality and are able to work with ideas and to plan and anticipate" (p. 6). In this stage, according to the Greenspans, a three-and-a-half-year-old child can say such things as "I dreamed there were witches under my bed. Tonight I'm going to dream about kittens" (p. 6).

It's important to emphasize here that the child's emotional development and his intellectual development go hand in hand, so to speak. As the Greenspans put it, the child

. . . will now begin to organize and manipulate his ideas into a cause-and-effect understanding of his own emotions and the world that *begins to take reality into account*. . . .

And,

. . . just as your child learned to combine blocks to make an original house, now he can combine emotional ideas. He may create new feelings of shame and, eventually, guilt based on his own feelings about his "bad" wishes and behavior.

Further,

He now emerges with the 'cause-and-effect' logic at the level of emotional ideas that he developed earlier at the level of behavior" (p. 173; italics added).

The Greenspans' work reveals the developmental course of the emotions, and it gives a hint of some of the changing content or focus of a child's emotional behavior. Therefore, part of your observation task will be to identify the specific content, character, and developmental level of children's emotional responses.

There is a broad range of emotions that children are ultimately capable of displaying. Since we have relied on such a considerable proportion of the Greenspans' work on this critical aspect of development, we shall adopt for use the seven areas of emotional functioning that they identify. These areas of functioning are "dependency, pleasure, love and intimacy, curiosity, assertiveness and exploration, protest and anger, and self-discipline." Also noted are the emotions that are related to these areas: "(feelings of) loss, sadness, anxiety, fear, shame, and guilt" (Greenspan and Greenspan 1985, p. 8).

We will briefly discuss only a few of the above-mentioned emotions or areas of emotional functioning. We want to deal with aggression (which, in the context of the Greenspans' terminology, can be thought of as assertiveness, protest, and anger), dependency, and fear. We hesitate to focus on the negative feelings or behaviors, but they are usually of some concern to parents and adults. Inappropriate aggression might be of particular concern to parents and teachers, especially aggression that threatens the safety of others or that is directed against adults.

Aggression, like some other types of behaviors, is used both to identify particular behaviors that have specific characteristics and to describe a particular personality *trait.* A trait is a tendency to behave in certain ways under certain circumstances. Each of these uses has accompanying problems. Aggressive behavior is frequently defined as behavior that is intended to physically or psychologically hurt another person (or oneself) or to damage or destroy property. An important issue is whether a behavior is *intentionally* aggressive or simply an accidental occurrence. Further, it is argued by some that in order for a behavior to be termed aggressive, the aggressor must feel anger or hostility toward the "victim" and must derive satisfaction from hurting the victim. This kind of aggression is called *hostile aggression.* In contrast to hostile aggression, there can be cases where the aggressor is interested only in getting some object from the victim or achieving some goal. This is called *instrumental aggression,* and it need not involve anger or hostility.

Be certain that you label as hostile aggression only those behaviors that you believe are purposely intended to hurt another person (include both physical and verbal aggression).

1. Observe the child's behavior for instances of aggression, either toward another child or an adult, or toward objects in the environment.

2. What kinds of situations or frustrations make the child angry? What behaviors by other people anger the child? How does she express her anger?

Dependency consists of such behaviors as clinging or maintaining proximity to adults or other children, seeking approval, recognition, assistance, attention, and reassurance, and striving for affection and support. It is important to recognize that all of us are dependent. The issue is to what degree and under what circumstances we show our dependency. It is also useful to distinguish between two basic types of dependency: (a) *instrumental dependency,* which essentially is the necessary reliance we have on others for certain things that are beyond our capacity to do;

and (b) *emotional dependency,* which is a need to be near others and to have their support, affection, and reassurance. It can also be the unwillingness or the self-perceived inability to do things for oneself that one can or should be able to do.

It is important that, where possible, you distinguish instrumental dependency from emotional dependency behaviors. It is also important to note that as children mature, the characteristics of their dependency behaviors change. Very young children are likely to show clinging and proximity-seeking behaviors, whereas older children, who also have greater cognitive abilities, will likely seek attention and approval.

3. In what situations or activities is the child dependent, and, for example, seeks the presence, direction, or assistance of others? In what situations is the child independent and does not seek direction or assistance from others?

    Fear is demonstrated by such behaviors as crying, withdrawing, seeking help, and avoiding the fear-producing situation. Fear can promote both dependency and aggressive behaviors. Nonetheless, fear can be expressed in such a way that it, and not aggression or dependency, is the primary emotion.

4. What kinds of objects or situations appear to scare the child? In what ways does the child express his fears? How does he deal with his fears (e.g., by withdrawing, confronting the fearful situation, seeking help)?

Figure 17-5   A face can say a lot to a teacher.

In addition to the emotional behaviors just discussed, there are other feelings that children are capable of experiencing and expressing. You should be alert to as many of the child's affective states as possible. For example, there are the feelings of pleasure and displeasure, frustration, boredom, and sadness. Like adults, children will differ as to how accurately they can identify what they feel.

Figure 17-6 Instrumental dependency. This child relies on her teacher to complete a task she cannot handle herself.

5. What kinds of things does the child find pleasant? What activities, play materials, stories, games, and so on, seem to be particularly attractive to the child? How does he express that pleasure?

6. What kinds of things are unpleasant or uncomfortable for the child? In what situations does the child appear to be ill at ease? How does she express her displeasure?

As a final topic, and one that pertains to all of the preceding, consider the following question:

7. Are all or most of the child's feelings expressed with equal strength, or does their intensity vary with the particular feeling or situation?

This exercise could get a bit complicated, essentially because you will be asked to attempt some conclusions regarding which of the Greenspans' stages of development your particular child or children can be placed. Additionally, in this exercise you will be trying to gain some general understanding of the child's emotional behaviors, of the range of her emotions and the kinds of situations that prompt these behaviors. Again, you can only infer what the child is feeling from the overt behaviors you have witnessed; you cannot observe emotions directly.

Observation Objectives

To learn about the differences in children's emotional behaviors and the range of emotional responses in preschool children. To determine the level of a child's emotional development according to stages five and six of Greenspan and Greenspan's six milestones or stages of emotional development.

Procedure

There are two parts to this exercise. In Part I, select three children and, using the event sampling technique, watch for and record behaviors or patterns of behavior that would indicate or reflect at which milestone a child's emotional development can be located. Objectively describe those behaviors, and specify as precisely as you can why you think the behaviors you've recorded do in fact indicate a particular level of emotional development.

In Part II, staying with the same three children as in Part I, and using the specimen record technique, observe and record each child's behavior for a period of 10 to 15 minutes. Record in as much detail as possible, and be sure to include descriptions of the physical and social context as they apply to the emotional behaviors observed. Interpret or comment on each child, using the questions and background information provided as guides.

Finally, compare the three children. Look at the range of emotional expression, intensity of expression, and what evokes emotional responses. In short, summarize how the children differ from one another in this area of functioning.

Observation Exercise 17-6

Part I: Level of Emotional Behavior or Development

Observer's Name _____

Child Observed (code name or number) _____

Children's Ages _____ Children's Sex _____

Observation Context (Home, preschool, playground) _____

Date of Observation _____ Time Begun _____ Time Ended _____

Brief Description of Setting/Situation

OBJECTIVE BEHAVIORAL DESCRIPTION   **JUSTIFICATION OF LEVEL CHOSEN**

(Event Sampling)

Child 1:

Child 2:

Child 3:

Summary of Differences in Level of Emotional Development (if any):

Observation Exercise 17-6

Part II: Emotional Behavior

Observer's Name _____

Child Observed (code name or number) _____

Children's Ages _____ Children's Sex _____

Observation Context (Home, preschool, playground) _____

Date of Observation _____ Time Begun _____ Time Ended _____

Brief Description of Setting/Situation

OBJECTIVE BEHAVIORAL DESCRIPTION	INTERPRETATIONS

Child 1:

Child 2:

Child 3:

Summary of Behavioral Differences:

Summary of Behavioral Similarities:

Exercise 17-7: Social Development and Peer Interactions

Background Information

Some believe that social development should be the most important concern of the preschool curriculum in particular, and the preschool years in general. It is during this period of life that the child's horizons are expanding dramatically, and his cognitive and emotional abilities are becoming more and more suited to interacting socially with others.

Social behaviors are behaviors that are oriented toward and influenced by other persons. A *social interaction* is a situation where two or more individuals take one another into account. So, for example, Alex and Thomas are in a social interaction when Alex influences Thomas and is also influenced by Thomas.

The concept of *social skills* is familiar to most of us. Social skills include such things as the ability to get along with others, to influence or persuade others without aggression, to resolve conflicts and disagreements in a socially approved way, and generally to be able to initiate and sustain friendships and social interactions. Social skills can involve the ability to be a leader in a group, as well as a follower who can work for the group's best interests.

Social skills are a product of decreasing egocentrism and increasing sociocentrism. Both of these are supported by increasing cognitive and intellectual skills, along with increased contact with others in social situations.

There are many areas of development and behavior that pertain to social behavior. It should also be noted that much of what the child does during the preschool day is done within a social context. Consequently, most if not all of your observation exercises in this chapter have a social component.

1. How does the child show awareness of and sensitivity to others? How does she express concern for others' feelings and needs?
2. How does the child respond in a situation in which he is a follower? Does he follow the directions of the leader or does he refuse to cooperate? Is the child sensitive to the needs of the group and is he willing to play a follower role where it is appropriate? In this regard, does the child follow whatever rules appear to be operating in the situation? Does the child share, take turns, and so on?
3. If the child is a leader, how does she behave in that role? Does she offer suggestions or does she make demands on others? How do the other children respond to her efforts to lead? Does the child instill confidence in others or does she tend to alienate them?
4. How does the child initiate contact with other children? That is, how does he try to join a group, start a new activity or participate in one already going on, or strike up a friendship? How do others respond to the child's efforts?
5. How does the child settle arguments or conflicts—with physical force, verbal threats, efforts to compromise, appeal to an adult, and so on?

Observation Objectives

To identify the social "statuses" of various children in a group. To learn about children's differing styles of social interaction.

Procedure

There are two parts to this exercise. In Part I, try to identify the leaders in particular social/peer interaction situations. Observe and record the behaviors of these leaders and the behaviors of the other children in the group. Do the following:

1. Compare and contrast the leadership styles or behaviors of the several different leaders you have observed. "Style" here simply refers to the way in which the child asserts his or her leadership: through force, verbal persuasion, "charisma" or sheer positive force of personality, and
2. Compare and contrast the behaviors of the leaders with the behaviors of the followers or others in the group. How are they different? How are they alike? How do the leaders get the others to follow them? Is a child a leader in one group or situation, and a follower in another?

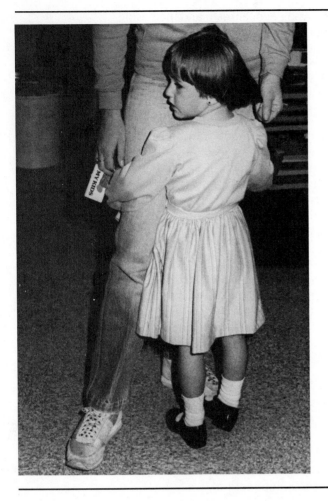

Figure 17-7 Proximity-seeking behavior, a sign of emotional dependency. (Photo by Karen Norton)

In Part II, construct a chart or diagram (perhaps the best such diagram would be a *sociogram*) that will enable you to determine who are the most and the least popular children in the group—popular in the sense of such indications as the number of social interactions in which they engage, and the number of other children who seek them out or show signs of wanting to be with them. Then observe and record the behaviors of the most popular child and the least popular child in the group. Examine your data record and compare the interaction styles and general behavioral characteristics of these children.

By the way, the sociogram was developed by a psychiatrist named J. L. Moreno. Sociograms, says sociologist Rodney Stark (1985), are "charts showing the social networks within a group" (p. 22). Networks are relationships within a group. Sociograms are often constructed by asking members of a group questions such as: Who are your closest friends? Whom do you admire the most? With whom would you most like to take a trip? Asking such questions may not be possible or desirable with preschoolers; you therefore may have to observe the interactions and social exchanges that occur among the children and calculate a sociogram from that data. A sample sociogram is given immediately below.

Observation Exercise 17-7

PART I: Social Development and Peer Interactions

Observer's Name _____

Child Observed (code name or number) _____

Children's Ages _____ Children's Sex _____

Observation Context (Home, preschool) _____

Date of Observation _____ Time Begun _____ Time Ended _____

Brief Description of Setting/Situation

OBJECTIVE BEHAVIORAL DESCRIPTION, PART I	INTERPRETIVE COMMENTS

Leader 1:

Leader 2:

Leader 3:

Followers, Situation 1:

Followers, Situation 2:

Followers, Situation 3:

Leader Comparisons:

Leader/Follower Comparisons:

Observation Exercise 17-7

PART II: Social Development and Peer Interactions

Observer's Name _____

Child Observed (code name or number) _____

Children's Ages _____ Children's Sex _____

Observation Context (Home, preschool) _____

Date of Observation _____ Time Begun _____ Time Ended _____

Brief Description of Setting/Situation

Least Popular Child: **Behavioral Descriptions**

Most Popular Child:

Comparison of Least Popular with Most Popular Child:

appendix I
Developmental Checklist

Child's Name _____ Age _____

Observer _____ Date _____

DEVELOPMENTAL CHECKLIST

	Yes	No	Sometimes
BY 12 MONTHS: Does the Child			
Walk with assistance?			
Roll a ball in imitation of an adult?			
Pick objects up with thumb and forefinger?			
Transfer objects from one hand to other hand?			
Pick up dropped toys?			
Look directly at adult's face?			
Imitate gestures: peek-a-boo, bye-bye, pat-a-cake?			
Find object hidden under a cup?			
Feed self crackers (munching, not sucking on them)?			
Hold cup with two hands; drink with assistance?			
Smile spontaneously?			
Pay attention to own name?			
Respond to "no"?			
Respond differently to strangers and familiar persons?			
Respond differently to sounds: vacuum, phone, door?			
Look at person who speaks to him or her?			
Respond to simple directions accompanied by gestures?			
Make several consonant-vowel combination sounds?			
Vocalize back to person who has talked to him or her?			
Use intonation patterns that sound like scolding, asking, exclaiming?			
Say "da-da" or "ma-ma"?			

Child's Name _____ Age _____

Observer _____ Date _____

DEVELOPMENTAL CHECKLIST

	Yes	No	Sometimes
BY TWO YEARS: Does the Child Walk alone?			
Bend over and pick up toy without falling over?			
Seat self in child-size chair? Walk up and down stairs with assistance?			
Place several rings on a stick?			
Place 5 pegs in a peg board?			
Turn pages 2 or 3 at a time?			
Scribble?			
Follow one-step direction involving something familiar: "Give me—." "Show me—." "Get a—."			
Match familiar objects?			
Use spoon with some spilling?			
Drink from cup holding it with one hand, unassisted?			
Chew food?			
Take off coat, shoe, sock?			
Zip and unzip large zipper?			
Recognize self in mirror or picture?			
Refer to self by name?			
Imitate adult behaviors in play—for example, feeds "baby"?			
Help put things away?			
Respond to specific words by showing what was named: toy, pet, family member?			
Ask for desired items by name: (cookie)?			
Answer with name of object when asked "What's that"?			
Make some two word statements: "Daddy bye-bye"?			

Child's Name _____ Age _____

Observer _____ Date _____

DEVELOPMENTAL CHECKLIST

	Yes	No	Sometimes
BY THREE YEARS: Does the Child			
Run well in a forward direction?			
Jump in place, two feet together?			
Walk on tiptoe?			
Throw ball (but without direction or aim)? Kick ball forward?			
String 4 large beads?			
Turn pages in book singly?			
Hold crayon: imitate circular, vertical, horizontal strokes?			
Match shapes?			
Demonstrate number concepts of one and two? (Can select one or two; can tell if one or two objects.)			
Use spoon without spilling?			
Drink from a straw?			
Put on and take off coat?			
Wash and dry hands with some assistance?			
Watch other children; play near them; sometimes join in their play?			
Defend own possessions?			
Use symbols in play—for example, tin pan on head becomes a space ship.			
Respond to "Put—in the box," "Take the—out of the box"?			
Select correct item on request: big vs little; one vs two?			
Identify objects by their use: show own shoe when asked, "What do you wear on your feet"?			
Ask questions?			
Tell about something with functional phrases that carry meaning: "Daddy go airplane." "Me hungry now"?			

Child's Name _____ Age _____

Observer _____ Date _____

DEVELOPMENTAL CHECKLIST

	Yes	No	Sometimes
BY FOUR YEARS: Does the Child			
Walk on a line?			
Balance on one foot briefly? Hop on one foot?			
Jump over an object 6 inches high and land on both feet together?			
Throw ball with direction?			
Copy circles and crosses?			
Match 6 colors?			
Count to 5?			
Pour well from pitcher? Spread butter, jam with knife?			
Button, unbutton large buttons?			
Know own sex, age, last name?			
Use toilet independently and reliably?			
Wash and dry hands unassisted?			
Listen to stories for a least 5 minutes?			
Draw head of person and at least one other body part?			
Play with other children?			
Share, take turns (with some assistance)?			
Engage in dramatic and pretend play?			
Respond appropriately to "Put it beside," "Put it under"?			
Respond to two step directions: "Give me the sweater and put the shoe on the floor"?			
Respond by selecting the correct object—for example, hard vs. soft object?			
Answer "if," "what," and "when" questions?			
Answer questions about function: "What are books for"?			

Child's Name _____ Age _____

Observer _____ Date _____

DEVELOPMENTAL CHECKLIST

	Yes	No	Sometimes
BY FIVE YEARS: Does the Child			
Walk backward, heel to toe?			
Walk up and down stairs, alternating feet?			
Cut on line?			
Print some letters?			
Point to and name 3 shapes?			
Group common related objects: shoe, sock and foot; apple, orange and plum?			
Demonstrate number concepts to 4 or 5?			
Cut food with knife: celery, sandwich?			
Lace shoes?			
Read from story picture book—in other words, tell story by looking at pictures?			
Draw a person with 3 to 6 body parts?			
Play and interact with other children; engage in dramatic play that is close to reality?			
Build complex structures with blocks or other building materials?			
Respond to simple three step directions: "Give me the pencil, put the book on the table, and hold the comb in your hand"?			
Respond correctly when asked to show penny, nickel, and dime?			
Ask "How" questions?			
Respond verbally to "Hi" and "How are you"?			
Tell about event using past and future tense?			
Use conjunctions to string words and phrases together—for example, "I saw a bear and a zebra and a giraffe at the zoo"?			

Child's Name _____ Age _____

Observer _____ Date _____

DEVELOPMENTAL CHECKLIST

	Yes	No	Sometimes
BY SIX YEARS: Does the Child			
Walk across a balance beam?			
Skip with alternating feet?			
Hop for several seconds on one foot?			
Cut out simple shapes?			
Copy own first name?			
Show well-established handedness; demonstrate consistent right or left handedness?			
Sort objects on one or more dimensions: color, shape or function?			
Name most letters and numerals?			
Count by rote to 10; know what number comes next?			
Dress self completely; tie bows?			
Brush teeth unassisted?			
Have some concept of clock time in relation to daily schedule?			
Cross street safely?			
Draw a person with head, trunk, legs, arms and features; often add clothing details?			
Play simple board games?			
Engage in cooperative play with other children, involving group decisions, role assignments, rule observance?			
Use construction toys, such as Legos, blocks, to make recognizable structures?			
Do 15 piece puzzles?			
Use all grammatical structures: pronouns, plurals, verb tenses, conjunctions?			
Use complex sentences, carry on conversations?			

appendix II
Social-Emotional Checklist

1. Initiation of Activity:

   _____ Almost always involves self in constructive activity of own choice; often rejects suggestions.

   _____ Occasionally needs help in initiating activity; accepts it readily.

   _____ Frequently spends long period before initiating activity; sometimes may reject suggestion.

   _____ Rarely initiates activities, or usually rejects suggestions.

2. Attention Span:

   _____ Can stay with a chosen activity for very long periods, even returning the next day.

   _____ Can remain with an age-appropriate task until it is finished.

   _____ Needs encouragement to stay with task until complete.

   _____ Rarely finishes task. Moves rapidly from one to another.

3. Curiosity:

   _____ Interested in new ideas—words and relationships as well as things.

   _____ Actively explores any new things in the room.

   _____ Can be intrigued by really exciting things, but usually uninterested.

   _____ Shows little or no interest in anything new.

4. Frustration Tolerance:

   _____ Is inventive in solving practical problems. If he is completely blocked, shows mature behavior.

   _____ Usually tries hard and accepts failure well, but if severely frustrated may behave immaturely.

   _____ Sometimes reacts to mild frustrations by giving up, crying, or behaving aggressively.

_____ Unable to tolerate any level of frustration; gives up, cries, or behaves aggressively.

5. Relationship with Teacher:

_____ Self sufficient; may volunteer help or support to teacher.

_____ Warm relationship, but asks for help or attention only when appropriate.

_____ Sometimes requires unusual amount of help or physical contact; or seeks attention through silly or wild actions; or is occasionally aggressive toward teacher.

_____ Continually seeks: help, contact, or attention; or frequently behaves aggressively; or ignores teacher entirely (but clings to avoid some situations).

6. Acceptance of Routines and Limits:

_____ Understands and obeys intelligently even when teacher is not present.

_____ Usually conforms to limits and routines but can deviate easily when appropriate.

_____ Frequently tests limits; or fails to follow routines; or somewhat anxious about changes in routine.

_____ Testing of limits and resisting of routines continuous problem; or compulsive about routine, becomes anxious at any deviation from schedule.

7. Reactions to Adults Other Than Teacher:

_____ Interested in new adults; will take lead in conversation but not try to monopolize.

_____ Does not initiate contact but will accept it and leave room with adult if teacher tells him to do so.

_____ Will not respond to initiation; or refuses to leave room until he knows person well; or overly eager for attention from strangers.

_____ Cries or hides when stranger approaches; or makes immediate demands for exclusive attention from new adults.

8. Interaction with Other Children:

_____ Initiates cooperative play regularly.

_____ Occasionally initiates play and usually accepts initiation from others.

_____ Often rejects advances of others; or plays more alone than with others.

_____ Avoids other children most of the time.

Reprinted, by permission, from Helen Chauvin, Director, Head Start Program, Plattsburgh State University College.

appendix III
Areas for Notice in Observing an Individual Child

Physical Appearance

What are the child's general physical features?

Does he seem in good physical health?

Body Movements and Use of Body

Does he move quickly or slowly?

Does he seem at ease with his body, or is he stiff or unsure?

Are his small and large muscle skills and movements about equally developed or is one area more developed than the other?

Does he express his feelings through his body—slouching shoulders, drooping head, slow movements; or quick, jaunty pace, chest puffed out, marked arm swing?

Facial Expressions

Does she use her face to express feelings?

Does her face register her minute-by-minute reactions to what she is experiencing and what is occurring around her?

Does her face show only intense feelings?

Does she typically show a "deadpan" expression?

Speech

How much of his feelings does he express through his tone of voice?

Does he generally keep his voice under control, or does it express changing moods?

When upset, does he talk more or less than usual?

Is speech an important means of communication to the child, or does he seldom speak, preferring to communicate in other ways?

Does he play with speech by making up chants, songs, puns, stories?

Is his speech fluent, average, inarticulate?

Emotional Reactions

How and when does she exhibit happiness, anger, sadness, doubt, enthusiasm, fear?

Does she seem to have too much control over her feelings, too little control, or a good balance?

Play Activities

What activities does he get involved in?

How does he become involved; how do the activities progress; what does he go to next?

Does he play for a long time at one thing or does he move from one activity to another?

Does he play only briefly in some activities but show prolonged attention in others?

Does she avoid any activities?

What does she seem to derive from an activity—the pleasure of being with other children, sensory stimulation or pleasure, a feeling of mastery or problem solving, a sense of creative expression of ideas and feelings?

Do any aspects of an activity seem to especially frustrate or especially please her?

Does the tempo or pace of his play remain even, speed up, slow down? Under what circumstances?

Does he prefer to play alone—never, always, sometimes? Under what circumstances?

Does she express fantasy in her play verbally, through gestures, through play materials?

If she engages in dramatic play, what kind of roles does she like to take—mother, baby, father, dog?

Does he try new things?

Does he show curiosity about his environment, equipment, people?

Does she prefer to confine her play to a relatively small space, or does she expand over a large area?

Does he seem more comfortable playing indoors or outdoors?

Does she have special skills (music, painting, puzzles, dramatic play)?

Basic Needs

Do you notice anything in particular about his habits and feelings about food? elimination? sexuality? sleep? rest?

appendix IV ===
Emotional Dependency Behavior: Time Sample Procedure

Observer's Name _____

Observation Setting (Home, day-care center, etc.) _____

Date _____ Time _____ Activity _____

Brief Description of Setting/Situation

Recording Intervals	1	2	3	4	5	6	Child

Behavior Signs

Proximity-Seeking

FT Follows Teacher
FC Follows Child
CT Cries when Teacher
     leaves area
RS Resists Strangers
CT Clings to Teacher

Positive Attention-Seeking

AT Seeks approval from
     teacher for specific
     acts done, work
     accomplished

Recording Intervals	1	2	3	4	5	6	Child
AC Seeks approval from child, for acts done, work accomplished							
GT Seeks general acknowledgement from teacher— no specific focus of efforts							
GC Seeks general acknowledgement from child— no specific focus of efforts							

Negative Attention-Seeking

WA Whines for attention
CA Cries for attention
TT Temper tantrum for attention, or if does not get attention
DG Disrupts group activities to get attention

Definitions of Behavior Signs and Procedure

Proximity-seeking consists of behaviors that (1) serve to keep the child physically close to the teacher or another child, or (2) indicate anxiety or displeasure at being apart from the teacher or other child. "Clings to teacher" (or child) involves actual physical contact, whereas "follows" indicates being close without actually touching. "Resists strangers" implies stranger anxiety and an accompanying desire on the part of the child to be near a *familiar* adult or child. Proximity is sought for its own sake and for the emotional security it provides the child.

Positive and *negative attention-seeking* are more specific in their focus, even though they usually require the child to be at least momentarily close to the adult or another child. "General acknowledgement" refers to attention-seeking that has no specific focus or intent; the child simply wants an adult or another child to know he is there or that he has done something. He does not demand actual approval for his accomplishment; and so a mere "I see" from the teacher may be sufficient. Approval-seeking demands a more specific kind of acknowledgement from the teacher or another child—"Yes, John, that's *very good!*" may be the response John wants to hear.

Negative attention-seeking behaviors are behaviors that adults (and sometimes children) usually define as unpleasant or unacceptable. Whining, crying, temper tantrums, and generally disruptive behaviors are usually considered negative. The child who displays such behaviors often does so for their attention-getting value; he will even risk punishment, if that is a form of attention he is willing to accept, or if it seems to him to be the only way he can get attention when he wants or feels he needs it. These behaviors can be viewed as attention-seeking if the child stops the behavior when he receives the attention.

Procedure   Observe for 10 seconds and note whether the child is displaying any of the behaviors listed on the observation sheet. Record the behavior using the coding abbreviations; give yourself 20 seconds to make the recording. Then move on to the next child; stay in column "1" until all the children have been observed once. Repeat this process until you have a total of six (6) separate recordings for each child. If you observe 10 children, it will take you five minutes to complete the first round of observations.

Always record the most complex behavior displayed by the child. For example, if the child follows the teacher to get her approval of a drawing she has just completed, mark the incident as AT, since the proximity-seeking only served the primary purpose of getting approval of the drawing.

appendix V
Observational Record (Social Skills)

Date _____

Frequency of Participation

Activities	9:00	9:15	9:30	9:45	10:00	10:15	10:30	10:45	11:00	11:15	**Total**
Easel-Markers turtle, printing, playdough											
Housekeeping											
Blocks Large Small											
Manipulative toys dominoes counting bears											
Calendar Weather											
Finger plays "8 pigs" "This little cow"											
Pig puppets art (group)											
Name bingo (group)											
Trikes Sand (group)											
Books Music											
Making snack											
Game: Guess who's tapping											

Comments:

Reprinted, with permission, from Susan Benzon

appendix VI
Observational Record 1

Totals: _____
_____
_____
_____

Date: _____   **Social Situations**

	Name	1	2	3	4	5	6	7	8	9	10	11	12
ART													
MUSIC													
SAND & WATER													
HOUSE KEEPING													
DRAMA PLAY													
BLOCKS													
BOOKS													
PUZZLES													

Reprinted, with permission, from Susan Benzon

appendix VII
Observational Record 2

Date _____

Group Activities

Name	Large Groups		%	Small Groups			%

Comments:

Note
Appendices labeled V, VI, and VII are used with permission of Susan Benzon, former Director, Humpty Dumpty Preschool, Plattsburgh Air Force Base, Plattsburgh, New York.

appendix VIII
Summary of Piaget's First Two Stages of Cognitive Development

Stage 1   Sensorimotor   Child learns to control his body in space. Behaves intelligently, but without use of language; uses his physical senses and his motor capacities to interact with and learn about the environment. Object permanence the capstone achievement of this stage.

Stage 2   Preoperational   Judgments of quantity based on perceptions. Various cognitive operations begin— seriation, classification, concepts of space, time, causality. Egocentric in some thinking and behavior. Language used to express thoughts. Still needs practical, concrete experiences; cannot reason hypothetically. Reasons from particular to particular; cannot reason from the general to the particular.

appendix IX
Havighurst's Development Tasks—Infancy Through Middle Childhood

Havighurst defined "developmental task" as "a task which arises at or about a certain period in the life of an individual, successful achievement of which leads to his happiness and to success with later tasks, while failure leads to unhappiness in the individual, disapproval by society, and difficulty with later tasks" (Havighurst, R. J. *Human Development and Education.* New York: Longmans, Green. 1953: 2).

Infancy and Early Childhood (first five years)

1. Learning to walk
2. Learning to take solid food
3. Learning to talk
4. Learning to control elimination of body wastes
5. Learning sex differences and sexual modesty
6. Achieving physiological stability
7. Forming simple concepts of social and physical reality
8. Learning to relate oneself emotionally to parents, siblings, and other people
9. Learning to distinguish right and wrong, and developing a conscience

Middle Childhood (from six to twelve years)

1. Learning physical skills necessary for ordinary games
2. Building wholesome attitudes toward oneself as a growing organism
3. Learning to get along with agemates
4. Learning an appropriate masculine or feminine social role
5. Developing fundamental skills in reading, writing, and calculating
6. Developing concepts necessary for everyday living
7. Developing a conscience, morality, and a scale of values
8. Achieving personal independence
9. Developing attitudes toward social groups and institutions

appendix X
Sources of Information, Support, and Training Material for Teachers and Parents of Children with Developmental Disabilities

PROFESSIONAL ORGANIZATIONS

Alexander Graham Bell Association for the Deaf
3417 Volta Place NW
Washington, D.C. 20007

American Association of Universiy Affiliated
    Programs (UAFs)
8605 Cameron Street
Silver Springs, Maryland 20910

American Association on Mental Retardation
    (AAMD)
1719 Kalorama Road NW
Washington, D.C. 20009

American Cleft Palate Foundation and Parent
    Committee
Louisiana State University School of Medicine
Department of Audiology and Speech
    Pathology
Shreveport, Louisiana 71130

American Foundation for the Blind
15 West 16th Street
New York, New York 10011

American Speech, Hearing, & Language
    Association (ASHA)
10801 Rockville Pike
Rockville, Maryland 20852

National Association for Retarded Citizens
    (NARC)
2510 Avenue J
Arlington, Texas 76011
(This association has large and active chapters
    in many of the 50 states.)

Council for Exceptional Children (CEC)
1920 Association Drive
Reston, Virginia 22091

Division of Early Childhood (DEC/CEC)
1920 Association Drive
Reston, Virginia 22091
(CEC has a number of other divisions, each
    focused on specific areas of exceptionality.
    The parent organization, CEC, will supply
    contacts for each.)

Epilepsy Foundation of America
4351 Garden City Drive
Landover, Maryland 20785

Muscular Dystrophy Association
810 Seventh Avenue
New York, New York 10019

National Association for Parents of the Visually
    Impaired
2011 Hardy Circle
Austin, Texas 78718

National Association of the Deaf
National Association of Parents of the Deaf
814 Thayer Avenue
Silver Springs, Maryland 20910

National Blindness Information Center
1346 Connecticut Avenue, NW
Room 212
Washington, D.C. 20036

National Down Syndrome Congress
1800 Dempster Street
Park Ridge, Illinois 60068

National Easter Seal Society for Crippled Children
and Adults
2023 Ogden Avenue
Chicago, Illinois 60612

National Foundation, March of Dimes
1275 Mamaroneck Avenue
White Plains, New York 10605

National Information Center for Handicapped
Children and Youth
P.O. Box 1492
Washington, D.C. 20013

National Society for Children and Adults with
Autism
1234 Massachusetts Avenue NW
Suite 107
Washington, D.C. 20005

Spina Bifida Association of America
343 South Dearborn
Suite 319
Chicago, Illinois 60604

The Association for Persons with Severe
Handicaps (TASH)
7010 Roosevelt Way Northeast
Seattle, Washington 98105

United Cerebral Palsy Association
66 East 34th Street
New York, New York 10016

FEDERAL AGENCIES FURNISHING INFORMATION AND RESOURCES

Handicapped Children's Early Education Program
(HCEEP)
Office of Special Education and Rehabilitation
Services
U.S. Department of Education
Donohue Building
400 Maryland Avenue SW
Washington, D.C. 20202

National Institute of Child Health and Human
Development
National Institute of Health
Public Health Service
U.S. Department of Health and Human Services
Bethesda, Maryland 20014

Office of Human Development Services
U.S. Department of Health and Human Services
309F Hubert H. Humphrey Building
200 Independence Avenue SW
Washington, D.C. 20201

President's Committee on Mental Retardation
Regional Office Building 3
7th and D Streets
Washington, D.C. 20201

OTHER ASSISTING AGENCIES

Head Start Resource Access Projects (RAPs). To
help Head Start programs fulfill their mainstreaming commitments, 15 RAP Centers have been
established throughout the country under the aus-
pices of the Administration for Children, Youth,
and Families. The RAP centers offer many kinds
of services to Head Start programs, including a
variety of resource materials. Local Head Start
centers can supply information on the location
of the RAP center in the region, contact:

Jane De Weerd, RAP Coordinator
Head Start Bureau
400 6th Street SW
Washington, D.C. 20013

**Technical Assistance Centers for Handicapped
Children's Early Education Projects.** Established
by the office of Special Education within the fed-
eral government, the current resource center is
in the Frank Porter Graham Center at the University of North Carolina in Chapel Hill. Referred to
as TADS (Technical Assistance Development System), the center provides many kinds of resource
materials for HCEEP projects as well as for general dissemination.

**National Information Center for Handicapped
Children and Youth (NICHCY).** This is a free information center and materials development program for anyone in need of particular kinds of
information about handicapping conditions and
the lives and needs of those who are handicapped.
NICHCY answers questions and sends materials
to requests made by mail. The address is Box 1492,
Washington, D.C. 20013.

Glossary

Accommodation

a mental process in which the person changes his cognitive structure or sensorimotor scheme to deal successfully with a new situation; for example, a child accommodates when he comes to understand that not every four-legged animal is a "doggie."

Action fragment

a sample of behavior that is not representative and therefore supplies no information about the larger behavior stream; the behavior sample is thus only a fragment of the total action that occurred.

Actions

behaviors; actions form a class or set of items that are recorded by checklists, what Brandt (1972) called action checklists.

Activity versus passivity in development

two opposing points of view regarding the extent to which the child participates in his own development. The passive view holds that the child is primarily a *reactor* to the environment and "soaks up" stimulation like a sponge; the active view sees the child as an *actor* who seeks stimulation rather than passively waiting for it to occur.

Anecdotal record

an informal observation method often used by teachers as an aid to understanding the child's personality or behavior. It provides a running account of behavior that is either typical or unusual for the child being observed.

Animism

a belief that non-living objects are actually alive and behave like humans.

Artificialism

the belief that everything that exists has been created by human beings or by a god who builds things the way people do according to a plan or blueprint.

Assimilation

a mental process in which the person attempts to make a stimulus or piece of information fit into what she already knows.

Attachment

a condition process in which one person is dependent on another for emotional satisfaction and support; attachment forms with specific other persons and is enduring over time.

Behavior

anything an individual does that can be directly observed by one or more of the five physical senses.

Behavior sampling

this is the general objective and characteristic of all observation; sampling involves taking some portion (sample) of the behaviors out of an individual's behavior stream. Different methods of observing and recording take different sized samples with different amounts and kinds of information.

Behavior stream

a metaphor used by Herbert Wright to capture the continuous quality of behavior; behavior is a lifelong continuum, a stream that can never be seen in its entirety.

Bias

a particular perspective or point of view; biases can be personal or based on a theory or philosophy.

Category system

a type of coding system in which the categories of behavior chosen for observation are both mutually exclusive and exhaustive; that is, each category excludes all other categories, and the categories include the total range of behaviors that a child can exhibit.

Cephalocaudal principle

the principle that describes motor development as progressing in a head-to-foot direction; the child first gains control over the head and neck and proceeds down the body to finally gain control over the legs and feet.

Checklist

an informal observation method that denotes the presence or absence of something. In studying children, checklists record whether specific behaviors have occurred.

Classical conditioning

a form of learning in which a neutral stimulus—one that evokes no response—becomes paired with a stimulus that does. Eventually, the neutral stimulus evokes the response; for example, a puff of air on the eye causes the individual to blink, a soft tone does not; if the tone and the puff of air are both administered very close together in time, eventually the tone by itself will cause the individual to blink.

Classification

a process of sorting objects into groups according to perceived similarities; for example, putting all green things into one group, and all red things into another group. Objects (and ideas) can be classified according to a number of dimensions at the same time; for example, according to shape, size, and color.

Closed method

a characteristic of any method that does not preserve descriptions of behavior and events as they originally occurred.

Coding scheme

a means of reducing complex, detailed descriptions of behavior to a simple mark or tally on an observation sheet; coding schemes often record categories of behavior, such as aggression, dependency, or quarrels.

Cognitive structure

Piaget's concept referring to one's mental organization of ideas and facts; an individual's cognitive structure determines his intellectual behavior and abilities at any given stage of development.

Collective monologue

a form of egocentric speech in which two or more persons are talking together but none of them is paying attention to what the others are saying; each conversation is independent of the other conversations.

Concept

a mental representation or memory of something; concepts bring together attributes that are common to several different events; e.g., the concept "dog" represents the attributes of fur-bearing, four-legged, mammal, and domesticated carnivore that characterize collies, terriers, German shepherds, and all other breeds of dog.

Confidentiality

a condition of research and observation in which the observer or researcher does not reveal information about any individual to anyone.

Conservation

a general principle that the physical appearance of a substance does not necessarily affect its quantity. The principle applies to such things as substance, volume, number, area, and length; for example, the principle of conservation of number dictates that the physical arrangement of a group of coins has no effect on their number.

Context

a term that combines setting and situation to include all aspects of an environment—time, space, circumstances, other people, and physical and psychological conditions.

Cumulative change

a characteristic of development in which behaviors build on one another and contribute to the overall character and direction of the developmental process.

Degree of observer inference required

a characteristic of observation and recording methods involving the amount of inference that is required in using a particular method; inference was also discussed in terms of when in the observation process inference is needed. Specimen records require no inferences at the time of initial recording; time sampling using a coding scheme requires inferences at the time of recording.

Degree of selectivity

a characteristic of observation and recording methods that determines how many behaviors are targeted for observing and recording. Methods vary from completely unselective (specimen record) to highly selective (such as the event sample).

Describe

to tell or write about; to give a word picture of some object, event, or idea.

Development

change over time in the structure, thoughts, and behaviors of an individual due to biological and environmental influences.

Diary description

an informal observation method in which records are made daily of selected aspects of a child's growth and development. The topical diary restricts itself to new behaviors exhibited by the child in a particular developmental area, such as language, social and emotional behavior, and so on; the comprehensive diary records in order as much of everything new as it can.

Differentiation

a process in which behaviors that are initially expressed in a diffuse, non-specific way, eventually separate out and become more skilled, specific, and independent of one another. Also refers to learning a new skill and, during that process, having to practice only that skill, isolating it from other skills already mastered.

Duration record

a variation of the frequency count in which the observer times how long a particular behavior lasts.

Egocentric speech

speech that does not take the other person into account and that, for all practical purposes, is private.

Egocentrism

the cognitive inability to take other people's points of view and to recognize their needs and interests; a preoccupation with one's own view of the world.

Environmentalism

a point of view that stresses the role of the environment in determining behavior and development, in contrast with the role of heredity.

Emotional dependency

a need to be near others and to have their support, affection, and reassurance; it can also involve the unwillingness or self-perceived inability to do things for oneself that one can or should be able to do.

Empirical

having to do with things that can be seen, heard, touched, smelled, and tasted; data obtained by direct observation and not through abstract thought processes or theory; tied to the "real" world.

Errors of commission

errors in which you include more information than is actually present in the situation; reporting behaviors and interactions that did not occur or persons as present who were not.

Errors of omission

errors in which you leave out information that is helpful or necessary to understanding the child's behavior.

Errors of transmission

errors in which you record observed behaviors in the wrong order.

Evaluation

the application of your own values and attitudes to the child's behavior, characteristics, and personality; generally, placing a value on, or judging the worth of something.

Event

behaviors that can be placed into particular categories; for example, hitting to get a toy away from another child is a behavior that can be put into the category "instrumental aggression."

Event sampling

a formal method that observes and records specific kinds of behaviors (events) whenever they occur. It is a sampling technique because it takes out of the behavior stream only preselected behaviors or categories of behaviors.

Explain

to give the meaning or interpretation of; to make clear or plain; to show the relationship among facts or ideas.

Filter

a term used metaphorically to illustrate the idea that things and events "pass through" our personalities, through our individual experiences, values, attitudes, and knowledge; these act as filters that allow certain information to get through to us, while excluding or screening out certain other information.

Formal observation method

a method of observing and recording behavior that is highly structured and controlled; it typically involves a great deal of prior preparation, including the construction of elaborate data forms and training of observers. Formal methods are often used in research studies.

Frequency count

an informal observation method in which the observer simply makes a mark or tally on an observation sheet every time a particular behavior occurs.

Group

a collection of individuals who are organized around a common purpose. Some groups are organized by an outside agency or authority—a school system or church, for example—and these are called institutional groups. Other groups form spontaneously on the basis of mutual interests and common characteristics; these are called peer groups.

Group observation

observations in which (1) the individual is observed in the context of a group and changes in her behavior as she participates in different groups are documented, or (2) the group itself is considered a single entity or unit and its behavior is observed and recorded.

Growth

increase in size, function, or complexity to some point of optimal maturity; associated with quantitative change.

Habituation

a situation where, after being exposed to a physical stimulus that originally evokes a response, the individual ceases paying attention to it;
getting used to a stimulus and losing interest in it.

Hierarchic integration

a process in which skills and behaviors that are initially separate and
independent of one another are combined and can work together as a
harmonious unit (e.g., the skill of grasping an object and the skill of
moving the hand toward an object, are combined to form the integrated skill of reaching and grasping).

Hostile aggression

aggression in which the aggressor feels anger or hostility toward the
victim and derives satisfaction from hurting the victim.

Inconspicuous observation

observation that imposes or introduces nothing into the observation
setting and situation (context) beyond what is required to achieve legitimate objectives.

Informal observation method

a method of observing and recording behavior that lacks the strict
research format of formal methods; it is less structured than a formal
method and is suitable for immediate use by teachers and others who
can use the method for day-to-day program operation and interactions
with children.

Instrumental aggression

aggression in which the aggressor is interested only in getting an object
from the victim or in achieving some goal, and he uses aggression to
do so; it need not involve anger or hostility.

Instrumental dependency

the necessary reliance we all have on others for certain things that are
beyond our own capacities to do.

Interobserver reliability

the degree to which two or more observers agree with one another as
to what occurred during an observation session. High interobserver
reliability indicates minimal disagreement and relatively few differences in observers' judgments and inferences.

Interpretation

going beyond your objective descriptions and trying to explain or give
them meaning; relating something that is directly observable to something that is not directly observable, but which is perhaps based on a
theory or hypothesis.

Invisible displacement

taking an object from one place of concealment (such as under a
piece of cloth) and moving it to another, but not allowing the child to
watch you make the change; this is a technique used to test a child's
concept of object permanence.

Learning history

an individual's life experiences, which form a unique set of learned associations or stimulus-response bonds; these constitute that person's distinctive history and make her different from everyone else.

Linguistic

vocalizations that include actual words.

Maturation

developmental changes over time that are the result of heredity; changes built into the individual that unfold naturally and sequentially with time.

Method

a set of instructions that specifies what one must do to accomplish some task; it may also describe how to do what needs to be done.

Monologue

a form of egocentric speech in which the individual talks only to herself, with no one else present.

Natural unit

a sequence of behaviors that forms a logical whole or segment within the overall behavior stream; the unit has a distinct beginning, behaviors in the middle that constitute a specific event, and a distinct ending. Event sampling structures the observation environment into natural units. (Wright 1960)

Objective description

description of behavior and events that does not contain interpretations, subjective impressions, or speculations, but describes only what you see and hear in such a way that another observer would agree with your report.

Object permanence

the understanding that objects continue to exist even when out of sight or hearing; this is the most important achievement of the sensorimotor period.

Observation

noting and recording facts and events; looking for something in a controlled, structured way.

Observation plan

a plan that guides all phases of the observation process. The plan determines what behaviors will be observed, how much of the behavior stream will be sampled, and which observation method will be used to achieve the other steps in the plan.

One-to-one correspondence

a matching of two groups of objects in which one object of one group is paired with one and only one object of the other group; for example, a child who has this ability can give each child at the snack table one cookie and one napkin.

Open method

a characteristic of any method that preserves descriptions of behavior and events as they originally occurred.

Operant conditioning
> a form of learning in which the consequences of a response determine whether that response is likely to be repeated under the same or similar circumstances; for example, if a child's whining gets her the attention from the teacher that she desires, the child is likely to whine in future situations when she wants attention.

Orienting response
> a response in which the individual turns toward the source of a sound or other stimulus.

Participant observation
> when an observer becomes part of the group she is observing and participates in as many of its activities as is appropriate, with the objective of reducing the effects of observation on the group's behavior.

Prelinguistic
> vocalizations that occur prior to actual speech (cooing and babbling, for example).

Process (noun)
> a series of related activities that require time to accomplish.

Process (verb)
> to think about, give a verbal label to, or to put a fact into some meaningful relationship with other facts.

Professional ethics
> standards of conduct that serve to protect the privacy, confidentiality, rights, and safety of anyone who is the subject of observation or research.

Proximodistal principle
> the principle that describes motor development as progressing from the midline of the body outward to the extremities; thus, chest, shoulders, and upper arms come under control before the hands and feet.

Psychosocial crisis
> a concept in Erikson's theory of personality development; a crisis is a conflict, a turning point or time of special sensitivity to particular social influences.

Qualitative change
> change in psychological functions such as speech, emotions, and intelligence; involves change in the fundamental organization of behaviors and behavior patterns; change in the child's cognitive structure.

Quantitative change
> growth; changes in the amount, number or quantity of something (e.g., increases in height and weight).

Raw data
> descriptions of behavior and events as they originally occurred.

Reflex
> a built-in, preprogrammed pattern of involuntary motor behavior that is elicited by a specific form of stimulation; e.g., the startle reflex is elicited by a sudden loud noise.

Reinforcement

a condition in which an individual's response to a stimulus has rewarding or satisfying consequences; those consequences provide reinforcement of the response, thus increasing the probability that, in the future, the individual will respond in similar fashion to a similar stimulus.

Repetition

a form of egocentric speech in which the individual repeats words and phrases over and over again as if to practice them or as if he simply enjoyed making the sounds.

Representativeness

a desirable feature of behavior samples; representative samples are those that exemplify or reflect the typical characteristics of the larger population or class of behaviors of which the sample is a part.

Role

recurring behaviors and behavior patterns that are associated with specific statuses; teacher's role behaviors include teaching, grading, and counseling students, for example; parents' role behaviors include nurturing, protecting, and socializing the child.

Schema

Piaget's term for a concept or mental representaion of events in the world.

Sensorimotor period

the first stage in Piaget's theory of cognitive development; in this stage, the infant learns about his environment by active manipulation of the objects in it; learning and intellectual development are accomplished by use of the physical senses and motor abilities.

Sensorimotor schemes

organized actions or sequences of actions that permit the individual to interact with the environment.

Sequential change

change that occurs in a lawful, orderly fashion and according to a predetermined series of steps or stages; stage theories hold that change is sequential.

Seriation

a process of arranging objects in some order according to a particular dimension; seriation requires the ability to compare and coordinate differences between objects—for example, arranging a collection of rocks in order of increasing weight, from the lightest to the heaviest.

Setting

the physical environment in which an observation takes place; it includes such factors as physical space, objects in that space, and opportunities and resources that permit people to behave in certain ways.

Sign system

a type of coding system in which the categories of behavior chosen for observation are mutually exclusive; that is, no given behavior can be put into more than one category because each category excludes all others.

Situation

   the social and psychological characteristics and conditions that exist in a particular setting—the nature of the children's play, events that occur that may change the character of the ongoing activities, and so on.

Social autonomy

   the ability to rely on oneself for the satisfaction of various needs and desires; self-sufficiency.

Social behavior

   behavior between two or more persons who take one another into account and influence one another in some way.

Sociocentric speech

   public speech; speech that is intended to communicate with someone, and each person takes into account what the others say and each responds accordingly.

Sociocentrism

   the opposite of egocentrism; the ability to take other's points of view and to recognize their needs and interests.

Soothability

   the ability of a crying or upset infant to be quieted by such adult responses as rocking, holding, swaddling, or giving a pacifier.

Spatial definition

   the concept that physical spaces or environments have particular meanings associated with them, and these meanings or definitions determine what one may do when in that space or environment.

Specimen record

   a formal method of observation and recording in which you continuously record in as much detail as possible what the child does and says, by herself and in interaction with other persons or objects.

Spontaneous behaviors

   behaviors that are internally generated and not responses to outside stimuli; they include behaviors such as random startles, fleeting smiles, and erections.

Stage theory

   a theory that holds that development occurs in a step-like fashion, with each step or level qualitatively distinct from, and more complex than, previous levels.

States

   levels of arousal such as asleep, alert, drowsy, and crying; as they are behavioral conditions that (1) are stable over a period of time, (2) occur repeatedly in an individual infant, and (3) are encountered in similar form in other individuals.

Static descriptor

   a descriptive item that pertains to a highly stable characteristic of research subjects or settings (Brandt 1972); age, sex, race, and socioeconomic are examples of static descriptors. These descriptors are often recorded by a checklist.

Status

a position within a social group or organization; teacher, student, child, adult, president, and parent, are examples of statuses.

Stimulus-response bond

a connection or association between an environmental stimulus and an individual's response to that stimulus; the connection is established because the consequences of the response are rewarding or reinforcing to the individual.

Temperament

a child's characteristic ways of responding to various situations; temperament is described by the child's responses on six personality dimensions: activity level, rhythmicity, approach/withdrawal, adaptability, intensity of reaction, and quality of mood.

Theory

a formal set of general statements or propositions that are supported by data and that attempt to explain a particular phenomenon.

Time sampling

a formal method of observation and recording in which you record selected behaviors during preset uniform time periods and at regularly recurring or randomly selected intervals.

Trait

a tendency or predisposition to behave in certain ways under certain circumstances.

Trust versus mistrust

the first crisis in Erikson's theory; the infant's experiences with his environment and the people in it will determine whether he resolves the crisis or conflict by establishing a stronger sense of trust than of mistrust. A sense of trust will enable the infant to see his world as a predominantly safe, nurturing and trustworthy place.

Validity

pertaining to the accuracy and soundness of an observation or interpretation; the degree to which something measures what it claims to.

Bibliography

Almy, Millie and Celia Genishi. *Ways of Studying Children,* Rev. ed. New York: Teachers College Press. 1979.

Ainsworth, Mary. *Infancy in Uganda: Infant Care and the Growth of Love.* Baltimore: Johns Hopkins University Press. 1967.

Ault, Ruth. *Children's Cognitive Development.* New York: Oxford University Press. 1977.

Barker, R.G. and H.F. Wright. *One Boy's Day.* New York: Harper and Row. 1951.

Beaty, Janice J. *Observing Development of the Young Child.* Columbus: Merrill Publishing Co. 1986.

Berger, Kathleen S. *The Developing Person.* New York: Worth Publishers, Inc. 1991.

Berk, Laura E. *Child Development.* Needham Heights, Mass.: Allyn and Bacon. 1989.

Bigner, Jerry J. *Human Development: A Life-Span Approach.* New York: Macmillan Publishing Company, Inc. 1983.

Bower, T.G.R. *A Primer of Infant Development.* San Francisco: W.H. Freeman and Company. 1977.

Brainerd, Charles J. *Piaget's Theory of Intelligence.* Englewood Cliffs: Prentice-Hall, Inc. 1978.

Brandt, Richard M. *Studying Behavior in Natural Settings.* New York: Holt, Rinehart and Winston, Inc. 1972.

Carpenter, G. Mother's Face and the Newborn. *New Scientist.* 1974. 61: 742-44.

Coombs, C.H. *A Theory of Data.* New York: Wiley. 1964.

Craig, Grace J. *Human Development,* 5th ed. Englewood Ciffs, New Jersey: Prentice-Hall, Inc. 1989.

Dworetzky, John P. *Introduction to Child Development* 3rd ed. New York: West Publishing Co. 1987.

Elkind, David. *The Hurried Child: Growing Up Too Fast Too Soon.* Reading, Mass.: Addison Wesley Publishing Co. 1981.

Faw, Terry and Belkin, Gary S. *Child Psychology.* New York: McGraw-Hill Publishing Co. 1989.

Federico, Ronald C. *Sociology,* 2nd ed. Reading, Mass.: Addison-Wesley Publishing Co. 1979.

Fogel, Alan. *Infancy: Infant, Family, and Society.* New York: West Publishing Co. 1984.

Gander, Mary J. and Harry W. Gardner. *Child and Adolescent Development.* Boston: Little, Brown and Company. 1981.

Gardner, D. Bruce. *Development in Early Childhood,* 2nd ed. New York: Harper and Row. 1973.

Gaver, Donna, and Herbert C. Richards. *Dimensions of Naturalistic Observation for the Prediction of Academic Success.* Journal of Educational Research. Jan./Feb. 1979.

Goodwin, William R. and Laura A. Driscoll. *Handbook for Measurement and Evaluation in Early Childhood Education.* San Francisco: Jossey-Bass Publishers. 1980.

Greenspan, Stanley and Greenspan, Nancy T. *First Feelings: Milestones in the Emotional Development of Your Baby and Child.* New York: Viking Penguin. 1985.

Hansen, Norwood Russell. *Patterns of Discovery.* Cambridge at the University Press. 1958.

Hutt, S.J., H.G. Lenard, and H.E.R. Prechtl. Psychophysiology of the newborn. *Advances in Child Development and Behavior.* New York: Academic Press. 1969.

Ihde, Don. *Experimental Phenomenology: An Introduction.* New York: Paragon Books. 1977.

Irwin, D. Michelle and M. Margaret Bushnell. *Observational Strategies for Child Study.* New York: Holt, Rinehart and Winston. 1980.

Izard, Carrol E. *Human Emotions.* New York: Plenum Press. 1977.

Kagan, Jerome. *Personality Development.* New York: Harcourt Brace Jovanovich, Inc. 1971.

Kagan, Jerome. *The Nature of the Child.* New York: Basic Books, Inc. 1984.

Kamii, Constance and Rheta DeVries. Piaget for Early Education. *The Preschool in Action: Exploring Early Childhood Programs,* 2nd ed. Boston: Allyn and Bacon, Inc. 1977: 365-420.

Langer, Jonas. *Theories of Development.* New York: Holt, Rinehart and Winston, Inc. 1969.

Lay, Margaret Z. and John E. Dopyera. *Becoming a Teacher of Young Children.* Lexington, Mass.: D.C. Heath and Company. 1977.

Lay-Dopyera, Margaret and John E. Dopyera. *Becoming a Teacher of Young Children.* 2nd ed. Lexington, Mass.: D.C. Heath and Company. 1982.

Lefrançois, Guy R. *Of Children.* Belmont, Calif.: Wadsmorth Publishing Co. 1992.

Lerner, Richard. *Concepts and Theories of Human Development.* Reading, Mass.: Addison-Wesley. 1976.

Martin, Patricia Y. and Gerald G. O'Connor. *The Social Environment: Open Systems Application.* New York: Longman. 1989.

Mussen, Paul H., John J. Conger, and Jerome Kagan. *Child Development and Personality,* 5th ed. New York: Harper and Row. 1979.

Mussen, Paul H., John J. Conger, Jerome Kagan, and Aletha Huston. *Child Development,* 6th ed. Philadelphia: Harper and Row. 1984.

Papalia, Diane E. and Sally W. Olds. *Human Development.* New York: McGraw-Hill Book Company. 1978.

Papalia, Diane E. and Sally W. Olds. *A Child's World: Infancy Through Adolescence.* 4th ed. New York: McGraw Hill. 1987.

Papalia, Diane E. and Sally W. Olds. *A Child's World: Infancy Through Adolescence,* 6th ed. New York: McGraw-Hill Book Co. 1993.

Papalia, Diane E. and Sally W. Olds. *Human Development,* 5th ed. New York: McGraw-Hill Book Company. 1992.

Parten, Mildred B. Social Participation Among Pre-school Children. *Journal of Abnormal and Social Psychology.* 1932-33. 27: 243-269.

Pillari, Vimala. *Human Behavior in the Social Environment.* Belmont, Calif.: Wadsworth Publishing Co. 1988.

Richarz, Ann Sherrill. *Understanding Children Through Observation.* New York: West Publishing Company. 1980.

Salkind, Neil. *Theories of Human Development.* New York: D. Van Nostrand Co. 1981.

Saunders, Ruth and Ann M. Bingham-Newman. *Piagetian Perspective for Preschools: A Thinking Book for Teachers.* Englewood Cliffs, New Jersey: Prentice-Hall, Inc. 1984.

Schiamberg, Lawrence B. *Human Development.* 2nd ed. New York: Macmillan Publishing Co. 1985.

Seifert, Kelvin L. and Robert J. Hoffnung. *Child and Adolescent Development.* Boston: Houghton Mifflin Co. 1987.

Sroufe, L. Alan and Robert G. Cooper. *Child Development: Its Nature and Course.* New York: Alfred A. Knopf. 1988.

Stark, Rodney. *Sociology.* Belmont, Calif.: Wadsworth Publishing Co. 1985.

Stone, L. Joseph and Joseph Church. *Childhood and Adolescence: A Psychology of the Growing Person,* 4th ed. New York: Random House. 1979.

Thomas, A., S. Chess, and H. Birch. *Temperament and Behavior Disorders in Children.* New York: New York University Press. 1968.

Thomas, A., S. Chess, and H. Birch. The Origin of Personality. *Scientific American.* 1970. 232, 2: 102-09.

Thorndike, R.L. and E.P. Hagan. *Measurement and Evaluation in Psychology and Education,* 4th ed. New York: Wiley. 1977.

Travers, John F. *The Growing Child,* 2nd ed. Dallas: Scott, Foresman and Company. 1982.

Vander Zander, James W. *Human Development,* 4th ed. New York: Alfred A. Kropf. 1989.

Wadsworth, Barry J. *Piaget's Theory of Cognitive and Affective Development,* 3rd ed. New York: Longman Inc. 1984.

Webster's New World Dictionary of the American Language, College Edition. Cleveland: The World Publishing Company. 1960.

Willemsen, Eleanor. *Understanding Infancy.* San Francisco: W.H. Freeman and Company. 1979.

Wolff, Peter H. The Classification of States. *The Competent Infant.* New York: Basic Books. 1973.

Wright, Herbert F. Observational Child Study. *Handbook of Research Methods in Child Development.* New York: John Wiley and Sons, Inc. 1960.

Annotated Bibliography

Children with Developmental Problems or at High-Risk for Developmental Problems (Identification and Intervention)

Adler, S. and King, D., eds. *A Multidisciplinary treatment program for the preschool exceptional child.* Springfield, IL: Charles C. Thomas, 1986.
This text is a comprehensive, interdisciplinary manual on the care, education and treatment of young children with developmental problems; directed to professionals, day care providers and parents.

Allen, K.E. *The Exceptional Child: Mainstreaming in early childhood education.* Albany, NY: Delmar Publishers, Inc, 1992.
This text provides a comprehensive overview of early intervention and early childhood education for children with developmental problems, as well as their inclusion in the integrated (mainstreamed) classroom.

Blackman, J.A. *Medical aspects of developmental disabilities in children birth to three.* Rockville, MD: Aspen Systems Corp., 1984.
This is an outstanding book for early childhood personnel as it provides well-illustrated and readily understood information about medical issues that affect the developmental progress of young children; highly recommended.

Fallen, N.F. & Umansky, W. *Young children with special needs.* Columbus, OH: Charles E. Merrill, 1985.
This text is especially useful for its focus on the developmentally different child as being in need of a "holistic" approach to early care and education just as is the normally developing child.

Hanson, M.J. and Harris, S.R. *Teaching the young child with motor delays.* Austin, TX: Pro-Ed, 1986.
This easy-to-read handbook bridges the gap between parents and professionals who work with motor-impaired children, birth to three, and includes teaching strategies and therapy activities to be used in the home and in the infant center.

Haslam, R.H.A. and Valletutti, P.J. *Medical problems in the classroom.* Austin, TX: Pro-Ed, 1985.
This book provides teachers and professionals from other disciplines with clues to early identification and points out ways that teachers can assist in the management of these problems.

Krajicek, M.J. and Tomlinson, A.I.T. *Detection of developmental problems in children.* Baltimore, MD: University Park Press, 1983.
  Practical and readable, this is a highly acclaimed pediatric nursing text that focuses on early identification, screening and beginning intervention strategies with children with potential or identified developmental problems.

McCormick, L. and Schiefelbusch, R.L. *Early language intervention.* Columbus, OH: Charles E. Merrill, 1984.
  A good introduction to both normal and atypical language development and overall communication development with practical examples of programs, procedures and materials for fostering communication skills in young children.

Peterson, N.L. *Early intervention for handicapped and at-risk children.* Denver, CO: Love Publishing Company, 1987.
  This is an excellent text for students and professionals in early childhood special education and related disciplines who are working with young children with developmental problems; gives an invaluable perspective on what early intervention actually entails.

Infants, Toddlers and Parents

Apgar, V. and Beck, J. *Is my baby all right? A guide to birth defects.* New York: Trident, 1972.
  This continues to be one of the best sources for information about genetic and environmental causes of developmental problems and what the progress and treatment of a problem is from birth on; sensitive and readable.

Brazelton, T.B. *Infants and mothers: Differences in development.* New York: Dell, 1969.
  Though this book was published a number of years ago it remains one of the best descriptions of the first year of life. It is written by a sensitive and observant pediatrician who has remained at the forefront of developmetnal pediatrics.

Brazelton, T.B. *Toddlers and Parents.* New York: Dell, 1974.
  Like Brazelton's infant book this is an exceptionally good book for parents and caregivers of young children; just as sensitively written as the earlier book, this one too, is a treasury of good advice and sensible suggestion about toddlers.

Bricker, D.D. *Early education of at-risk and handicapped infants, toddlers, and preschool children.* Glenview, IL: Scott, Foresman, and Company, 1986.
  Written by one of the leading infant specialists, this text offers both students and practitioners a contemporary view of the field with examples of application for those working with atypical infants and children.

Bromwich, R.M. *Working with parents and infants*. Austin, TX: Pro-Ed, 1981.
This remains one of the best books in the field for helping parents learn to work with their handicapped or high-risk children; particularly noteworthy is the inclusion of case histories covering successful, partly successful, and unsuccessful interventions; invaluable for those working with parents.

Caplan, F. and Caplan, T. *The first twelve months of life* and *The second twelve months of life*. New York: Putnam Publishing Co., 1982.
Very readable books that provide excellent descriptions of normal growth and development although their emphasis on month to month changes rather than on developmental sequence may contribute to some undue anxiety in new parents. Includes many practical suggestions for dealing with daily behaviors and routines.

Hanson, M.J. *Atypical infant development*. Austin, TX: Pro-Ed, 1984.
This interdisciplinary text presents students and professionals with a current review of research and literature on both normal and atypical infant developmental problems.

Leach, P. *Your baby and child from birth to age five*. New York: Alfred A. Knopf, 1986.
This book offers parents and caregivers excellent developmental explanations as well as practical suggestions for daily caregiving routines, appropriate play equipment and behavior management.

Marotz, L.; Rush, J. and Cross, M. *Health, safety and nutrition for the young child*. Albany, NY: Delmar Publishers, Inc., 1993.
This book provides a comprehensive overview of the factors that contribute to maximizing the growth and development of each child. It includes some of the most current research information and knowledge concerning each of these areas and is especially useful for teachers, caregivers and parents.

Wilson, L.C. *Infants and toddlers*. Albany, NY: Delmar Publishers, Inc., 1990.
Parents and caregivers will find this book particularly useful in understanding developmental sequences, creating enriching environments and providing appropriate learning experiences for infants and toddlers based on their developmental needs.

index